Magento 1.4 Development Cookbook

Extend your Magento store to the optimum level by developing modules and widgets

Nurul Ferdous

[PACKT] open source*
community experience distilled
PUBLISHING

BIRMINGHAM - MUMBAI

Magento 1.4 Development Cookbook

Copyright © 2010 Packt Publishing

All rights reserved. No part of this book may be reproduced, stored in a retrieval system, or transmitted in any form or by any means, without the prior written permission of the publisher, except in the case of brief quotations embedded in critical articles or reviews.

Every effort has been made in the preparation of this book to ensure the accuracy of the information presented. However, the information contained in this book is sold without warranty, either express or implied. Neither the author, nor Packt Publishing, and its dealers and distributors will be held liable for any damages caused or alleged to be caused directly or indirectly by this book.

Packt Publishing has endeavored to provide trademark information about all of the companies and products mentioned in this book by the appropriate use of capitals. However, Packt Publishing cannot guarantee the accuracy of this information.

First published: December 2010

Production Reference: 1081210

Published by Packt Publishing Ltd.
32 Lincoln Road
Olton
Birmingham, B27 6PA, UK.

ISBN 978-1-849511-44-5

www.packtpub.com

Cover Image by Fillipo (filosarti@tiscali.it)

Credits

Author
Nurul Ferdous

Reviewer
Jose Argudo Blanco

Acquisition Editor
Dilip Venkatesh

Development Editor
Meeta Rajani

Technical Editor
Aditi Suvarna

Copy Editor
Laxmi Subramanian

Indexer
Tejal Daruwale

Editorial Team Leader
Aditya Belpathak

Project Team Leader
Lata Basantani

Project Coordinator
Vincila Colaco

Proofreader
Aaron Nash

Production Coordinator
Melwyn D'sa

Cover Work
Melwyn D'sa

About the Author

Nurul Ferdous is an open source enthusiast and IT specialist from Bangladesh who is currently working for TM Secure Inc. as a LAMP consultant. In fact, he is a soldier turned programmer. He started his career with the Bangladesh Air Force. He has also served in RAB as an intelligence staff where he was nominated for the President's Police medal for his contribution to national security. He is a true passionate programmer. He started his run on software development back in 2004, while he was working in the Bangladesh Air Force.

His primary skills are as a PHP developer. He is a Zend Certified PHP 5 Engineer, and contributes to a number of PHP projects, blogs on PHP-related topics, and presents talks and tutorials related to PHP development and the projects to which he contributes. He also contributes on open source community regularly. He is also a certified professional on TDD and Code Refactoring.

He has served in some top notch software companies both at home and abroad such as BIPL, Right Brain Solutions Ltd., TM Secure Inc., NameDepot.com Inc., and so on as a programmer, software engineer, and consultant. He also writes at his personal blog `http://dynamicguy.com` when he is not baking with codes.

> The very first person whom I would like to thank who made this happen is Dilip Venkatesh along with Meeta Rajani, Aditi Suvarna, and all PACKT personnels who worked on this book. I am also thankful to my wife, Ferdousy Chowdhury and my kid, Riva. They have helped me a lot during the whole writing process!

About the Reviewer

Jose Argudo is a web developer from Valencia, Spain. After finishing his studies he started working for a web design company. After six years of working for that company, and some others, he decided to start working as a freelancer.

Now, after some years have passed, he thinks it's the best decision he has ever taken, a decision that has let him work with the tools he likes, such as CodeIgniter, Joomla!, CakePHP, JQuery, and other well-known open source technologies.

For the last few months, he has also been reviewing some Packt Publications books, such as *Magento 1.3 Sales Tactics, Openx Ad server, Joomla! 1.5 Beginners Guide*, and many more.

He has also been the author of the *CodeIgniter 1.7* book, and *Joomla! 1.5 JavaScript jQuery*.

> To my girlfriend Silvia whose support helps me every day.

www.PacktPub.com

Support files, eBooks, discount offers and more

You might want to visit www.PacktPub.com for support files and downloads related to your book.

Did you know that Packt offers eBook versions of every book published, with PDF and ePub files available? You can upgrade to the eBook version at www.PacktPub.com and as a print book customer, you are entitled to a discount on the eBook copy. Get in touch with us at service@packtpub.com for more details.

At www.PacktPub.com, you can also read a collection of free technical articles, sign up for a range of free newsletters and receive exclusive discounts and offers on Packt books and eBooks.

PACKTLIB

http://PacktLib.PacktPub.com

Do you need instant solutions to your IT questions? PacktLib is Packt's online digital book library. Here, you can access, read and search across Packt's entire library of books.

Why Subscribe?

- Fully searchable across every book published by Packt
- Copy and paste, print and bookmark content
- On demand and accessible via web browser

Free Access for Packt account holders

If you have an account with Packt at www.PacktPub.com, you can use this to access PacktLib today and view nine entirely free books. Simply use your login credentials for immediate access.

Table of Contents

Preface	**1**
Chapter 1: Getting Started with Magento Development	**7**
Introduction	7
Preparing the platform with a virtual host	8
Setting up a Subversion/SVN	11
Getting the latest copy of Magento with the SVN checkout	13
Setting up MySQL tools	15
Setting up a Magento project with NetBeans	16
Working with Magento code	20
Chapter 2: CMS and Design	**23**
Introduction	23
Adding a home link to the menu bar	23
Changing any page title in Magento	26
Customizing a Magento error page	28
Adding AdWords tracking code to order confirmation page in Magento	31
Adding a custom CMS layout template	32
Adding an RSS feed (last five tweets!)	36
Placing the trusty old contact form in CMS	38
Integrating JW Image Rotator 3.17 in Magento	40
Chapter 3: Adding Extra Functionalities	**45**
Introduction	45
Integrating WordPress in Magento	45
Creating a new page	49
Adding jQuery support	51
Adding Lightbox2 in Magento	55
Adding an accepted payment banner at the footer	61

Table of Contents

Chapter 4: Customizing a Store — 65
Introduction — 65
Creating a custom "Twitter handle" field in a registration form — 65
Deleting orders in Magento — 70
Using Google Website Optimizer — 73
Creating a custom variable and using its own e-mail templates — 76
Using Google analytics for Magento — 78
Creating Catalog and Shopping Cart Price Rules — 79
Creating a featured product and showing it in the home page — 81
Creating a custom admin theme — 84

Chapter 5: Playing with Products — 87
Introduction — 87
Setting up the Catalog defaults — 87
Adding a Facebook 'Like' button in product page — 90
Setting up Table Rates shipping — 91
Adding a product to the cart through Querystring — 94
Creating a configurable product — 97
Embedding a YouTube video in product details — 101

Chapter 6: Adding a Professional Touch to Your Site — 105
Introduction — 105
Installing Magento 1.4 in PHP 5.3.2 (without mcrypt) — 106
Optimizing Magento store for search engines — 110
Implementing PayPal Website Payments — 114
Pro and Express Checkout into Magento — 114
Preventing a CSRF attack in Magento — 117

Chapter 7: Database Design — 121
Introduction — 121
Resources and database connections — 122
Magento database replication using Master Slave setup — 124
Using the Magento's Singleton method — 129
Repairing the Magento database — 130
Working with Magento's EAV design — 132

Chapter 8: Creating a Module — 135
Introduction — 135
Creating an empty module with a Module Creator — 136
Creating the required directories — 138
Activating a module — 139
Creating a controller for the module — 140
Creating a configuration XML file for the module — 149

Creating a helper for the News module	153
Creating models for the module	153
Setting up SQL for the News module	156
Designing a template for the News module	157
Adding required blocks for the News module	159

Chapter 9: Creating a Shipping Module — 171
Introduction	171
Initializing module configuration	171
Writing an adapter model	180
Adding a module in backend	181
Adding a module in frontend	183

Chapter 10: Writing a Social Widget — 185
Introduction	185
Creating an empty module and an enabler file	186
Creating a config file and declaring the widgets	188
Writing the default module helper Data.php	190
Creating a source model for services multi select in widget configuration	191
Creating frontend block for our widget	192
Creating templates	196

Chapter 11: Performance Optimization — 199
Introduction	199
Measuring/benchmarking your Magento with Siege, ab, Magento profiler, YSlow, Page Speed, GTmetrix, and WebPagetest	200
Optimizing Magento database and MySQL configuration	208
Optimizing Apache web server configuration	210
Tuning Magento configurations	213
Using APC/Memcached as the cache backend	215
Accelerating PHP: php.ini configuration	220
Applying YSlow and Page Speed rules	221

Chapter 12: Debugging and Unit Testing — 231
Introduction	231
Installing and configuring Xdebug	231
Using FirePHP with Zend Wildfire plugin	239
Installing PHPUnit and necessary PHP CLI binaries	242
Writing your first Magento test case	244

Index — 249

Preface

Magento is the fastest growing PHP-based eCommerce solution based on the Zend Framework. This robust CMS helps developers to enrich their store with more useful functionalities with custom modules. Developing a Magento store to get the desired look and feel is not as easy as you might believe, and may take hours due to the wealth of features available for you.

This book will provide unparalleled guidelines to develop a much faster and captivating Magento store by writing custom modules and powerful customizations. This book covers everything from common development tasks to customization of your store as per your needs.

If you choose to work through all the recipes from the beginning, you will have a development platform ready to work with Magento. You will also explore different ways to customize the look and feel of a Magento store to facilitate your customers and create a better user experience. Integration of Magento with WordPress to add striking functionality to your store will be accomplished in just a few steps. The Magento security measures have been taken care of in some cool recipes by editing the parameters in the admin panel. Setting up a master slave setup for Magento database is discussed along with other database optimizations in the database section. Developing new modules and widgets for Magento is elaborately described in many recipes. Magento's performance optimization is the most important part of this book, which is armed with some easy and incredible recipes dealing with YSlow, Page Speed, Siege, Apache bench, Apache configuration, php.ini optimization, and caching with APC or Memcached. The work procedure behind the wall is explained in an easy manner so that both a novice as well as an experienced developer could benefit from it. This book also has some recipes which are not only useful for Magento but also for any other LAMP-based project.

Preface

What this book covers

Chapter 1, Getting Started with Magento Development, introduces Magento and describes how to set up different tools required for a Magento project. It also illustrates how to work with Magento code.

Chapter 2, CMS and Design, describes how to customize the look and feel of a Magento store to change the default appearance of Magento to satisfy our corporate identity.

Chapter 3, Adding Extra Functionalities, illustrates how to design an eCommerce store in a user-friendly way so that any customer feels comfortable while browsing the shop, by adding some cool functionalities in the shop.

Chapter 4, Customizing a Store, focuses on some of the vulnerable features that are a must for any successful online store such as customizing Twitter handle field, deleting orders in Magento, creating Catalog and Shopping Cart Price Rules, among others.

Chapter 5, Playing with Products, helps you set up some important settings in Magento to enhance the usability of your store such as adding a Facebook 'Like' button in the product page, embedding a video in the product details page, and so on.

Chapter 6, Adding a Professional Touch to Your Site, covers topics such as installing Magento 1.4 in PHP 5.3.2 (without mcrypt), optimizing Magento store for search engines, among others.

Chapter 7, Database Design, covers the resources and database connections, database replication using Master Slave setup, and also explains how to work with Magento's EAV design.

Chapter 8, Creating a Module, covers how to create a module, design a template, and set up SQL for the module.

Chapter 9, Creating a Shipping Module, describes the steps on how to create the configuration file for a new shipping module along with adding a module in the backend and the frontend.

Chapter 10, Writing a Social Widget, explains how to make your own widget and also share this widget with various social network links.

Chapter 11, Performance Optimization, describes how to ensure the optimum performance of your Magento store and overcome the most common pitfalls by applying the techniques described in the different recipes in this chapter.

Chapter 12, Debugging and Unit Testing, guides you through installing, configuring, and using Xdebug, Zend Wildfire, and PHPUnit in an easy way.

What you need for this book

- Magento 1.4 source code
- Apache installation
- MySQL server
- PHP5
- PHP IDE preferably Netbeans
- MySQL client such as MySQL Query Browser
- PHPUnit
- Standard web browser such as Firefox
- Firebug (add-on of Firefox)
- FirePHP
- YSlow (add-on of Firefox)
- Page Speed (add-on of Firefox)
- Siege (a benchmarking tool)
- Lightbox2 library
- jQuery library
- TortoiseSVN (a GUI client for subversion)
- JW Image Rotator
- APC and Memcached to be installed

Who this book is for

If you are a PHP developer or a novice or an experienced software engineer, who is interested in achieving high impact in a fast-paced development environment and want to boost your (PHP/Magento) development skills to the next level, then this book is for you. No prior experience with Magento is required but basic knowledge of PHP is needed.

Conventions

In this book, you will find a number of styles of text that distinguish between different kinds of information. Here are some examples of these styles, and an explanation of their meaning.

Code words in text are shown as follows: "You can override the default `$` function using `jQuery.noconflict()` at any point in JQuery."

Preface

A block of code is set as follows:

```php
<?php $_menu = $this->renderCategoriesMenuHtml(0,'level-top') ?>
<?php if($_menu): ?>
<div class="nav-container">
  <ul id="nav">
    <?php echo $_menu ?>
  </ul>
</div>
<?php endif ?>
```

When we wish to draw your attention to a particular part of a code block, the relevant line or item is set in bold:

```
<Mage_Page>
  <active>true</active>
  <codePool>local</codePool>
  <depends>
    <Mage_Core/>
  </depends>
</Mage_Page>
```

Any command-line input or output is written as follows:

```
sudo aptitude install apache2 apache2.2-common apache2-mpm-prefork apache2-utils libexpat1 ssl-cert
```

New terms and **important words** are shown in bold. Words that you see on the screen, in menus or dialog boxes for example, appear in the text like this: "clicking the **Next** button moves you to the next screen".

> Warnings or important notes appear in a box like this.

> Tips and tricks appear like this.

Reader feedback

Feedback from our readers is always welcome. Let us know what you think about this book—what you liked or may have disliked. Reader feedback is important for us to develop titles that you really get the most out of.

To send us general feedback, simply send an e-mail to feedback@packtpub.com, and mention the book title via the subject of your message.

If there is a book that you need and would like to see us publish, please send us a note in the **SUGGEST A TITLE** form on www.packtpub.com or e-mail suggest@packtpub.com.

If there is a topic that you have expertise in and you are interested in either writing or contributing to a book, see our author guide on www.packtpub.com/authors.

Customer support

Now that you are the proud owner of a Packt book, we have a number of things to help you to get the most from your purchase.

> **Downloading the example code for this book**
>
> You can download the example code files for all Packt books you have purchased from your account at http://www.PacktPub.com. If you purchased this book elsewhere, you can visit http://www.PacktPub.com/support and register to have the files e-mailed directly to you.

Errata

Although we have taken every care to ensure the accuracy of our content, mistakes do happen. If you find a mistake in one of our books—maybe a mistake in the text or the code—we would be grateful if you would report this to us. By doing so, you can save other readers from frustration and help us improve subsequent versions of this book. If you find any errata, please report them by visiting http://www.packtpub.com/support, selecting your book, clicking on the **errata submission form** link, and entering the details of your errata. Once your errata are verified, your submission will be accepted and the errata will be uploaded on our website, or added to any list of existing errata, under the Errata section of that title. Any existing errata can be viewed by selecting your title from http://www.packtpub.com/support.

Piracy

Piracy of copyright material on the Internet is an ongoing problem across all media. At Packt, we take the protection of our copyright and licenses very seriously. If you come across any illegal copies of our works, in any form, on the Internet, please provide us with the location address or website name immediately so that we can pursue a remedy.

Please contact us at `copyright@packtpub.com` with a link to the suspected pirated material.

We appreciate your help in protecting our authors, and our ability to bring you valuable content.

Questions

You can contact us at `questions@packtpub.com` if you are having a problem with any aspect of the book, and we will do our best to address it.

Getting Started with Magento Development

In this chapter, we will cover:

- Preparing the platform with a virtual host
- Setting up a Subversion/SVN
- Getting the latest copy of Magento with the SVN checkout
- Setting up MySQL tools
- Setting up a Magento project with NetBeans
- Working with Magento code

Introduction

Most probably you have heard the hype about *Magento*. It's an award winning open-source eCommerce stack with smart features such as layered navigation, auto-complete search, multiple language support, multiple stores, smart browsing, RSS product feeds, tagging and reviewing products, reviewing search terms, reviewing customer tags, poll manager, currency exchange rates, Google sitemap integration, abandoned shopping cart report, catalog-wide product comparisons, product wish lists, and even zooming the product image. It was created by *Varien*, based on the top notch MVC framework—*Zend Framework,* on March 31, 2008. As with other MVC applications, Magento keeps the display logic separated from the application's business logic. A dedicated team works on updating Magento regularly.

Magento Developer is a very hands-on role for both a novice and experienced software engineer who is interested in achieving high impact in a fast-paced development environment with an ambitious mission. Magento gives a very handy way to deal with its features faster than any other alternatives, whether you know a little or a lot about PHP programming. Let's see how these things happen.

Getting Started with Magento Development

We will make our development platform ready to cook some mouth-watering recipes for Magento in this chapter. If you are a newbie, this is the right place to start. If you are a pro, this is still the right place to start as we have tried to follow some best practices for Magento development that you might not be aware of. Let's get our hands dirty with Magento Development! Good luck!

Preparing the platform with a virtual host

Magento is built on the de facto PHP framework—**Zend Framework**. We need to set up our development environment properly to get most out of it. In this recipe, we will set up a **Fully Qualified Domain Name** (**FQDN**) and a virtual host. We could use the domain as `http://localhost/magento` or something like this, but in that case accessing the admin panel might be cumbersome. In most cases, you have to access through the local IP address. Using a FQDN, you don't have to worry about it. A FQDN will make the debugging process much easier also.

Getting ready

We need to have the following things installed before kicking off the setup of a **virtual host** a.k.a. **vhost**:

- Apache2
- PHP5
- MySQL server 5.0

If we want to install the previously mentioned tools from Ubuntu Linux CLI, we can easily do that by running the following commands. We will be using Linux commands based on Ubuntu throughout the book.

The following command is a basic Apache installation command:

```
sudo aptitude install apache2 apache2.2-common apache2-mpm-prefork
apache2-utils libexpat1 ssl-cert
```

The following command is a basic PHP5 installation command:

```
sudo aptitude install libapache2-mod-php5 php5 php5-common php5-curl
php5-dev php5-gd php5-imagick php5-mcrypt php5-memcache php5-mhash php5-
mysql php5-pspell php5-snmp php5-sqlite php5-xmlrpc php5-xsl
```

Enter the following command to begin with a simple MySQL installation:

```
sudo aptitude install mysql-server mysql-client libmysqlclient15-dev
```

> Note that we have installed the development libs and headers with the `libmysqlclient15-dev` package. You can leave that out but it has been found that they are useful in many situations.

Alternately, we can use an all-in-one package, such as the XAMPP, to get all the aforementioned tools in one click. The XAMPP package can be downloaded from `http://www.apachefriends.org/en/xampp.html`.

How to do it...

1. To test the domain without creating a DNS zone and record(s) on some Internet nameserver(s), let's modify the `/etc/hosts` file on our local computer to include some entries mapping the `magento.local.com`, and so on to the local machine's public IP address (in most cases, 127.0.0.1). Open the `/etc/hosts` file with any text editor or run the following command in terminal:

   ```
   sudo nano /etc/hosts
   ```

2. Add the following line as a similar entry in `/etc/hosts` file:

   ```
   127.0.0.1         magento.local.com
   ```

   > The location of the host file depends on the OS loaded. If it's a Windows OS, it should be `c:\windows\system32\drivers\etc\hosts`.

3. Now let's create the layout for our domain. Open terminal and change your location to the WEBROOT directory by running the following command:

   ```
   cd /var/www/
   ```

   If you are using XAMPP, it would be `c:\xampp\htdocs`.

4. Now for our domain, we want to host/create a folder with a standard set of subfolders:

   ```
   mkdir -p magento.local.com/{public,private,log,cgi-bin,backup}
   ```

5. Let's create an `index.html` file for our domain:

   ```
   sudo nano /var/www/magento.local.com/public/index.html
   ```

6. It's time to put some content in our index file:

    ```html
    <html>
      <head>
        <title>Welcome to magento.local.com</title>
      </head>
      <body>
        <h1>Welcome to magento.local.com</h1>
      </body>
    </html>
    ```

7. We've set up the basics and now we're ready to add our own virtual hosts, so that we can start to serve our domain. Let's go ahead and create the vhost file for `magento.local.com`:

    ```
    sudo nano /etc/apache2/sites-available/magento.local.com
    ```

8. The contents should look like this:

    ```
    # Place any notes or comments you have here
    # It will make any customization easier to understand in the weeks to come
    # domain: magento.local.com
    # public: /var/www/magento.local.com/public
    <VirtualHost *:80>
        # Admin email, Server Name (domain name) and any aliases
        ServerAdmin webmaster@magento.local.com
        ServerName  magento.local.com
        # Index file and Document Root (where the public files are located)
        DirectoryIndex index.php index.html
        DocumentRoot /var/www/magento.local.com/public
        # Custom log file locations
        LogLevel warn
        ErrorLog  /var/www/magento.local.com/log/error.log
        CustomLog /var/www/magento.local.com/log/access.log combined
    </VirtualHost>
    ```

9. Now we have the site available, we need to enable it:

    ```
    sudo a2ensite magento.local.com
    ```

10. It seems like good advice to reload the apache:

    ```
    sudo /etc/init.d/apache2 reload
    ```

11. With such changes made, we can now navigate to our site in a web browser on our local computer, as seen in the following screenshot:

Tada! We now have the contents of `public/index.html` being shown.

How it works...

The *Getting ready* recipe describes the installation process of Apache, PHP, and MySQL from Linux command line. If you have already installed those, you can skip it and start configuring the layout and vhost directly.

The Magento source files will be put in the public directory. Other directories represent as their name suggest. Usually in production server, we don't have to write the domain name manually as we wrote here, as the DNS zone is there. The rest of this recipe is the same as the production server. The virtual host contents has some inline comments starting with # to describe the purpose.

Setting up a Subversion/SVN

A Subversion is a popular version control system initiated in 2000 by CollabNet Inc. We will use this tool throughout the book for source controlling. Its goal is to be a mostly-compatible successor to the widely used **Concurrent Versions System** (**CVS**).

Getting ready

If you are a Windows user, please download the *TortoiseSVN* client from here: `http://tortoisesvn.tigris.org/` and if you are a Linux user, fire up your terminal.

Getting Started with Magento Development

How to do it...

1. Execute the following command in the terminal to install Subversion:

   `sudo apt-get install subversion`

   > Make sure you have an active Internet connection as aptitude will install the package from Ubuntu repository.

   If you are using windows and intended to use TortoiseSVN you may get a Windows binary from http://tortoisesvn.tigris.org.

2. After downloading the TortoiseSVN installer file, double-click on the TortoiseSVN installer file and follow the on screen instructions.

3. Now let's add a new group called Subversion to our system and add current username to Subversion group.

   `sudo addgroup subversion`

   `sudo adduser <your_username_here> subversion`

   > If you don't a have a clue about your current username, issue the command whoami in your terminal.

4. Once the Subversion installation is completed, let's create our repository for Magento project. Now issue the following command in the terminal:

   `sudo mkdir /home/svn`

   `cd /home/svn`

   `sudo mkdir magento`

   `sudo chown -R www-data:subversion magento`

   `sudo chmod -R g+rws magento`

5. Now initiate an SVN repository with the following command:

   `sudo svnadmin create /home/svn/magento`

6. In the case of TortoiseSVN, open the folder where you want to put your Magento repository and right-click and find **create repository here...** from the context menu TortoiseSVN. Enter a name for your repository, in this case the repository name would be magento.

7. It's time to change your current working directory in terminal to:

   `cd /var/www/magento.local.com`

8. We will checkout the Magento project by issuing the following command in the terminal:

   `svn co file:///home/svn/magento public`

How it works...

When we execute any `apt-get` command, the aptitude will take care of the installation process. The aptitude will look for the package from Ubuntu central repository—and download it if necessary—and perform the necessary tasks.

After completion of the installation process, we've created a new group named `subversion` and added the username to the newly created group subversion. Then we've created a directory under `/home/location` to hold all repositories. After that, we've created a new repository for our Magento project named `magento`. Finally, we've checked out the repository in our site location in the public directory.

Getting the latest copy of Magento with the SVN checkout

We have already installed Subversion and prepared the environment for firing up our Magento project. Let's grab the latest and greatest version of Magento 1.4 through SVN.

Getting ready

You need to have an active Internet connection to check out Magento from its repository and about 250 MB free space on your hard drive. Fire up your terminal and be ready to issue some necessary commands to grab Magento files in your box.

To create a directory for holding up all the SVN, check out the files and create a lib directory under `/var/location` as follows:

`sudo mkdir /var/lib`

Getting Started with Magento Development

How to do it...

We will now get the Magento 1.4 package from its repository and insert it into our local Magento repository.

Checking out Magento:

1. Change your current directory to `/var/lib/` by issuing the following command on your terminal:

   cd /var/lib

2. Magento source is available at `http://svn.magentocommerce.com/source/branches/1.4-trunk`. Issue the following command to check out Magento 1.4 version name as Magento-1.4:

   svn checkout http://svn.magentocommerce.com/source/branches/1.4-trunk magento-1.4

Exporting checked out files:

1. Let's export the checked out files to our local Magento project's public directory. Issue the following command to export the checked out files to your local Magento project:

   svn --force export /var/lib/magento-1.4/ /var/www/magento.local.com/public/

   > We forced the export process as we already have a directory there, named `public`.

2. Let's add it to our local Magento repository's working copy. Execute the following command to add the exported files to the Magento's working copy:

   cd /var/www/magento.local.com/public

   svn add *

   > `svn add` will add all files recursively.

3. Now commit the changes to local Magento repository:

   svn ci -m 'Magento-1.4 files added'

Chapter 1

> Don't be upset if this takes a bit more time than you expected. There are too many files there in Magento you know!

How it works...

We've created a library for keeping Subversion checkout files for Magento in `/var/directory` and will grab the files through SVN checkout command from terminal. Then we exported the content to our Magento repository's working copy. Finally, we added and committed it to the local repository. We didn't SVN merge or import as Magento doesn't support it.

There's more...

You may read about other SVN commands from `http://svnbook.red-bean.com/`.

Setting up MySQL tools

We will use MySQL Query Browser for MySQL GUI tool as Magento uses MySQL database. It's the official tool for handling MySQL databases. Let's get it.

Getting ready

Get your MySQL Query Browser installer from `http://dev.mysql.com/downloads/gui-tools/5.0.html`.

How to do it...

1. Run the installer that you downloaded from `http://dev.mysql.com/downloads/gui-tools/5.0.html` and follow the onscreen instructions.
2. If you want to install it from Ubuntu terminal, fire up the terminal and execute this command:

   `sudo apt-get install mysql-query-browser`

3. Now, we will create a database for our Magento project with MySQL Query Browser. Fire up MySQL Query Browser and create a new database named `magento`. Alternately, you can run this command in your MySQL terminal:

```
CREATE DATABASE `magento` DEFAULT CHARACTER SET utf8 COLLATE utf8_general_ci;
```

How it works...

Let's assume that you already know the basics of MySQL and any generic installation process. We simply installed the GUI tools to handle our MySQL database here and created a database named `magento`.

Setting up a Magento project with NetBeans

NetBeans is a powerful free and Open Source IDE, which you can use for almost any language. We will use this IDE throughout this book. You can have a look why should we use it at http://netbeans.org/switch/why.html.

Getting ready

Get your copy of NetBeans from `http://netbeans.org/downloads/index.html` and install it. Make sure that you have installed the right download bundle, which is either **PHP** or **All**.

How to do it...

Now you should have everything ready and set up to create a Magento project in NetBeans.

1. Start **NetBeans**. When the IDE comes up, create a new PHP project (**File | New Project | PHP | PHP Application with Existing Sources; PHP Application from Remote Server**). Note that we chose the second one, that is, **PHP Application with Existing Sources,** as we have the Magento source code already at hand.

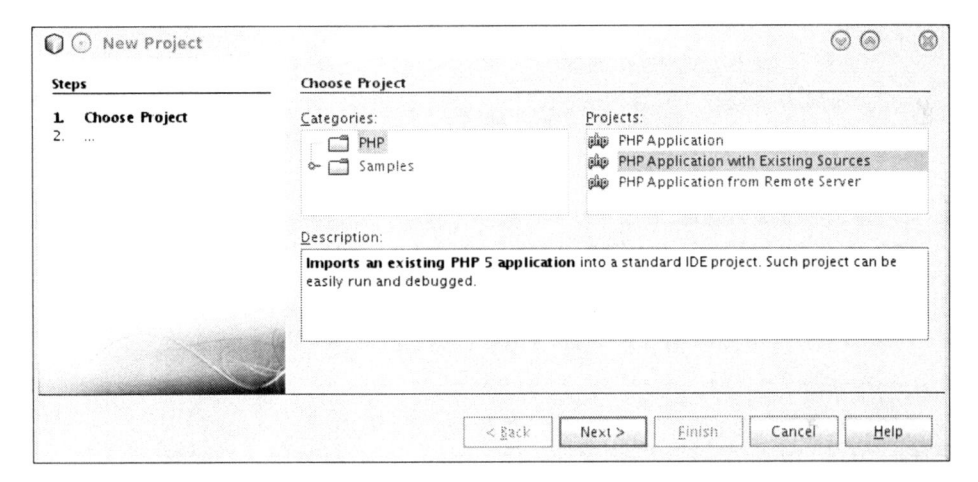

2. Then click **Next**.

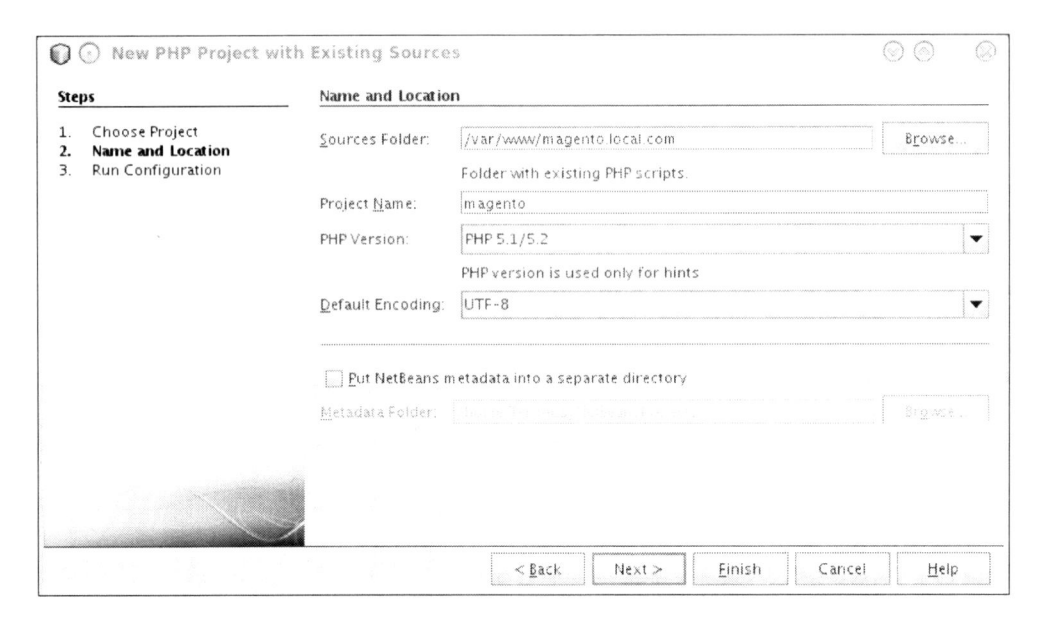

3. In the **Sources Folder** field, enter or select the directory where you previously exported the Magento sources (`/var/www/magento.local.com`).
4. Next, choose the **Project Name** (`magento`).
5. Then click **Next**. The **Run Configuration** dialog will appear.

Chapter 1

6. In the **Run Configuration** step, select **Local Web Site(running on local web server)** in the **Run As** field.

7. Enter the URL to open the main Magento page in the browser (http://magento.local.com/).

8. Click the **Finish** button now to complete the project setup. Now you should have got something like this:

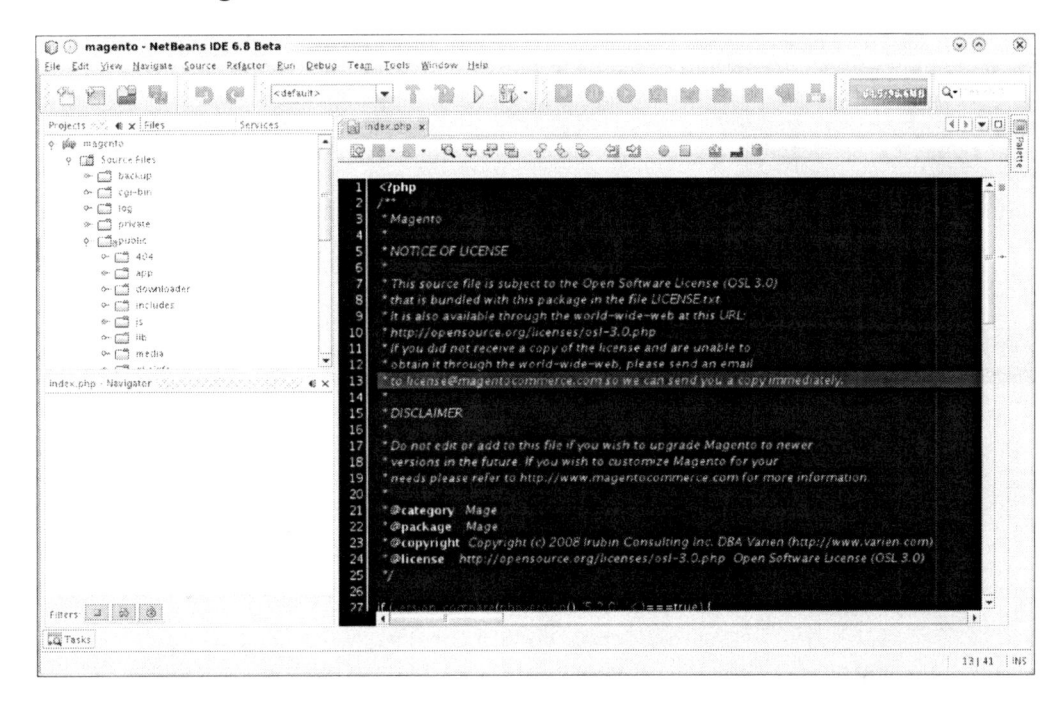

How it works...

With the NetBeans IDE for PHP, you get the best of both worlds: the productivity of an IDE (code completion, real-time error checking, debugging, and more) with the speed and simplicity of your favorite text editor in a less than 30 MB download.

Upon completion of project setup, NetBeans will open Magento project files and scan the files for debugging information and Subversion history. This could take some time.

Getting Started with Magento Development

Working with Magento code

Somebody might tell you that Magento has too many files to deal with and its naming convention is crazy! Yes it is!!

But together they have a nice harmony. If you come to know the glitches to deal with this HUGE file structure, I bet you will love it. So, what are the glitches?

At first, let's know the file structure of Magento.

Getting ready

Start **NetBeans** and press *Ctr + 1* or select **Window | Project** from the menu. Look at the file structure. We kept all Magento source files under the public directory. There are some other directories to help keep those necessary files.

How to do it...

- Our Magento project paths:

  ```
  / -private: Keeps the private files.
  / -cgi-bin: Here should be some cgi binaries if required.
  / -backup: Keep backup data.
  / -public: This is the Directory Root of Magento in our project.
      /app      This is where all the PHP code for the application
      resides.
      /lib     - The external code library.
      /skin    - This is where css and other images resides.
  ```

- A quick overview of `app` directory:

  ```
  /app
      /code       - Where all types of modules resides.
      /design     - Contains both layout xml files and template
      .phtml files.
      /etc        - Global configuration.
      Mage.php   - Static class Mage, where everything is held
      together.
  ```

- Before moving on to the other directories, let's see the directories in this (`/app/code`) dir:

  ```
  /code
      /community - Downloaded modules built by Magento community.
      /core          - The core modules 'out of the box' build
      by Magento.
      /local         - Any module we build ourselves.
  ```

- What about the `/app/design` directory?

  ```
  /app
      /design
          /adminhtml    - Admin designs.
          /frontend     - Front End designs.
              /default - This is the default Interface.
                  /default - This is the default theme.
                      /layout     - Contains all the layout xml
                                    files.
                      /template    - Contains all the template
                                    .phtml files.
  ```

- Lastly, let's overview the `/public/skin` directory:

  ```
  /public
      /skin
          /adminhtml    - Admin styles directory.
          /frontend     - frontend styles directory.
              /default - Our default interface.
                  /default    - Our default theme.
                      /css
                      /images
                      /js
  ```

How it works...

Magento class names follow a strict convention, which is *Camel case* and separated by underscores. You can easily interpret any class name to its location by replacing the underscores to forward slashes.

We are not compelled to follow Magento conventions, but if we follow Magento conventions, we will get some extra benefits such as—Magento will take the name, replace underscores with forward slashes, include that file, then load the requested class, and return an instance of that class. Pretty cool!

There's more...

If you want to download the sample data in another format, visit this page and download your own:

http://www.magentocommerce.com/knowledge-base/entry/installing-sample-data-archive-for-magento-120.

Getting Started with Magento Development

> Make sure you have run the SQL and pasted the media directory before starting the Magento installation.

Some notes on installation and sample data

You can now point your browser `http://magento.local.com` to kick off the Magento installation process. If this is your first time in Magento, you should also install the sample data provided by Magento. You may download the sample data for Magento 1.4 version from here: `http://www.magentocommerce.com/downloads/assets/1.2.0/magento-sample-data-1.2.0.tar.gz`.

2
CMS and Design

In this chapter, we will cover some cool recipes on how to customize the look and feel of a Magento store. In real life, we all need to change the default appearance of Magento to satisfy our corporate identity. Let us take a glance over the recipes titles, which we will be working on:

- Adding a home link to the menu bar
- Changing any page title in Magento
- Customizing a Magento error page
- Adding AdWords tracking code to order confirmation page in Magento
- Adding a custom CMS layout template
- Adding an RSS feed
- Placing the trusty old contact form in CMS
- Integrating JW Image Rotator 3.17 in Magento

Introduction

Magento has a well-organized file structure. We have to work on several files to make the necessary changes. We will add some extra features to facilitate our customers with a better user experience.

Adding a home link to the menu bar

Magento has linked the home link with the logo at the top-left corner. A user can easily navigate to the home page by clicking on the logo. Still a user might look for the home link at the top navigation bar. This is why we will add a new menu at the top navigation bar.

CMS and Design

Getting ready

Magento has a strong caching mechanism to serve the pages faster. By default, Magento sets the caching as `enabled`. We have to disable the caching feature to view the changes after necessary modification. At development, the environment will keep the caching disabled. To disable the caching, go through the following steps:

1. Log in at your **Magento Admin Panel** and point your browser to **System | Cache Management**.
2. Click on the **Select All** link to select all rows.
3. Select **Disable** from the **Actions** dropdown.
4. Click on the **Submit** button to save the changes.

We need to make some small changes to the catalog template and skin. Let's fire up the Magento project in our IDE.

How to do it...

1. Now look for the `top.phtml` file in `app/design/frontend/YOUR_PACKAGE/YOUR_THEME/template/catalog/navigation/` directory. In my case, the absolute path of `top.phtml` file for active default theme is: `/var/www/magento.local.com/public/app/design/frontend/base/default/template/catalog/navigation/`.

2. The code should look like this:
   ```
   <?php $_menu = $this->renderCategoriesMenuHtml(0,'level-top') ?>
   <?php if($_menu): ?>
   <div class="nav-container">
     <ul id="nav">
       <?php echo $_menu ?>
     </ul>
   </div>
   <?php endif ?>
   ```

3. Next, let's add the new alternative home link now. Add the following code snippet before the `foreach` loop:
   ```
   <!-- NEW HOME LINK -->
   <li class="home"><a href="<?php echo $this->getUrl('')?>"><?php echo $this->__('Home') ?></a></li>
   <!-- NEW HOME LINK -->
   ```

4. After the changes, now the `top.phtml` file should look like this:
   ```
   <?php $_menu = $this->renderCategoriesMenuHtml(0,'level-top') ?>
   <?php if($_menu): ?>
   ```

```
<div class="nav-container">
  <ul id="nav">
    <!-- NEW HOME LINK -->
    <li class="home"><a href="<?php echo $this-
>getUrl('')?>"><?php echo $this->__('Home') ?></a></li>
    <!-- NEW HOME LINK -->
    <?php echo $_menu ?>
  </ul>
</div>
<?php endif ?>
```

5. Next, we will add some CSS style for the active state of our home link like other menus in the top navigation bar. Find the `styles.css` file from the `skin/frontend/YOUR_PACKAGE/YOUR_THEME/css/` directory and open it. In my case, the location of `styles.css` file is: `/var/www/magento.local.com/public/skin/frontend/default/default/css`.

6. Now append the following line at the end of `styles.css` file:

   `body.cms-home #nav li.home a { color:#d96708; }`

7. Reload the home page and see the changes. A new home menu will appear:

CMS and Design

How it works...

Let's explain how these steps allow us to add a new alternative home link. We have added a new `<li>` item to the navigation bar with a new class named `home` as the active theme. The file path of `top.html` and `styles.css` might be different, if your theme name is not `default`. Replace `yourtheme` word with your theme folder from paths.

Prior to Magento version 1.4.x, the file structure has been changed. Now Magento has got a base directory as package. You can create your own package there instead of using the base. By default, Magento has a package in the base folder inside `app/design/frontend`. Magento's own four themes reside in `app/design/frontend/default` location. By default, `app/design/frontend/default/default` theme is activated; but this location has no template files as all those are coming from `app/design/frontend/base/default` directory. In fact, a theme extends a package, which is the base in this case. If you want to override a template from the base package, you need to create a file with the same name and path. This is how it works.

After adding the list item `<li>`, which has the `<a>` tag for our home link, we have added a new CSS style to the newly added menu so that it looks like the other menus in the top navigation bar when it's in the active state.

Changing any page title in Magento

Magento sets the page automatically through the controller. If you need to set the page title with your own custom title then this could be cumbersome if you don't know how to do that. In this recipe, we will change the page title with the help of layout and template files as we cannot go with `setTitle` through layout, as the controller sets the title right before rendering it.

Getting ready

Fire up your IDE and open the Magento project. Now expand the following directory: `app/design/frontend/YOUR_PACKAGE/YOUR_THEME`. In my case, it is: `app/design/frontend/base/default`.

How to do it...

We will change the page template and related layout file to set our custom page title:

1. Find and open the `head.phtml` file from your active theme directory. In my case, the `head.phtml` file is located in the `/var/www/magento.local.com/public/app/design/frontend/base/default/template/page/html/` directory.

2. Look for the following line:

   ```
   <title><?php echo $this->getTitle() ?></title>
   ```

3. Now replace the line with the following:

   ```
   <title><?php echo ($this->getMyTitle()) ?
   Mage::getStoreConfig('design/head/title_prefix').' '.$this-
   >getMyTitle().' '.Mage::getStoreConfig('design/head/title_suffix')
   : $this->getTitle(); ?></title>
   ```

4. Now let's change the template to set our own custom page title. Let's say, we shall change the page title for the customer's login page.

5. Find and open the file `customer.xml` from the `app/design/frontend/YOUR_PACKAGE/YOUR_THEME/layout/` directory. In my case, it's located in the `/var/www/magento.local.com/public/app/design/frontend/base/default/layout/` directory.

6. The code inside `customer.xml` has a block something like this:

   ```
   <!--
   Layout for customer login page
   -->
   
     <customer_account_login translate="label">
       <label>Customer Account Login Form</label>
       <!-- Mage_Customer -->
       <remove name="right"/>
       <remove name="left"/>
   
       <reference name="root">
         <action method="setTemplate"><template>page/1column.phtml</template></action>
       </reference>
       <reference name="content">
         <block type="customer/form_login" name="customer_form_login" template="customer/form/login.phtml"/>
       </reference>
     </customer_account_login>
   
   <!--
   Layout for customer log out page
   -->
   ```

7. We shall add a new custom reference to this block. After adding the new reference, the `customer_account_login` block should look like this:

   ```
   <!--
   Layout for customer login page
   -->
   ```

CMS and Design

```
<customer_account_login translate="label">
  <label>Customer Account Login Form</label>
  <!-- Mage_Customer -->
  <remove name="right"/>
  <remove name="left"/>

  <reference name="root">
     <action method="setTemplate"><template>page/1column.phtml</template></action>
  </reference>
  <reference name="content">
     <block type="customer/form_login" name="customer_form_login" template="customer/form/login.phtml"/>
  </reference>
  <!-- New reference for page title starts -->
  <reference name="head">
     <action method="setMyTitle" translate="title"><title>Buyer Login</title></action>
  </reference>
  <!-- // New reference for page title ends -->
</customer_account_login>

<!--
Layout for customer log out page
-->
```

8. We are done!

How it works...

We have modified the `head.phtml` file to render our custom page title in any page overriding the page title that was automatically rendered by the controller.

Finally, we changed the specific layout file to show our custom page title. We can set custom page title in any page by just adding a new head reference with the action `setMyTitle`.

Notice the translate labels we added. If we want our store to be in different languages, then this would help you translate your string with the translate attribute as we have set here.

Customizing a Magento error page

Magento has a built-in error page. Whenever a customer visits a non-existing page, he is automatically redirected to a built-in 404 error page. However, we can change the default error page to our own custom error page. It's not a tough dance to dance. Let's do it.

How to do it...

1. Magneto has a strong CMS section. We can set our own error page by using it. We can also set a custom error page by changing the no-route template. Log in to your Magento Admin Panel and point your browser to **CMS | Pages**.
2. Now open the page named **404 not found 1**.
3. You will see that the **Page information** menu is active. Check the status as to whether it's enabled or not. If it's enabled then the content on this page will be shown or else the error page will show the content of `no-routee.phtml` file from your template directory or as specified in your layout file.
4. From the left navigation panel, click on **content**. The content will be shown in the editor.
5. Click on **Show/Hide Editor** button to disable the visual editor.
6. Now replace the content from the editor with your own content. In my case, I used the following html:

```html
<div class="page-head-alt">
  <h3>D'oh! That page can't be found.</h3>
  <p><strong>Don't get angry, and don't cry.</strong> Let us take that burden. It's not your fault. No, really, listen to me. It's not your fault. We have a 24 hour hotline to deal with things just like this.   Okay, its not really a hotline, its really just some encouraging words to keep trying,    but hotline sounds so much .</p>
  <p>Sorry but the page you are looking for cannot be found. If you're in denial and think this is a conspiracy that cannot possibly be true,</p>
</div>
<dl> <dt>Perhaps you are here because:</dt> <dd>
    <ul class="disc">
      <li>The page has moved</li>
      <li>The page is no longer exists</li>
      <li>You were looking for your puppy and got lost</li>
      <li>You like 404 pages</li>
    </ul>
  </dd>
</dl>
<dl>
  <dt>What can you do?</dt> <dd>Have no fear, help is near! There are many ways you can get back on track with Magento Demo Store.</dd> <dd>
    <ul class="disc">
      <li><a onclick="history.go(-1);" href="#">Go back</a> to the previous page.</li>
```

CMS and Design

```
        <li>Use the search bar at the top of the page to search for
your products.</li>
        <li>Follow these links to get you back on track!<br /><a
href="/">Store Home</a><br /><a href="/customer/account/">My
Account</a></li>
      </ul>
  </dd>
</dl>
```

7. Now save the changes and see them in action by typing a wrong URL in your browser!
8. Your error page should be something like this:

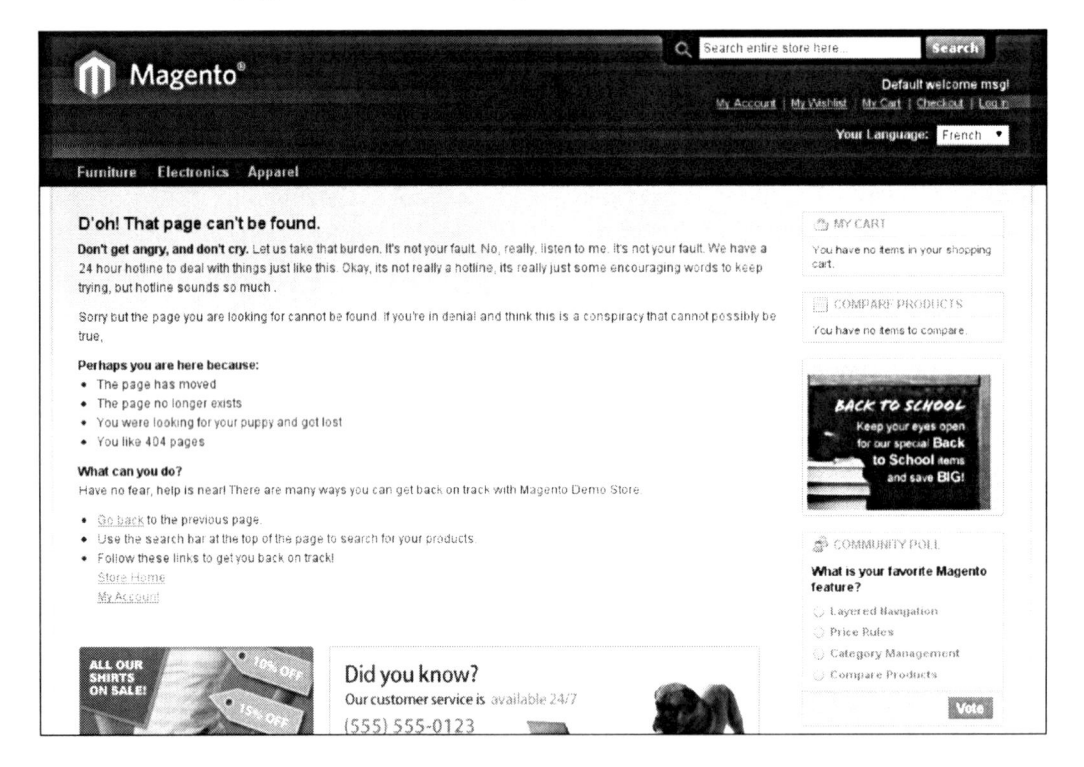

How it works...

Using Magento CMS, setting up a custom error page is pretty easy. We just need to replace the old content with the new one. The CMS will take care of it.

> Remember to keep the 404 no-route page enabled if you want to show error page content from CMS rather than your template.

There's more...

We can also set a custom error page in a different way by modifying the template. At first, we need to disable the CMS 404 page.

Then, we should change the content of the error page from the `no-route.phtml`. Locate the `no-route.phtml` file from the `app/design/frontend/YOUR_PACKAGE/YOUR_THEME/template/cms/default` directory.

In my case, the `no-route.phtml` file is located at the `/var/www/magento.local.com/public/app/design/frontend/base/default/template/cms/default` directory.

Now change the content with the new one.

From the layout directory, you can even change the `no-route.phtml` file with a new one by changing the template attribute of the content block tag.

Adding AdWords tracking code to order confirmation page in Magento

Google AdWords tracking code is an awesome way to manage and optimize advertisement campaign. If you have the Google AdWords tracking code, you can easily add it to your Magento store's page.

Getting ready

Let's say, we want to add the AdWords tracking code in order to our confirmation page. Fire up your IDE and open Magento project.

How to do it...

1. Find and open the `checkout.xml` file from your theme's layout directory. The possible location of `checkout.xml` file is (if your theme name is `yourtheme`): `app/design/frontend/default/yourtheme/layout/checkout.xml`. In my case, it is `app/design/frontend/base/default/layout/checkout.xml`

2. Look for the block `<checkout_onepage_success>` and replace it with the following code block:

```
<checkout_onepage_success translate="label">
<label>One Page Checkout Success</label>
   <reference name="root">
     <action method="setTemplate"><template>page/2columns-right.phtml</template></action>
   </reference>
```

CMS and Design

```
        <reference name="content">
          <block name="checkout.success" template="checkout/success.
    phtml" type="checkout/onepage_success" />
          </reference>
        <!-- Google adwords tracking code block -->
          <reference name="before_body_end">
            <block name="google_adwords_tracking" template="checkout/
    googleadwords/tracking.phtml" type="core/template" />
          </reference>
        <!-- Google adwords tracking code block -->
        </checkout_onepage_success>
```

3. Now create a new directory named `googleadwords` in `app/design/frontend/YOUR_PACKAGE/YOUR_THEME/templates/checkout` directory in your template and create a file named `tracking.phtml` file in `googleadwords` directory. In my case, the full path is `app/design/frontend/base/default/template/checkout/googleadwords/tracking.phtml`.
4. Paste the Google AdWords tracking code in `tracking.phtml`.
5. Save and close this file. View the source of checkout success page and look for the AdWords code that you added.

How it works...

We added a new reference named `before_body_end` at our `checkout.xml` file, which will be invoked right before the end of the body tag.

Make sure that your template called the following code snippet from your `1column.phtml`, `2columns-left.phtml`, `2columns-right.phtml`, and `3columns.phtml` template's page directory:

```
<?php echo $this->getChildHtml('before_body_end') ?>
```

Adding a custom CMS layout template

We are already acquainted with Magento CMS templates, which could be used in different pages. We shall create a new custom CMS template to use in different pages. While working in the backend with CMS, you might have noticed that you can choose from some predefined layouts. If you want to add a new layout in that dropdown, this recipe will help you to do this. The following is a screenshot after completion of this recipe:

Getting ready

We can easily create and edit pages from Magento admin area, unfortunately we have to make some small changes to our code base for creating a new CMS layout. Here is how:

How to do it...

Enabling the local directory:

1. Find and open `Mage_All.xml` file from `app/etc/modules/directory`.

2. At line number 41, you will see a code block like this:

   ```
   <Mage_Page>
     <active>true</active>
     <codePool>core</codePool>
     <depends>
       <Mage_Core />
     </depends>
   </Mage_Page>
   ```

3. Replace the previously-mentioned code block with the following:

   ```
   <Mage_Page>
     <active>true</active>
     <codePool>local</codePool>
     <depends>
       <Mage_Core />
     </depends>
   </Mage_Page>
   ```

CMS and Design

Creating a local `config.xml` file:

For some update/upgrading issues, we won't bother with core `config` file. We will create our own `config.xml` in the local directory. You will notice that inside `app/code`, there are three folders:

- community—this is for installed extension from third party extensions.
- core—this is where Magento core code resides. Don't modify any code here.
- local—this is your folder. Place all code here for modules, extensions, and so on.

Keeping code in the local directory prevents custom module from overriding during Magento upgrade, we should place the custom module in the local folder.

We have enabled the local directory. We can create the `config` file in the local directory now:

1. Fire up your terminal and change your current directory at Magento project's root directory. Now issue the following command to create the `config.xml` file in `app/code/local` directory recursively:

   mkdir -p app/code/local/Mage/Page/etc/

2. Issue the following command in your terminal to create `config.xml` in the `app/code/local/Mage/Page/etc/` directory. If you are a Windows user, just create new xml file named `config.xml` in the `app/code/local/Mage/Page/etc/` folder.

   touch app/code/local/Mage/Page/etc/config.xml

3. Now copy the content of `app/code/core/Mage/Page/etc/config.xml` file to the newly created `app/code/core/Mage/Page/etc/config.xml` file.

4. Find and open the `config.xml` file from the `app/code/local/Mage/Page/etc/` directory.

5. After `three_columns` layout, we will add our own custom layout named `packt`. Append the following block after `three_columns` and save this file:

   ```
   <!-- new layout for packt -->
   <packt module="page" translate="label">
     <label>packt</label>
       <template>page/packt.phtml</template>
       <layout_handle>page_packt</layout_handle>
   </packt>
   <!-- new layout for packt -->
   ```

6. Let us create the template file now in the `app/design/frontend/base/default/template/` directory as `packt.phtml` and put the following content:

   ```
   <!--- put your template code here --->
   <!DOCTYPE html PUBLIC "-//W3C//DTD XHTML 1.0 Strict//EN" "http://www.w3.org/TR/xhtml1/DTD/xhtml1-strict.dtd">
   ```

```
<html xmlns="http://www.w3.org/1999/xhtml" xml:lang="<?php echo
$this->getLang() ?>" lang="<?php echo $this->getLang() ?>">
<head>
<?php echo $this->getChildHtml('head') ?>
</head>
<body<?php echo $this->getBodyClass()?' class="'.$this-
>getBodyClass().'"':'' ?>>
<?php echo $this->getChildHtml('after_body_start') ?>
<div class="wrapper">
  <?php echo $this->getChildHtml('global_notices') ?>
  <div class="page">
    <?php echo $this->getChildHtml('header') ?>
    <div class="main-container col3-layout">
      <div class="main">
        <?php echo $this->getChildHtml('breadcrumbs') ?>
        <div class="col-wrapper">
          <div class="col-main">
            <?php echo $this->getChildHtml('global_messages') ?>
            <?php echo $this->getChildHtml('content') ?>
          </div>
          <div class="col-left sidebar"><?php echo $this-
          >getChildHtml('left') ?></div>
        </div>
        <div class="col-right sidebar"><?php echo $this-
        >getChildHtml('right') ?></div>
      </div>
    </div>
    <?php echo $this->getChildHtml('footer') ?>
    <?php echo $this->getChildHtml('before_body  </div>
</div>
<?php echo $this->getAbsoluteFooter() ?>
</body>
</html>
```

7. Now you can log in to the admin area and add or edit a page in CMS and assign it to your new layout file named `packt`.

How it works...

We added a new layout named `packt` inside the layouts block in `config.xml`. We can add our new layout in the core `config.xml`, which is strongly discouraged as in case of upgrading, the core `config.xml` might be replaced.

Thus, we created the `config.xml` in our local directory. Before that we enabled the local directory from `Mage_All.xml`.

CMS and Design

Adding an RSS feed (last five tweets!)

You might have heard about the much hyped *Twitter* and might have an account with it. You will be glad if we could add it to your eCommerce store powered by Magento, probably in the sidebar.

We will add the last five tweets from a given Twitter account's username and Twitter feed. It's not a tough dance to dance! We can add it within a couple of minutes!

Getting ready

We will use `Zend_Feed_Rss` library to parse the RSS feed, which came with Magento and Zend Framework. Open your favorite PHP IDE and fire up the Magento project.

How to do it...

1. Create a new file named `tweets.phtml` in the `app/design/frontend/YOUR_PACKAGE/YOUR_THEME/template/callouts` directory. In my case, it's `app/design/frontend/base/default/template/callouts`.
2. Now paste the following code inside it and change the Twitter username and feed URL with your desired one:

```php
<?php
/**
 * @var String $twitterUsername
 * change $twitterUsername with your desired username
 */
$twitterUsername = 'packtpub';
/**
 * @var String $twitterFeedUrl
 * change it with your twitter feed. you will find it at the right side of your twitter page
 */
$twitterFeedUrl = 'http://twitter.com/statuses/user_timeline/17778401.rss';

$tweets = new Zend_Feed_Rss($twitterFeedUrl);
?>

<div class="box base-mini mini-compare-products">
    <div class="head">
        <h4>Tweet! Tweet!!</h4>
    </div>
    <?php foreach ($tweets as $key=>$tweet): ?>
    <?php if($key <= 4): ?>
```

```
    <div class="content"><p><?php echo str_
replace("$twitterUsername:", "", $tweet->title); ?></p></div>
    <?php endif; ?>
    <?php endforeach; ?>
</div>
```

3. Now log in to your Magento backend. Navigate to the page **CMS | Pages | Home page | Design | Layout Update XML**.

4. Let's add the following content at the end and save these changes:

```
<reference name="right">
<block type="core/template" name="tweets" as="getTweets"
template="callouts/tweets.phtml"  translate="label">
   <label>Twitter updates</label>
</block>
</reference>
```

5. Guess what! We are done! Now check your Magento home page. Your home page should look something like this:

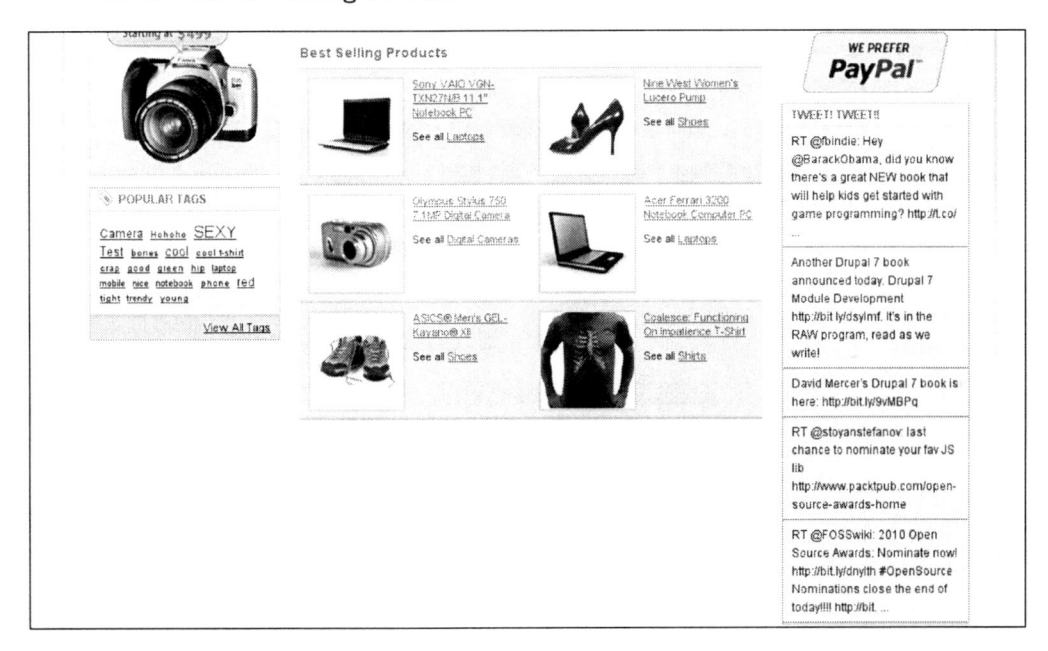

How it works...

We used `Zend_Feed_Rss` class to parse the RSS feed, which returns an array of feeds. We have iterated through the array and rendered it in the content of the sidebar.

We have modified the home page from CMS section, more specifically the layout template xml to call the newly created template `tweets.phtml`.

CMS and Design

Placing the trusty old contact form in CMS

A contact form is an effective way to interact with the user. We will place the trusty old contact form in CMS so that the store owner can edit the content any time.

Magento has a built-in contact form, which can be used to accept user's feedback through e-mail specified in the admin area.

If you want to provide an option in the admin area to edit the content of the contact form with some additional data like contact address, and so on, here is how to do it...

Getting ready

Magento's built-in contact form is hardcoded; this form is located in the `app/design/frontend/YOUR_PACKAGE/YOUR_THEME/template/contacts` directory. There is no option to edit the content from CMS.

How to do it...

1. Log in to Magento's admin area and point your browser to **CMS | Pages**.
2. Now click on the **Add New Page** button located at the top-right corner. A new page form will be shown.
3. Let's enter the contact form details as per the following screenshot:

Chapter 2

4. We will add the content now. Click on the content link from the left sidebar. Click on the **Show/Hide Editor** button to hide the editor and paste the following code inside the textarea:

   ```
   <p>{{block type='core/template' name='contactForm'
   template='contacts/form.phtml'}}</p>
   <h4>Other forms of contact</h4>
   <p>Packt Publishing Ltd</p>
   <p>32 Lincoln Road</p>
   <p>Olton</p>
   <p>Birmingham B27 6PA</p>
   <p>UK</p>
   <p>You can reach us by mail with info{at}packtpub{dot}com</p>
   <script type="text/javascript">
   element = $("contactForm");
   element.writeAttribute('action', '/contacts/index/post');
   </script>
   ```

5. Let's add some design information in it. Click on **Design link** from the left panel and select two columns with left bar from the Layout select box.

6. Save the newly added contact page.

7. Add a new menu named Contact in the `app/design/frontend/base/default/template/catalog/navigation/top.phtml` file.

   ```
   <!-- NEW CONTACT BUTTON LINK -->
   <li class="contact">
     <a href="<?php echo $this->getUrl('contact')?>">
       <?php echo $this->__('Contact') ?>
     </a>
   </li>
   <!-- NEW CONTACT BUTTON LINK
   ```

8. It's time to add some CSS stuff in the `menu.css` file from `skin/frontend/YOUR_PACKAGE/YOUR_THEME/css/` directory. Let us add some style for active state on contact link like the others in the top menu bar:

   ```
   body.cms-contact #nav li.contact a { color:#d96708; }
   ```

CMS and Design

9. We are done! Now point your browser to the newly added contact page. In my case, it's `http://magento.local.com/contact` and it looks like the following screenshot:

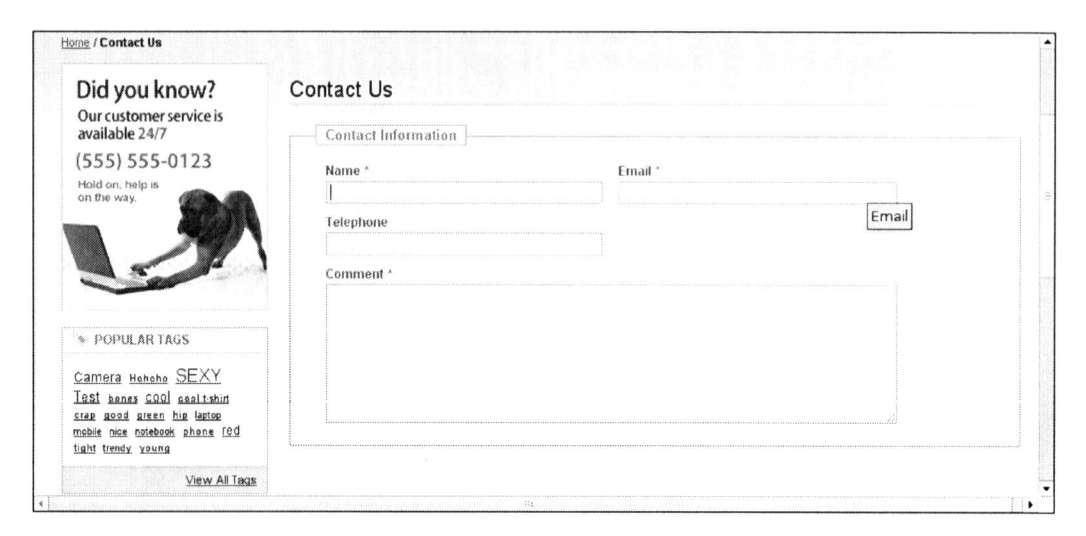

How it works...

We have created a new page in Magento CMS named `Contact` with URL key contact. Finally, we added a new link at the top menu bar and pointed it to the newly created URL key.

Magento has got a contact form by default. This is one of the most forgotten features as it's not seen in the default layout easily. You can navigate this page at contacts.

In fact, we are submitting our contact form to forms to use the configurations from `Mage_contacts` module. From the backend, the sender's reply to e-mail and templates could be modified. Alternately, you can modify the contents of `form.phtml` instead of creating a new page in CMS.

Integrating JW Image Rotator 3.17 in Magento

JW Image Rotator is a very popular Adobe Flash-based image gallery with many options to modify the look and feel, and smooth effects and transitions. You can grab it from `http://www.longtailvideo.com/players/jw-image-rotator/`.

Getting ready

Grab the latest release of JW Image Rotator from `http://www.longtailvideo.com/players/jw-image-rotator/`.

How to do it...

1. Extract the downloaded files and copy the `imagerotator.swf` in the `/media/content/flash/` directory.
2. Create a new directory named `imagerotator` in `/js` directory and paste the extracted `swfobject.js` file in it.
3. Drop some images in `media/content/images/` folder for showing in JW Image Rotator, which will be linked in `packt.xml` file. Create a new XML file named `packt.xml` in the `media/content/flash/` directory and paste the following code:

```xml
<?xml version="1.0" encoding="utf-8"?>
<playlist version="1" xmlns="http://xspf.org/ns/0/">
  <trackList>
    <track>
      <title>Amisha patel</title>
        <creator>PACKT PUBLISHERS</creator>
          <location>http://magento.local.com/media/content/images/
          amisha.jpg</location>
          <info>http://www.packtpub.com</info>
    </track>
    <track>
      <title>Gold fish</title>
        <creator>PACKT PUBLISHERS</creator>
          <location>http://magento.local.com/media/content/
          images/fish.jpg</location>
          <info>http://www.packtpub.com</info>
    </track>
    <track>
      <title>Bolt</title>
        <creator>PACKT PUBLISHERS</creator>
          <location>http://magento.local.com/media/content/
          images/bolt.jpg</location>
          <info>http://www.packtpub.com</info>
    </track>
  </trackList>
</playlist>
```

4. Replace the title location and other information as required.

CMS and Design

5. We have to add the `swfobject.js` file from the `js/imagerotator/` directory through the `page.xml` file, which is located in the `app/design/frontend/YOUR_INTERFACE/YOUR_THEME/layout/` directory. In the head block, add this line to load the `swfobject.js` file (possibly in line 37):

   ```
   <action method="addJs"><script>imagerotator/swfobject.js</script></action>
   ```

6. Let's add this gallery to our home page now. Log in to Magento admin area and open the home page from **CMS | Pages | Home Page | Content**.

7. Paste the following code inside the `<div class="home-spot">` tag:

   ```
   <div id="packtGallery" style="text-align:center;"><a href="http://www.adobe.com/go/getflashplayer" target="_blank"> <img src="http://www.adobe.com/macromedia/style_guide/images/160x41_Get_Flash_Player.jpg" alt="" /> </a>
   <p>Hey! To view the section below as an interactive content feed</p>
   <p>please install the latest version of the Adobe Flash Player clicking <a href="http://www.adobe.com/go/getflashplayer" target="_blank">here</a></p>
   </div>
   <script type="text/javascript">// <![CDATA[
     var gallery = new SWFObject("http://magento.local.com/media/content/flash/imagerotator.swf","packtGallery","470","230","9","#FFFFFF", "http://magento.local.com/media/content/flash/expressInstall.swf");
     gallery.addParam("allowfullscreen","true");
     gallery.addParam("wmode","transparent");
     gallery.addParam("allowscriptaccess","always");
     gallery.addParam("flashvars", "file=http://magento.local.com/media/content/flash/packt.xml&autostart=true&allowscriptaccess=always&showicons=false&transition=slowfade&shownavigation=true&overstretch=true&backcolor=0x000000&repeat=true&rotatetime=5&shuffle=false&linktarget=_self&linkfromdisplay=true&width=470&height=230");
     gallery.write("packtGallery");
   // ]]></script>
   ```

8. Save the home page now and see it in action. You should see something like this:

How it works...

JW Image Rotator is a very simple tool to use. We just downloaded and extracted it. Then we copied the `swfobject.js` and `imagerotator.swf` files to the `/js/imagerotator/` and `/media/content/flash/` directories respectively.

After that we created a new `packt.xml` file to add the image tracks there to show in the gallery. We also replaced the home page static skin image with our JW Image Rotator by using a small code snippet. This snippet simply invokes the flash player to render the image gallery.

There's more...

You can see more information on this tool from the LongTail Ad Solutions website: `http://www.longtailvideo.com/players/jw-image-rotator/`.

3
Adding Extra Functionalities

In this chapter, we will cover:

- Integrating WordPress in Magento
- Creating a new page
- Adding jQuery support
- Adding Lightbox2 in Magento
- Adding an accepted payment banner at the footer

Introduction

We always need to design an eCommerce store in a user-friendly way so that any customer feels comfortable while browsing the shop. We will add some cool functionality in our shop within this chapter for making our shop more user friendly.

Integrating WordPress in Magento

WordPress has been a very popular CMS. Integrating WordPress in Magento has become a hot topic in Magento forum. We will integrate and modify the look and feel of our blog just like the main shop.

Getting ready

We need to download the latest WordPress from `http://wordpress.org/latest.tar.gz`. I have used WordPress 3.0.1 version.

Adding Extra Functionalities

How to do it...

1. After downloading the WordPress, we have to extract it to our Magento project's directory and rename it to `blog`.

2. Let's point our browser to the blog. In my case, it's `http://magento.local.com/blog`, and then fire up the installation process.

3. All the installation steps are self-explanatory, so follow them and complete the installation process.

4. We will create a theme for our new WordPress blog. For a standard WordPress theme skeleton, let's copy the default theme (Twenty Ten) and paste it as Magento folder name in `/blog/wp-content/themes/` directory.

5. Remove all files except those with `*.php` extensions from `blog/wp-content/themes/magento` folder.

6. Copy the CSS files and images of your Magento active theme from `skin/frontend/default/default/` and paste them in `blog/wp-content/themes/magento/` folder.

7. Okay, let's play with the code now! Fire up your Editor IDE and open the `style.css` file from `blog/wp-content/themes/magento` directory.

8. The `style.css` content should be something like this (if you use the default Magento theme):

```
/*
Theme Name: Magento
Theme URI: http://dynamicguy.com/
Description: The Magento theme for wordpress created with magento
default theme based on Twenty Ten
Author: Your Name
Version: 1.0
Tags: black, blue, white, two-columns, fixed-width, custom-header,
theme-options, threaded-comments, sticky-post, translation-ready,
microformats, rtl-language-support
*/
@import 'css/styles.css';
#s{
  border-color: 1px solid #5C7989;
  margin-right: 4px;
  width: 140px;
}
```

9. Let's modify the header and footer to make it look like our main Magento store. Find and open the `header.php` file from `/blog/wp-content/themes/` directory and assign the required classes and IDs to the relevant nodes. I have added a left sidebar in `header.php` file to show some widget stuff.

> You will find the final theme source code with this book as archive.

10. Open the `footer.php` as we did before with `header.php` and make the changes.
11. You will find `<?php get_sidebar(); ?>` in almost every PHP file in the theme directory, we have to disable this function with a preceding comment like this: `<?php //get_sidebar(); ?>`. Let's hunt it down as we have already shown a left sidebar in `header.php` file.
12. After activating your new Magento theme, we might be interested to add the menus from Magento store in our blog. You can add any number of custom menus in your WordPress admin panel. Here is a screenshot after adding some custom menus in WordPress admin panel:

13. When you are done with all the steps mentioned previously, give it a go!

Adding Extra Functionalities

How it works...

Let's explain how these steps allow us to integrate WordPress. We just installed a new WordPress installation like any other web installer in the same database of Magento. Then we modified the theme structure to fit it in our current store by adding some CSS ID and classes.

There's more...

Though there are some other practices that make WordPress fall under the same hood in Magento, like parsing the RSS feed, pointing all 404 pages to the blog with default no-route block, this is still way better to keep them in their own place. Redirecting a 404 page to the blog is not a very good decision.

A typical blog in Magento might look like this:

See Also

If you want to add a blog menu in the main navigation then the *Adding a home link to the menu bar* recipe of *Chapter 2, CMS and Design* in this book would be helpful.

Creating a new page

Creating a new page in Magento is pretty easy to do. In this recipe, we are going to create a new page and add it to the footer block by using Magento CMS.

Getting ready

Log in to Magento admin panel for creating a **Terms of Service** page from Magento admin area.

How to do it...

1. Enter the Magento admin area and point your browser to **CMS | Pages** menu.
2. Click the **Add New Page** button from the top-right corner.
3. You should see an empty field for newly created page. Fill it up and save the changes you made.
4. Let me tell you what I entered there in the **Page Information** menu:
   - **Page Title**: Terms of Service
   - **URL Key**: tos
   - **Store view**: All Store Views
   - **Status**: enabled
5. Enter some data in **Content**, **Design**, and **Meta Data** sections.
6. Save all changes.
7. Now, we will add this newly created page into our store footer menu block. Point your cursor to **CMS | Static Blocks**. You will see a listing page with all the static blocks.
8. Click on **Footer Links** to open it.
9. Find and click on the button **Show/Hide Editor**.
10. Append the following line at the end of the `<ul>` tag:
    ```
    <li class="last">
      <a title="TOS" href="{{store direct_url="tos"}}">Terms of service</a>
    </li>
    ```
11. The final source code for **Footer Links** block should be something like this:
    ```
    <ul>
    <li><a href="{{store direct_url="about-magento-demo-store"}}">About Us</a></li>
    <li><a href="{{store direct_url="customer-service"}}">Customer Service</a></li>
    ```

```
<li class="last"><a title="TOS" href="{{store direct_
url="tos"}}">Terms of service</a></li>
</ul>
```

12. Click on the **Save Block** button from the top-right corner.
13. Give it a go! Point your browser to any one of your Magento store pages; you will see a new link has arrived in the footer named **Terms of Service**, click on it!
14. You should see the page you created in action now!

How it works...

Magento CMS has been evolved to version 1.4.0.0 with a great content management system. One can easily create a new page and add it to any block as he/she needs with a user-friendly graphical interface by TinyMCE. Now creating a gorgeous page in Magento store and linking it to a block is just a matter of couple of mouse clicks and keystrokes.

Magento uses its own replacement tags to render dynamic content in CMS pages, e-mail templates, and static blocks. You might have noticed that in CMS pages and static blocks there are some `{{ double curly brace wrapped }}` items with some attributes. These are known as template tags. In this recipe, we used the store tag only while there were five other tags. Some of the template tags are as follows:

- **Block**: This creates a static block with specified ID. For example: `{{block type='core/template' template='cms/your_page.phtml'}}`
- **Layout**: This renders an HTML layout output for the specified layout. The handle attribute expects the name of a layout handle. For example: `{{layout handle="default"}}`
- **Media**: This retrieves path of files from `root/media` folder. For example: `{{media url="images/logo.png"}}`
- **Skin**: This gets files from active theme in `skin/frontend` folder. For example: `<img src="{{skin url='images/media/about_us.png'}}"/>`
- **Store**: This creates routes and custom URLs for Magento store. For example: `{{store url="contact"}}` would render the full URL for that path.
- **htmlescape**: This escapes html characters as its name suggests. For example: `{{htmlescape var=""}}`
- **var**: This renders a variable. For example: `{{var my_variable}}`
- **protocol**: This renders the proper protocol (HTTP or HTTPS) depending on current context. For example: `{{protocol url="www.domain.com/"}}`

If you want to see the methods that handle this stuff you can have a look on `app/code/core/Mage/Core/Model/Email/Template/Filter.php`.

Adding jQuery support

jQuery is a very popular JavaScript framework among the developers with a small footprint. DOM Programming does bring in its challenges while handling the browser-specific quirks. JQuery provides quite a few utilities to help working in a browser agnostic environment. jQuery has a wide variety of plugins. If we can add jQuery in Magento, we can also use some cool jQuery plugins as well.

Magento has already three `js` frameworks (prototype, scriptaculous, and extjs) for handling the frontend logics. Adding yet another JS framework like jQuery will cause a conflict with their factory methods. JQuery library and virtually all of these plugins are wrapped within the JQuery namespace. *Global* objects are stored inside JQuery namespace and there shouldn't be any name conflict with prototype. Let's cite an example:

```
Prototype example: $('comments').addClassName('active').show();
jQuery example: $("div.slide").slideup("slow").addClass("removed");
```

Note that both libraries are using $ as factory method. You can override the default $ function using `jQuery.noconflict()` at any point in JQuery and other libraries like this:

```
<html>
    <head>
        <script type="text/javascript" src="prototype.js"></script>
        <script type="text/javascript" src="jquery.js"></script>
        <script type="text/javascript">
            jQuery.noConflict();
            // Use jQuery via jQuery(...)
            jQuery(document).ready(function()
            {
                jQuery("div").hide();
            });
            // Use Prototype with $(...).
            $('HTMLid').hide();
        </script>
    </head>
    <body>

    </body>
</html>
```

At the end of this recipe, we will get a 3D rotating tag cloud for our Magento store. Let's assume that we have a tag cloud in our home page and we are going to make it a ROTATING 3D TAG CLOUD!!

Adding Extra Functionalities

Getting ready

We will use jQuery and one jQuery plugin to make it done. Let us grab these files from the following location:

- **jQuery**: http://jquery.com
- **tagoSphere plugin**: http://plugins.jquery.com/project/tagosphere

How to do it...

1. Create a new folder named `jquery` in `/js/` directory.
2. Create another folder in `/js/jquery/` directory with name `plugins`.
3. Drop the latest jQuery file in `/js/jquery` directory. I used the minified one: `jquery-1.4.2.min.js`.
4. Place the downloaded plugin file named `jquery.tagosphere.js` in the `/js/jquery/plugins` folder.
5. Okay, let's include it in our layout then! Open the file named `page.xml` from `app/design/frontend/YOUR_PACKAGE/YOUR_THEME/layout` folder and add the following two lines in the block with the name `head`. Add two actions in the head block by adding the following two lines at the beginning of block. Make sure that you added it before prototype.

    ```
    <action method="addJs"><script>jquery/jquery-1.4.2.min.js</script></action>
    <action method="addJs"><script>jquery/plugins/jquery.tagosphere.js</script></action>
    ```

6. After adding these two lines the head block should look like this:

    ```
    <block type="page/html_head" name="head" as="head">
       <action method="addJs"><script>jquery/jquery-1.4.2.min.js</script></action>
       <action method="addJs"><script>jquery/plugins/jquery.tagosphere.js</script></action>
       <action method="addJs"><script>prototype/prototype.js</script></action>
       <action method="addJs" ifconfig="dev/js/deprecation"><script>prototype/deprecation.js</script></action>
       <action method="addJs"><script>lib/ccard.js</script></action>
       <action method="addJs"><script>prototype/validation.js</script></action>
       <action method="addJs"><script>scriptaculous/builder.js</script></action>
       <action method="addJs"><script>scriptaculous/effects.js</script></action>
    ```

```xml
<action method="addJs"><script>scriptaculous/dragdrop.js</script></action>
<action method="addJs"><script>scriptaculous/controls.js</script></action>
<action method="addJs"><script>scriptaculous/slider.js</script></action>
<action method="addJs"><script>varien/js.js</script></action>
<action method="addJs"><script>varien/form.js</script></action>
<action method="addJs"><script>varien/menu.js</script></action>
<action method="addJs"><script>mage/translate.js</script></action>
<action method="addJs"><script>mage/cookies.js</script></action>
<action method="addCss"><stylesheet>css/styles.css</stylesheet></action>
<action method="addItem"><type>skin_css</type><name>css/styles-ie.css</name><params/><if>lt IE 8</if></action>
<action method="addCss"><stylesheet>css/widgets.css</stylesheet></action>
<action method="addCss"><stylesheet>css/print.css</stylesheet><params>media="print"</params></action>
<action method="addItem"><type>js</type><name>lib/ds-sleight.js</name><params/><if>lt IE 7</if></action>
<action method="addItem"><type>skin_js</type><name>js/ie6.js</name><params/><if>lt IE 7</if></action>
</block>
```

7. Open both the JavaScript files that we have added now and append the following line at the end of each file to resolve conflicts:

   `jQuery.noConflict();`

8. Let us modify the template file now for popular tags. Look for the file `popular.phtml` from `app/design/frontend/base/default/template/tag/` directory and replace the existing code with the following code:

```
<div class="block block-tags">
  <div class="block-title">
    <strong><span><?php echo $this->__('Popular Tags'); ?></span></strong>
  </div>
  <div class="block-content content" id="tagoSphere">
    <ul>
      <?php foreach ($this->getTags() as $_tag): ?>
        <li><a href="<?php echo $_tag->getTaggedProductsUrl() ?>" style="font-size:<?php echo $_tag->getRatio()*70+75 ?>%;"><?php
```

Adding Extra Functionalities

```
      echo $this->htmlEscape($_tag->getName()) ?></a></li>
        <?php endforeach; ?>
      </ul>
      <div class="actions">
        <a href="<?php echo $this->getUrl('tag/list') ?>"><?php echo
$this->__('View All Tags') ?></a>
      </div>
    </div>
</div>
<script type="text/javascript">
  var settings = {
    //height of sphere container
    height: 193,
    //width of sphere container
    width: 193,
    //radius of sphere
    radius: 45,
    //rotation speed
    speed: 3,
    //sphere rotations slower
    slower: 0.97,
    //delay between update position
    timer: 10,
    //dependence of a font size on axis Z
    fontMultiplier: 15,
    //tag css stylies on mouse over
    hoverStyle: {
      border: 'none',
      color: '#6f0b0b'
    },
    //tag css stylies on mouse out
    mouseOutStyle: {
      border: '',
      color: ''
    }
  };

  jQuery(document).ready(function(){
    jQuery('#tagoSphere').tagoSphere(settings);
  });
</script>
```

How it works...

Like any other jQuery plugins the tagoSphere plugin deals with jQuery. I have written this plugin earlier. We just added the jQuery file and the plugin in our layout and added an extra line to resolve the conflict between prototype and jQuery, which is a jQuery function:

```
jQuery.noConflict();
```

Thus, we wrote jQuery codes with jQuery rather than $ in `popular.phtml` file. We set a settings variable to pass as parameter for our plugin. You can play with the settings to make it as you want. Give it a go now!

Adding Lightbox2 in Magento

"Lightbox is a simple, unobtrusive script used to overlay images on the current page. It's a snap to setup and works on all modern browsers." This the slogan that has been used on its project overview page by its creator *Lokesh Dhakar*.

It's a popular and widely used tool in modern web applications for its elegant styles and easy implementation. While it was initially developed from scratch, Lightbox has since been modified to use a number of *JavaScript libraries* (such as the *Prototype JavaScript Framework* and *script.aculo.us* for its animations and positioning), in order to reduce the size of the code and the ultimate result is Lightbox2.

Integrating Lightbox2 in Magento is pretty simple if you know the Magento files and codes to handle it. The good news is Magento has already included the JavaScript libraries, which were required for Lightbox2.

In a short while, we shall integrate Lightbox2 for our shop's product images in the product details page.

Adding Extra Functionalities

Getting ready

Go and grab a copy of Lightbox2 from `http://www.lokeshdhakar.com/projects/lightbox2/`.

How to do it...

1. We have the Lightbox2 archive that we downloaded from `http://www.lokeshdhakar.com/projects/lightbox2/`. Let's extract it.

2. Open `/skin/frontend/YOUR_PACKAGE/YOUR_THEME/js/` and create a new directory named `lightbox` (in my case, it's `/skin/frontend/default/default/js/`) and put `lightbox.js` in this directory.

3. Open `lightbox.js` file in your editor and replace the last line with the following code:

   ```
   var myLightbox;
   document.observe('dom:loaded', function () { myLightbox = new Lightbox(); });
   ```

4. Find these two lines in `lightbox.js` and replace them with the following highlighted code:

   ```
   fileLoadingImage: 'images/loading.gif',
   fileBottomNavCloseImage: 'images/closelabel.gif',

   fileLoadingImage: SKIN_URL + 'images/lightbox/loading.gif',
   fileBottomNavCloseImage: SKIN_URL + 'images/lightbox/closelabel.gif',
   ```

5. Now copy `lightbox.css` to the `/skin/frontend/YOUR_PACKAGE/YOUR_THEME/css/` directory (in my case, it's `/skin/frontend/default/default/css/`).

6. Let's add the required images. Find and open the `/skin/frontend/YOUR_PACKAGE/YOUR_THEME/images` directory (in most cases, it would be `/skin/frontend/default/default/images/`).

7. Create a new directory named `lightbox` and paste all the images from the lightbox into it.

8. We shall modify the `lightbox.css` file now to load UI images correctly.

9. Open: `/skin/frontend/default/default/css/lightbox.css` and then apply these find and replace as specified:

   Replace:
   ```
   background: transparent url(../images/blank.gif) no-repeat;
   ```

Chapter 3

With:

```
background: transparent url(../images/lightbox/blank.gif) no-repeat;
```

Replace:

```
#prevLink:hover, #prevLink:visited:hover { background: url(../images/prevlabel.gif) left 15% no-repeat; }
```

With:

```
#prevLink:hover, #prevLink:visited:hover { background: url(../images/lightbox/prevlabel.gif) left 15% no-repeat; }
```

Replace:

```
#nextLink:hover, #nextLink:visited:hover { background: url(../images/nextlabel.gif) right 15% no-repeat; }
```

With:

```
#nextLink:hover, #nextLink:visited:hover { background: url(../images/lightbox/nextlabel.gif) right 15% no-repeat; }
```

10. Okay, let's modify the template files now. Open /app/design/frontend/YOUR_PACKAGE/YOUR_THEME/template/page/html/head.phtml.

11. Find this code snippet and replace it with the following highlighted code:

```
<!--[if lt IE 7]>
<script type="text/javascript"//<![CDATA[
    var BLANK_URL = '<?php echo $this->helper('core/js')->getJsUrl('blank.html') ?>';
    var BLANK_IMG = '<?php echo $this->helper('core/js')->getJsUrl('spacer.gif') ?>';
//]]>
</script>
<![endif]-->
```

Replace it with:

```
<script type="text/javascript">
    var SKIN_URL = '<?php echo $this->helper('core/js')->getJsSkinUrl('') ?>';
</script>
<!--[if lt IE 7]>
<script type="text/javascript">
//<![CDATA[
    var BLANK_URL = '<?php echo $this->helper('core/js')->getJsUrl('blank.html') ?>';
    var BLANK_IMG = '<?php echo $this->helper('core/js')->getJsUrl('spacer.gif') ?>';
//]]>
</script>
<![endif]-->
```

Adding Extra Functionalities

12. Notice that we added another script block to declare our new `SKIN_URL` variable.

13. We have to add the `lightbox2.js` and CSS files in Magento template's head section. We can do this by modifying the `page.xml` file from `/app/design/frontend/YOUR_PACKAGE/YOUR_THEME/layout/` directory. Find and open `page.xml` file and look for the following line:

    ```
    <action method="addJs"><script>mage/cookies.js</script></action>
    ```

14. Then add the following lines before it. In my case, it's at line number 50.

    ```
    <!--lightbox specific-->
    <action method="addItem">
    <type>skin_js</type><name>js/lightbox.js</name>
    </action>
    <action method="addCss">
    <stylesheet>css/lightbox.css</stylesheet>
    </action>
    <!--end lightbox specific-->
    ```

15. It's okay now to edit the `/app/design/frontend/bases/default/template/catalog/product/view/media.phtml` file. Open it and look for the following code:

    ```
    <?php foreach ($this->getGalleryImages() as $_image): ?>
    <li>
    <a href="#" onclick="popWin('<?php echo $this->getGalleryUrl($_image) ?>', 'gallery', 'scrollbars=yes,width=200,height=200,resizable=yes');return false;">
    <img src="<?php echo $this->helper('catalog/image')->init($this->getProduct(), 'thumbnail', $_image->getFile())->resize(68,68); ?>" alt="<?php echo $this->htmlEscape($_image->getLabel()) ?>" title="<?php echo $this->htmlEscape($_image->getLabel()) ?>"/>
    </a>
    </li>
    <?php endforeach; ?>
    ```

    Replace it with:

    ```
    <?php foreach ($this->getGalleryImages() as $_image): ?>
      <li>
        <a href="<?php echo $this->helper('catalog/image')->init($this->getProduct(), 'image', $_image->getFile())->resize(640, 480); ?>" rel="lightbox[rotation]" title="<?php echo $_product->getName();?>">
          <img src="<?php echo $this->helper('catalog/image')->init($this->getProduct(), 'thumbnail', $_image->getFile())->resize(68, 68); ?>" width="68" height="68" alt=""/>
        </a>
      </li>
    <?php endforeach; ?>
    ```

16. In `media.phtml` you should replace:

    ```php
    <?php
    $_img = '<img id="image" src="'.$this->helper('catalog/image')-
    >init($_product, 'image').'" alt="'.$this->htmlEscape($this-
    >getImageLabel()).'" title="'.$this->htmlEscape($this-
    >getImageLabel()).'" />';
    echo $_helper->productAttribute($_product, $_img, 'image')
    ?>
    ```

    With:

    ```php
    <?php
    $_img = '<img id="image" src="'.$this->helper('catalog/
    image')->init($_product, 'image').'" alt="'.$this-
    >htmlEscape($this->getImageLabel()).'" title="'.$this-
    >htmlEscape($this->getImageLabel()).'" ondblclick="myLightbox.
    start($(\'imageLink\'));"/>';
    echo $_helper->productAttribute($_product, $_img, 'image')
    ?>
    <a href="<?php echo $this->helper('catalog/image')->init($_
    product, 'image'); ?>" id="imageLink" rel="lightbox"></a>
    ```

    Next find:

    ```
    <script type="text/javascript">
    Event.observe(window, 'load', function() {
    product_zoom = new Product.Zoom('image', 'track', 'handle', 'zoom_
    in', 'zoom_out', 'track_hint');
    });
    </script>
    ```

    Replace with:

    ```
    <script type="text/javascript">
     Event.observe(window, 'load', function() {
     product_zoom = new Product.Zoom('image', 'track', 'handle',
    'zoom_in', 'zoom_out', 'track_hint');
     Event.stopObserving($('image'), 'dblclick', null);
     });
    </script>
    ```

17. It's time to refresh the cache (if it's enabled). Log in to **Admin Dashboard** then point your browser to **System | Cache Management** and be sure to change **All cache** settings from **No change** to **REFRESH** and then click the **Images Cache—Clear** button.

18. Navigate to any product details page now and try to click on any of the *more images* or double-click on the product main image to see the lightbox2 in action!

Adding Extra Functionalities

How it works...

Lightbox2 is pretty straightforward to use. If you want to display the large image in the same page without page reload and with an elegant style, all you have to do is add the required JavaScript libraries such as the Prototype JavaScript framework and script.aculo.us for its animations and positioning. Magento comes with these libraries by default. So, we added only the `lightbox.js`, `lightbox.css`, and lightbox images for the previous and next navigation. Finally, we added a `rel="lightbox"` attribute to initiate the image opening in lightbox. In the more images section, we added the `rel` attribute as `rel="lightbox[rotation]"` as a group for previous and next navigation. The caption for each image is extracted from the anchor title attribute.

We have also disabled the observe event by calling the following:

```
Event.stopObserving($('image'), 'dblclick', null);
```

Now, if we double-click on a product's main image in the product details page, it will be opened in lightbox2 with a larger size. If the product image has more views that can also be viewed in lightbox2. You can try clicking on the product images in any product details page now.

If everything goes well, you should see a page something like the following:

Adding an accepted payment banner at the footer

Credit card icons are an essential part of every online shop. They are often used to indicate available payment conditions and purchasing options. The clearer they are presented in the online shop, the easier it is for potential customers to figure out if they actually can pay online in this shop or not. Therefore, when it comes to the design of an online shop, there is no way to get around using some credit card icons.

Getting ready

Collect required specific credit card icons, for instance, the icons of a regional bank in your country; make sure to visit the official site of the bank first to get the most recent icons. They are usually presented in the sections titled *logo center*, *brand materials*, *media center*, and so on. Credit cards may also look different depending on the country they are supposed to be used in. I have used some typical free credit card icons from `http://www.virtuallnk.com/credit-card-icons.aspx`.

How to do it...

1. Let's assume that you have already collected the credit card icons that will be shown in the accepted payment banner.

2. Fire up your file explorer and point it to the `skin/frontend/default/default/images/` directory. Now, create a new directory there named `payment_logos` and paste your logos in it.

3. Find and open the file named `footer.phtml` from `app/design/frontend/base/default/template/page/html/` directory. Look for the block as:

   ```
   <!-- start footer -->
     <div class="footer-container">
       <div class="footer">
         <?php echo $this->getChildHtml('footer') ?>
       </div>
     </div>
   <!-- end footer -->
   ```

4. Modify this block and make it like this one:

   ```
   <!-- start footer -->
     <div class="footer-container">
       <div class="footer">
         <?php echo $this->getChildHtml('footer') ?>
       </div>
       <div id="payment-logos">
   ```

Adding Extra Functionalities

```
            <ul class="mini-product-tags">
            <li><img src="<?php echo $this-
            >getSkinUrl('images/payment_logos/amex.png'); ?>"
            alt="amex"/></li>
            <li><img src="<?php echo $this-
            >getSkinUrl('images/payment_logos/discover.png'); ?>"
            alt="discover"/></li>
            <li><img src="<?php echo $this-
            >getSkinUrl('images/payment_logos/eCheck.png'); ?>"
            alt="eCheck"/></li>
            <li><img src="<?php echo $this-
            >getSkinUrl('images/payment_logos/masterCard.png'); ?>"
            alt="master card"/></li>
            <li><img src="<?php echo $this-
            >getSkinUrl('images/payment_logos/paypal.png'); ?>"
            alt="paypal"/></li>
            <li><img src="<?php echo $this-
            >getSkinUrl('images/payment_logos/visa.png'); ?>"
            alt="visa"/></li>
            </ul>
        </div>
    </div>
<!-- end footer -->
```

5. Repeat steps 3 and 4 in other template files such as `2columns-left.phtml`, `1column.phtml`, and `3columns.phtml`, if you want it or you can put it in `app/design/frontend/base/default/template/page/html/footer.phtml`, so that it would be called in every page.

6. Reload your shop home page to see the accepted payment banner in action. It should be something like the following screenshot:

How it works...

We added the credit card logos in our skin's images directory. Then we added an unordered list with credit card images, after the footer block, to show as an accepted payment banner. We used predefined class from `boxes.css` to show the list items inline with a little bit of padding.

Alternatively, you can and should add the markup in `app/design/frontend/base/default/template/page/2columns-right.phtml` file just for the purpose of adding it in a specific template file. I put this in `footer.phtml` just to give you an idea and bypassing some extra CSS tweaks.

4
Customizing a Store

In this chapter, we will cover:

- Creating a custom "Twitter handle" field in a registration form
- Deleting orders in Magento
- Using Google Website Optimizer
- Creating a custom variable and using its own e-mail templates
- Using Google analytics for Magento
- Creating Catalog and Shopping Cart Price Rules
- Creating a featured product and showing it in the home page
- Creating a custom admin theme

Introduction

It's very important to customize the Magento store for making a successful online store. Magento comes without some features that we need while we customize our store. In this chapter, we will focus on those vulnerable features, which are a must for any successful online store.

Creating a custom "Twitter handle" field in a registration form

Magento came up with a simple account creation page, which sometimes is not enough for some shop owners who want some more user information. If we want to add a new registration field like user's Twitter ID or something like that, then we have no option in the admin panel to add such a field. We can do it by writing some code. It's easy!

Customizing a Store

In this recipe, we will add a new optional registration field for collecting user's Twitter handle, as nowadays people are crazy for the much-hyped Twitter. Furthermore, we can use Twitter for marketing and product analysis purposes.

Getting ready

Let's fire up our IDE and open the Magento project, where we will write some code for adding the Twitter handle registration field.

How to do it...

1. Magento uses the **Entity-Attribute-Value** (**EAV**) data model for manipulating data in a more flexible way. In an EAV data model, data is usually stored in three columns:
    - **Entity**: This is the item being described
    - **Attribute** or **parameter**: A foreign key into a table of attribute definitions
    - **Value**: This is the value of the attribute

2. We have to add a new EAV attribute for the new Twitter field to save the user's Twitter field with registration data. We will add it by executing a code snippet from `register.phtml` file located in:

    `app/design/frontend/YOUR_PACKAGE/YOUR_THEME/template/customer/form/`

3. Open the aforementioned file (in my case, the file location is `app/design/frontend/base/default/template/customer/form`).

4. Now paste the following code snippet at the beginning of the file:

    ```php
    <?php
      $setup = new Mage_Eav_Model_Entity_Setup('core_setup');
      $setup->addAttribute('customer', 'twitter', array(
        'label'    => 'Twitter handle',
        'type'     => 'varchar',
        'input'    => 'text',
        'visible'  => true,
        'required' => false,
        'position' => 1
      ));
    ?>
    ```

5. Let's find a place to put our Twitter field. Look for the following lines:

    ```
    <li>
      <label for="email_address"><?php echo $this->__('Email Address')
      ?> <span class="required">*</span></label><br/>
    ```

Chapter 4

```
<input type="text" name="email" id="email_address" value="<?php 
echo $this->htmlEscape($this->getFormData()->getEmail()) ?>" 
title="<?php echo $this->__('Email Address') ?>" class="validate-
email required-entry input-text" />
    </li>
```

6. Now replace the preceding code with the following (actually we added a new `<li>` element with our new Twitter field):

```
<li>
  <label for="email_address" class="required"><em>*</em><?php echo 
$this->__('Email Address') ?></label>
  <div class="input-box">
    <input type="text" name="email" id="email_address" 
value="<?php echo $this->htmlEscape($this->getFormData()-
>getEmail()) ?>" title="<?php echo $this->__('Email Address') ?>" 
class="input-text validate-email required-entry" />
  </div>
</li>
<li>
  <label for="twitter"><?php echo $this->__('Twitter handle') ?></
label>
  <div class="input-box">
    <input type="text" name="twitter" id="twitter" value="<?php 
echo $this->htmlEscape($this->getFormData()->getTwitter()) ?>" 
title="<?php echo $this->__('Twitter') ?>" class="input-text" />
    <label for="twitter" style="color: #ccc;font-size: 
85%;">Example: @packtpub</label>
  </div>
</li>
```

7. We have to modify the `edit.phtml` file as well so that the user can edit the Twitter information from his account information page. Let's open it from here:

   `app/design/frontend/YOUR_PACKAGE/YOUR_THEME/template/customer/form/`

8. Now find the code snippet (in my case, it is at line number 39):

```
<li>
  <label for="email" class="required"><em>*</em><?php echo $this-
>__('Email Address') ?></label>
  <div class="input-box">
    <input type="text" name="email" id="email" value="<?php 
echo $this->htmlEscape($this->getCustomer()->getEmail()) ?>" 
title="<?php echo $this->__('Email Address') ?>" class="input-text 
required-entry validate-email" />
  </div>
</li>
```

67

Customizing a Store

9. Then replace it with the following (we added another field for our Twitter wrapped in a `<li>` element):

   ```
   <li>
     <label for="email" class="required"><em>*</em></?php echo $this->__('Email Address') ?></label>
     <div class="input-box">
       <input type="text" name="email" id="email" value="<?php echo $this->htmlEscape($this->getCustomer()->getEmail()) ?>" title="<?php echo $this->__('Email Address') ?>" class="input-text required-entry validate-email" />
     </div>
   </li>
   <li>
     <label for="twitter"><?php echo $this->__('Twitter handle') ?></label>
     <div class="input-box">
       <input type="text" name="twitter" id="twitter" value="<?php echo $this->htmlEscape($this->getCustomer()->getTwitter()) ?>" title="<?php echo $this->__('Twitter') ?>" class="input-text" />
       <label for="twitter" style="color: #ccc;font-size: 85%;">Example: @ferdous</label>
     </div>
   </li>
   ```

10. Now that we have added the field in the form, let's add it in our layout config file. Open the `config.xml` file from `app/code/core/Mage/Customer/etc/` directory.

11. Look for the `<global>` block and modify it as shown in the following code snippet (in my `config.xml` file, the global block is at line number 81):

    ```
    <global>
      <fieldsets>
      <customer_account>
        <prefix><create>1</create><update>1</update><name>1</name></prefix>
        <firstname><create>1</create><update>1</update><name>1</name></firstname>
        <middlename><create>1</create><update>1</update><name>1</name></middlename>
        <lastname><create>1</create><update>1</update><name>1</name></lastname>
        <suffix><create>1</create><update>1</update><name>1</name></suffix>
        <email><create>1</create><update>1</update></email>
        <twitter><create>1</create><update>1</update></twitter>
        <password><create>1</create></password>
    ```

```
            <confirmation><create>1</create></confirmation>
            <dob><create>1</create><update>1</update></dob>
            <taxvat><create>1</create><update>1</update></taxvat>
            <gender><create>1</create><update>1</update></gender>
        </customer_account>
    </fieldsets>
```

12. The last step is adding an entity attribute in the setup model. Open the `Setup.php` file from the `app/code/core/Mage/Customer/Model/Entity/` directory. At line number 120 after the email field as:

```
'email' => array(
    'type'          => 'static',
    'label'         => 'Email',
    'class'         => 'validate-email',
    'sort_order'    => 60,
),
```

13. Add the following code snippet for the newly created **Twitter** field, right after the e-mail setup:

```
'twitter' => array(
    'label'         => 'Twitter',
    'required'      => false,
    'sort_order'    => 65,
),
```

14. We are done. Point your browser to create the customer account URL and try to create a new account. You should see a page something like the following screenshot:

Customizing a Store

How it works...

Let's explain how these steps allow us to complete the task or solve the problem. We added a new EAV attribute for the new field Twitter by writing a code snippet in `register.phtml` file and running it.

We added one new text field for our newly created Twitter field in both register and edit form.

Finally, we modified the configuration file and entity model setup for taking care of our newly created **Twitter** field.

Some important gotchas about Twitter for store owners:

- Would you like a way to connect and network with others in your industry or others who share you views?
- Would you like a way to get instant access to what's being said, this minute, about your organization, people, products, or brand?
- Would you like a steady stream of ideas, content, links, resources, and tips focused on your area of expertise or interest?
- Would you like to monitor what's being said about your customers to help them protect their brands?
- Would you like to extend the reach of your thought leadership—blog posts and other content?
- Would you like to promote your products and services directly to a target audience?

If your answer for the previously mentioned questions is YES, then this will help a lot. So, if we can harvest a good amount of Twitter usernames who are our clients, we can communicate with them more conveniently.

Deleting orders in Magento

We got to place some test orders for the sake of development. But when the development process is over, we got to delete those junk orders. Unfortunately, Magento has no such option in the admin panel to delete an order. In the admin panel, what we can do only is—cancel an order.

We will install a cool Magento extension through **Magento Connect** named `Delete Orders` developed by *Boutik Circus*. In fact, the motto of this recipe is to learn "how to install a Magento extension from the admin panel through Magento connect?"

Getting ready

For installing an extension, you got to be a member of the Magento community. If you are not already a member of it, then please register yourself from here: `http://www.magentocommerce.com/boards/member/register/`.

How to do it...

1. Fire up your favorite browser and navigate to `http://www.magentocommerce.com/magento-connect`.
2. Log in with your Magento community username and password.
3. Now look for the **Search for Extensions** textbox from the right-side bar and write `delete orders` in it and hit *Enter/Return* key from your keyboard. The extension search box should be like this:

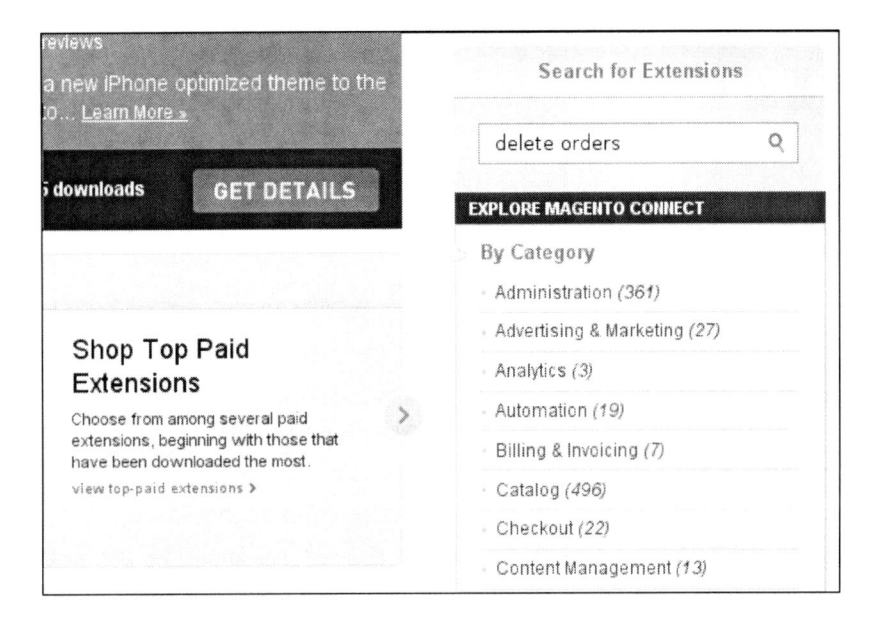

Customizing a Store

4. Now look for the title **Delete Orders** in the result page. You should see it in the first page. Click it to navigate to the **details** page.

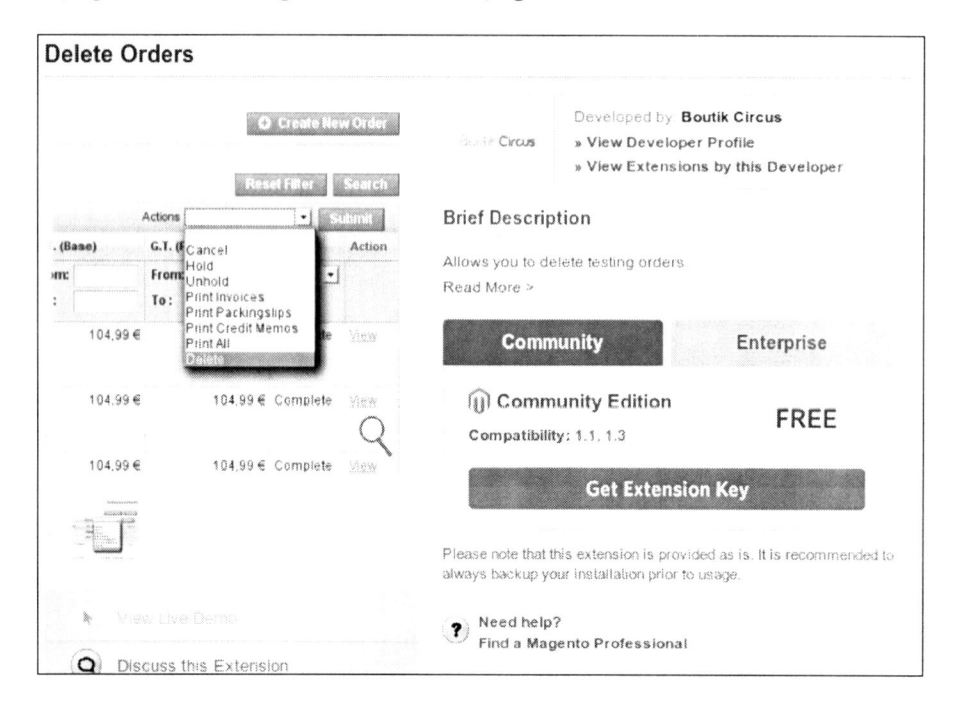

5. Click on the **Get Extension Key** button for retrieving the extension key. If you are not logged in at Magento Connect, please log in now as this is required for getting the extension key. If you don't have an account, please create one. It's free.

6. Agree to the terms, and then copy the extension key. In my case, the key for delete orders extension was: `magento-community/BoutikCircus_DeleteOrders`.

7. Now sign in to your Magento store admin panel.

8. Navigate to **System | Magento Connect | Magento Connect Manager**.

9. Paste in the extension key and click **Install**. The installer should be self explanatory, still if you run into any issues, consult the extension documentation forums on Magento Community.

How it works...

One of the popular features of Magento is its Magento Connect, which really made the store owner's life easier than any other CMS did while installing a new extension. No download things to be done here. Look for the desired extension in Magento Connect site, grab the extension key and paste it in your Magento admin panel, follow the installation steps and voila! You are done! No jail break required!

There's more...

By default, Magento Connect is equipped with stable releases. If you need to install a beta or alpha release, carry out the following procedure:

1. Sign in to your Magento store admin panel.
2. Point your browser to **System | Magento Connect | Magento Connect Manager**.
3. Select the **Settings** tab, and choose the **Preferred State** as **Beta** or **Alpha**.
4. Let's save these settings by clicking on **Save Settings** button.
5. Return to the **Extension** tab, paste the extension key and click **Install**.

Using Google Website Optimizer

What is **Google Website Optimizer** (**GWO**), you might ask? It is Google's free website testing and optimization tool, which allows you to increase the value of your existing websites and traffic without spending a cent.

It's a powerful tool that allows you to test various page concepts directly on your visitors and see which of your ideas works best in practice.

Using Website Optimizer to test and optimize site content and design, you can quickly and easily increase revenue and ROI whether you're new to marketing or an expert.

Magento came up with an easy integration with Website Optimizer in the admin panel. In Magento 1.4 version, we can test the conversion rate for the following pages:

- Shopping Cart
- One Page Checkout
- Multi-Address Checkout
- Order Success (One-Page Checkout)
- Order Success (Multi-Address Checkout)
- Account registration page

Getting ready

All we need is a Google account to use this free service from Google. So, fire up your favorite web browser and get it (if you don't have one!).

Customizing a Store

How to do it...

Let's fire up our favorite browser, log in to our Magento store admin panel, and sign up in GWO:

1. Visit the home page for GWO: `http://www.google.com/websiteoptimizer`.

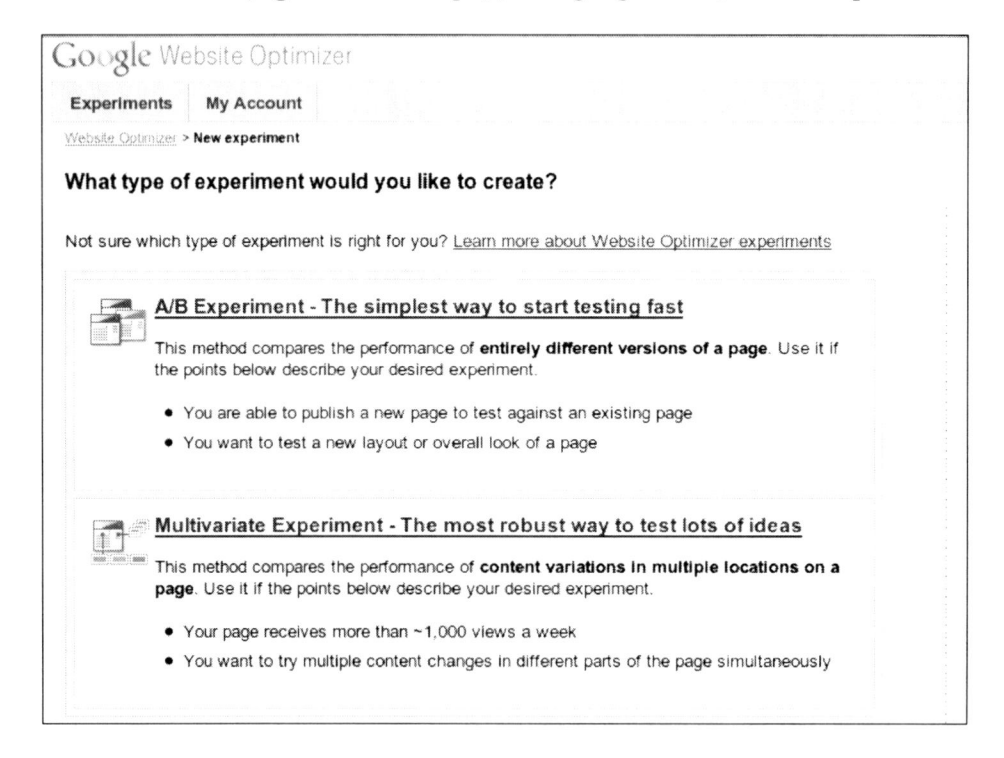

2. Log in to your Magento store admin panel. Now point your browser to **System | Configuration | Google API**. Look for the link GWO and click it. You should see a page something like this:

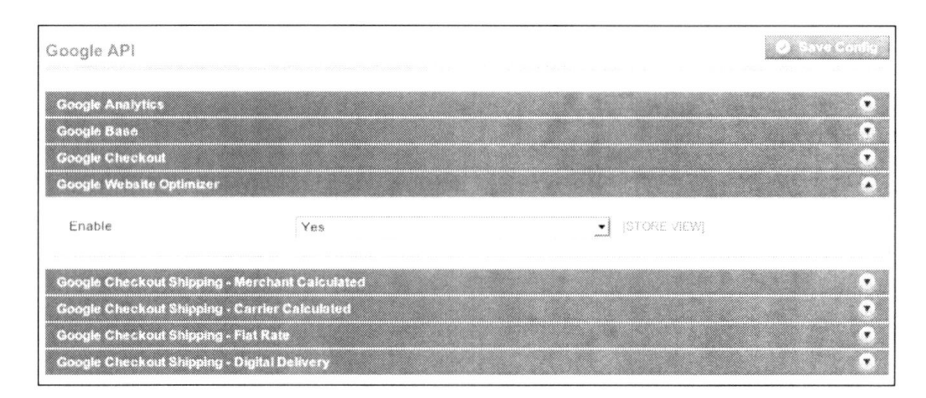

3. Select **Yes** and save the configuration.
4. Now visit the **Category Management** page from **System | Catalog | Manage Categories**.
5. Select a category. Let's select the **Furniture** category.
6. Navigate to the last tab named **Category View Optimization**.
7. Let's select **Shopping Cart** from **Conversion** page drop-down.
8. It's time to go back to GWO page to collect the **Scripts Install URL**.
9. Click on **Multivariate Experiment** link from GWO page.
10. Select the checkbox and click on the **Create** button.
11. We got to identify experiment pages now. Let's assume that we will test the furniture category and the URL will be as shown in the following screenshot:

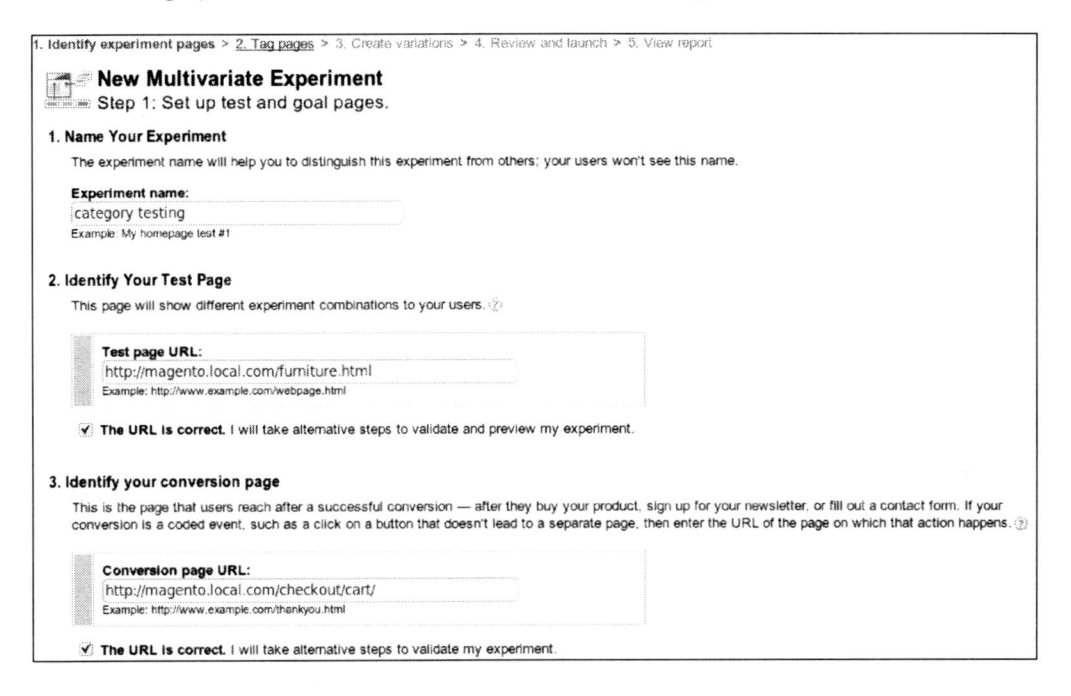

1. Identify experiment pages > 2. Tag pages > 3. Create variations > 4. Review and launch > 5. View report

New Multivariate Experiment
Step 1: Set up test and goal pages.

1. Name Your Experiment
The experiment name will help you to distinguish this experiment from others; your users won't see this name.

Experiment name:
category testing
Example: My homepage test #1

2. Identify Your Test Page
This page will show different experiment combinations to your users.

Test page URL:
http://magento.local.com/furniture.html
Example: http://www.example.com/webpage.html

☑ **The URL is correct.** I will take alternative steps to validate and preview my experiment.

3. Identify your conversion page
This is the page that users reach after a successful conversion — after they buy your product, sign up for your newsletter, or fill out a contact form. If your conversion is a coded event, such as a click on a button that doesn't lead to a separate page, then enter the URL of the page on which that action happens.

Conversion page URL:
http://magento.local.com/checkout/cart/
Example: http://www.example.com/thankyou.html

☑ **The URL is correct.** I will take alternative steps to validate my experiment.

12. Click on the **Continue** button. In the next form, click on **Your webmaster will install and validate JavaScript tags.** radio button.
13. Upon clicking you will be given the installation URL within the same page in a textbox, which will be like this:

```
http://www.google.com/analytics/siteopt/install?experiment
=EAAAAAN1RwfVB2XKRBaP0kudZ1I&account=8351934&user=AN_xLxd0_
R2mDzmRHRDVMWdMX5N7hOmuqQ&hl=en_us&portal=0&t=Kma6M9xqZ90
```

Customizing a Store

14. Copy this URL and go back to the Magento admin panel in the **Category view optimization** page.
15. Paste the URL in the **Scripts Install URL** textbox and click on **Install Scripts** button.
16. Upon clicking on the button the rest of the text areas in this form will be filled automatically by GWO.
17. Save the changes we made and go to the GWO page.
18. Now check the installation status of your test. If it's successful then edit the category title, photo, and description and set it to what your marketing team suggested.
19. Finally, launch the experiment.

How it works...

Magento 1.4 is closely integrated with GWO. Once you are done with the aforementioned steps, Google will collect the required data and provide you with conversion-related data to optimize your store.

There's more...

You can also optimize other pages of your store. Here are some possible pages:

- Home page to cart page funnel
- General checkout process funnel including the cart page
- General checkout process funnel excluding the cart page
- Checkout process funnel for different payment types including the cart page
- Checkout process funnel for different payment types excluding the cart page

Further reading

For further information on GWO, you can read about the best practices here:

`http://websiteoptimizer.blogspot.com/`.

Creating a custom variable and using its own e-mail templates

Magento 1.4 introduced custom variables, which we can use only on **CMS** pages and e-mail templates. Custom variable is a great feature for newsletter/e-mail marketing, it eliminated the tedious hassles to customize various e-mail templates. A custom variable can hold both html and plain text to represent your Twitter handle, coupon code, promotional ad images, and so on.

In this recipe, we will create a new custom variable and use it on a newly created e-mail template for new account activation e-mail.

Getting ready

Fire up your browser and log in to your Magento admin panel.

How to do it...

1. From the Magento admin panel, visit **System | Custom Variables**.
2. Click on the **Add New Variable** button.
3. Enter `store_twitter` in the **Variable Code** textbox.
4. Type `Store Twitter` in the **Variable Name** labeled textbox.
5. In the **Variable HTML Value**, enter `Follow us: <a href="http://twitter.com/packtpub">@packtpub</a>`.
6. Enter `@packtpub` or your own Twitter handle in the **Variable Plain Value** field and save it. Here is a screenshot:

7. Now move to the **System | Transactional Emails** section in the Magento admin panel.
8. Click on the **Add New Template** button. From the **Load Default Template** section load a template. This recipe will use **New Account** from **Template** drop-down.
9. Modify the form values as you need. Place the cursor in the position where you want to insert a variable.
10. Let's click the **Insert Variable** button now and look for the newly created variable **Store Twitter** under **Custom Variables**.
11. Click it to insert the variable in the template.

Customizing a Store

12. Save and preview the template.
13. It's time to use the newly created e-mail template in the new account activation e-mail.
14. Point your browser to **System | Configuration | Customer Configuration**.
15. Click the **Create New Account** option to expand it.
16. Look for the drop-down labeled **Default Welcome Email** and select your newly created e-mail template. In my case, it's `My New Account`.
17. Click on the **Save Config** button to save it.
18. Check with registering a new customer account.

How it works...

Magento 1.4 is equipped with **Custom Variables** management at the admin panel. We have created a new custom variable named `store_twitter`, which can be accessed in any CMS and templates. We used it in our newly created e-mail template for new account activation. Magento takes care to keep this operation functional.

Using Google analytics for Magento

An eCommerce store needs some special care for converting the site visitor to buyer. Site analytics data is very important to help this out. In this recipe, we will use **Google Analytics** (**GA**), which is a free service that generates detailed statistics about the visitors to a website offered by **Google**. This service was developed from Urchin Software Corporation's analytics system, **Urchin on Demand**, which was later acquired by Google. It has some cool features, which are obvious for an eCommerce store.

Getting ready

Sign up for a GA account, if you don't already have one, from `http://www.google.com/analytics`.

How to do it...

1. Log in to your GA home page.
2. Create a new profile for your store if you haven't already done the same.
3. During profile creation, you will see a value name with **Web Property ID**, which should look something like this:

UA-1234567-1

4. Copy this text from **GA's Analytics Settings | Tracking Code page**.
5. Log in to your Magento admin panel.
6. Select a configuration scope for your store.
7. Point your browser to **System | Configuration | Google API**.
8. Expand the **Google Analytics** tab.
9. Set **Enable** to **Yes**.
10. Put your **Web Property ID** (which looks like **UA-1234567-1**) from GA in the **Account Number** text field.
11. Save the configuration.

How it works...

If you follow the steps described previously, then Magento will grab the JavaScript code from GA and put it in pages to help populate analytics data and reports. If you are curious enough to see where Magento actually puts this JS snippet then after saving the configuration view—the source of your store's frontend and have a look where the body tag started.

There's more...

Users can officially add up to 50 site profiles. It is limited to sites, which have a traffic of fewer than five million page views per month (roughly two page views per second), unless the site is linked to an AdWords campaign.

Creating Catalog and Shopping Cart Price Rules

Sometimes, we as a store owner need to deal with some promotional activities to boost our sales up. The promotional offers could be for some special events with some percentage of the total price, subtotal, or a fixed amount, or buy one, get one free offers.

Magento has two types of price rules: Catalog Price Rules and Shopping Cart Price Rules, which will be described in this recipe. Catalog Rules are applied to products before they are added to the shopping cart, while Shopping Cart Price Rules are applied to products in the shopping cart.

Getting ready

We've got to know about the Catalog and Shopping Cart Price Rules before we proceed further. Catalog Price Rules are applied to products before they are added to a shopping cart. They can be used to create sales and discounts that do not require that a discount code be entered by the customer.

Customizing a Store

Shopping Cart Price Rules, as the name implies, are applied when a customer reaches the shopping cart. They can be applied either with or without the customer entering a coupon code. This feature can not be found in traditional coupon tools.

Log in to your Magento admin panel.

How to do it...

Setting up Catalog Price Rules:

1. From the **Promotions** menu, select the **Catalog Price Rules** option and then select the **Add New Rule** button.
2. Fill up the form as you like. Remember to set the status as active. You can use the **Priority** field (**1** is the highest priority) when there are multiple rules. This determines which rule takes effect when more than one Catalog Price Rule applies.
3. Click on **Conditions** and set one or more conditions. You can add more conditions by clicking the plus (**+**) icon.
4. In actions, set the discount amount and other related information.
5. Click on the **Save** and **Apply** button.

Setting up Shopping Cart Price Rules:

1. From the **Promotions** menu, select the **Cart Price Rules** option and then select the **Add New Rule** button.
2. Fill up the form with relevant data.
3. Enter the coupon code if you want. In the **Coupon** field, enter 1 and even in the **Uses Per Customer** field, enter 1. If we would like to create a limited offer, the coupon can be limited to be used 10 times by entering the value 10 in the **Uses per coupon** field.
4. Click the **Save Rule** button.

How it works...

Magento handles the data you entered while creating Catalog and Shopping Cart Price Rules.

> It is good practice to test the effect of these rules yourself before trying them out on the public. Either use a discount code that only you know or assign your test customer to a testing customer group and limit the cart rules to only that customer group.

Creating a featured product and showing it in the home page

In some cases, we need to promote some products as featured so that they would stay sticky in the home page. Unfortunately, Magento had no such feature until 1.4 version.

In this recipe, we will do it in a very simple way!

Getting ready

Fire up your favorite IDE and open your Magento project. Visit your Magento store's admin area.

How to do it...

1. Log in to your Magento admin panel.
2. Go to **Catalog | Manage Categories**.
3. We will add a new subcategory under the **Root** category named Featured Products. Click on the **Add Subcategory** button.
4. In the **General Information** tab, enter the following data:
    - **Name ***: Featured Products
    - **Description**: <empty>
    - **Image**: <empty>
    - **Page title**: Featured Products
    - **Meta Keywords**: <empty>
    - **Meta Description**: <empty>
    - **Is Active ***: Yes
    - **Include in Navigation Menu**: No
    - **URL key**: featured
5. Leave the other tabs, except **General Information**, as they are.
6. Click on the **Save Category** button.
7. After completing the **Save** process you'll see the category ID at the top-left side of your page, which should look something like this:

    Featured Products (ID: 35)

8. Notice the category ID **35** (in my case it's 35, it may vary on your box). Write this category ID somewhere to use it in future.

Customizing a Store

9. Add some products to the newly created category from Magento admin panel.
10. Copy the file `/app/design/frontend/default/default/template/catalog/product/list.phtml` to `/app/design/frontend/default/default/template/catalog/product/featured.phtml`.
11. We won't provide any filtering or sorting for featured products. So let's remove the following line:

    ```
    <?php echo $this->getToolbarHtml() ?>
    ```

12. The final content of `featured.phtml` should be something like this:

    ```
    <?php
      $_productCollection=$this->getLoadedProductCollection();
      $_helper = $this->helper('catalog/output');
    ?>
    <div class="block block-tags">
      <div class="block-title">
        <strong><span>Featured Products at <?php echo Mage::getStoreConfig('design/head/default_title') ?></span></strong>
      </div>
    <?php if(!$_productCollection->count()): ?>
    <div class="note-msg"><?php echo $this->__('There are no featured products now.') ?></div>
    <?php else: ?>
    <div class="category-products">
      <?php $_iterator = 0; ?>
      <ol class="products-list" id="products-list">
      <?php foreach ($_productCollection as $_product): ?>
        <li class="item<?php if( ++$_iterator == sizeof($_productCollection) ): ?> last<?php endif; ?>">
          <?php // Product Image ?>
            <a href="<?php echo $_product->getProductUrl() ?>" title="<?php echo $this->stripTags($this->getImageLabel($_product, 'small_image'), null, true) ?>" class="product-image"><img src="<?php echo $this->helper('catalog/image')->init($_product, 'small_image')->resize(135); ?>" width="135" height="135" alt="<?php echo $this->stripTags($this->getImageLabel($_product, 'small_image'), null, true) ?>" /></a>
          <?php // Product description ?>
            <div class="product-shop">
                <div class="f-fix">
                    <h2 class="product-name"><a href="<?php echo $_product->getProductUrl() ?>" title="<?php echo $this->stripTags($_product->getName(), null, true) ?>"><?php echo $_helper->productAttribute($_product, $_product->getName(), 'name') ?></a></h2>
    ```

```php
                        <?php if($_product->getRatingSummary()): ?>
                        <?php echo $this->getReviewsSummaryHtml($_product) ?>
                        <?php endif; ?>
                        <?php echo $this->getPriceHtml($_product, true) ?>
                        <?php if($_product->isSaleable()): ?>
                            <p><button type="button" title="<?php echo $this->__('Add to Cart') ?>" class="button btn-cart" onclick="setLocation('<?php echo $this->getAddToCartUrl($_product) ?>')"><span><span><?php echo $this->__('Add to Cart') ?></span></span></button></p>
                        <?php else: ?>
                            <p class="availability out-of-stock"><span><?php echo $this->__('Out of stock') ?></span></p>
                        <?php endif; ?>
                        <div class="desc std">
                            <?php echo $_helper->productAttribute($_product, $_product->getShortDescription(), 'short_description') ?>
                            <a href="<?php echo $_product->getProductUrl() ?>" title="<?php echo $this->stripTags($_product->getName(), null, true) ?>" class="link-more"><?php echo $this->__('Learn More') ?></a>
                        </div>
                        <ul class="add-to-links">
                <?php if ($this->helper('wishlist')->isAllow()) : ?>
                    <li><a href="<?php echo $this->helper('wishlist')->getAddUrl($_product) ?>" class="link-wishlist"><?php echo $this->__('Add to Wishlist') ?></a></li>
                <?php endif; ?>
                <?php if($_compareUrl=$this->getAddToCompareUrl($_product)): ?>
                    <li><span class="separator">|</span> <a href="<?php echo $_compareUrl ?>" class="link-compare"><?php echo $this->__('Add to Compare') ?></a></li>
                <?php endif; ?>
            </ul>
         </div>
      </div>
    </li>
  <?php endforeach; ?>
  </ol>
  <script type="text/javascript">decorateList('products-list', 'none-recursive')</script>
</div>
```

Customizing a Store

```
<?php endif; ?>
<div class="actions">
  <a href="/featured.html">View All Featured products</a>
</div>
</div>
```

13. Navigate to the Magento admin panel, go to **CMS | Manage Pages**, and edit the home page to include the following code where you want to display the featured products:

    ```
    {{block type="catalog/product_list" category_id="2"
    template="catalog/product/featured.phtml"}}
    ```

14. If everything goes well you should see a page something like this:

15. That's it!

How it works...

All we did was create a new category for **Featured Product** and then create a template for it. Finally, we added a block from our store admin panel to hold it in the store home page.

Creating a custom admin theme

Sometimes, we need to change the admin theme as well to meet the store owner's requirement. This is identical to the frontend theme. In this recipe, we will create our own admin theme. This is the simplest way to hack into the Magento admin theme.

Getting ready

Open your code editor and load the Magento project there. Open the Magento project in your file explorer too. Log in to your Magento admin panel to test the change you made.

How to do it...

1. Open the `/app/design/adminhtml/default/` directory.
2. Copy the default directory and paste it in the same location with the name `packt` (you can name it as your own instead of `packt`).
3. Let's open the file `local.xml` from `/app/etc/` directory.
4. Paste the following code just before the ending of the `config` tag:

   ```
   <stores>
     <admin>
       <design>
         <package>
           <name>default</name>
         </package>
         <theme>
           <default>packt</default>
         </theme>
       </design>
     </admin>
   </stores>
   ```

5. Open the location `/skin/adminhtml/default/`.
6. Copy the default folder and paste it in the same location with the name `packt`.
7. Now, modify the template files to fit your needs. For testing purposes, I modified the `header.phtml` and `footer.phtml` files from `/app/design/adminhtml/default/packt/template/page/` directory.
8. Reload your admin panel and see how it goes with the new theme we created.

How it works...

By adding some code in the `local.xml` as described previously, we told Magento to change the admin theme to our own, which we have created by copying the default admin theme.

5
Playing with Products

In this chapter, we will cover:

- Setting up the Catalog defaults
- Adding a Facebook 'Like' button in the product page
- Setting up Table Rates shipping
- Adding a product to the cart through Querystring
- Creating a configurable product
- Embedding a YouTube video in product details

Introduction

Decorating a store by displaying products is the most important part of any store. Turning a potential viewer to a customer is the main goal of our Magento store. We have to display the products in that way. Magento is a robust CMS. If we cannot set it up professionally, our goal will not be accomplished. This chapter will help you set up some important settings in Magento. There is a recipe for adding a Facebook 'Like' button in the product page. There is also a recipe for embedding video in the product details page. The ultimate goal of this chapter is to enhance the usability of our store.

Setting up the Catalog defaults

The very first step to creating a successful online store is setting up the Catalog system defaults. In this recipe, we will set up the Catalog system and the required categories.

Playing with Products

Getting ready

Fire up your web browser and log in to your Magento store admin panel.

How to do it...

1. Log in and visit the page **System | Configuration** at the Magento store admin panel.
2. Click on the **Catalog** from the left sidebar.
3. Under the **Product Review** accordion, select **yes** to allow unregistered users to write reviews.
4. Under the **Frontend** accordion, here is what I set:
    - **List Mode**: **Grid (default) / List**
    - **Products per Page on Grid Allowed Values**: **9,15,30**
    - **Products per Page on Grid Default Value**: **9**
    - **Products per Page on List Allowed Values**: **5,10,15,20,25**
    - **Products per Page on List Default Value**: **10**
    - **Allow All Products per Page**: **Yes**
    - **Product Listing Sort by**: **Best Value**
    - **Use Flat Catalog Product**: **No**
    - **Use Flat Catalog Category**: **No**
5. In the **Sitemap** area, enter text as:
    - **Use Tree Like Category Sitemap**: Yes
    - **Minimum Lines per Page**: 30
6. The **Product alert** settings is as:
    - **Allow Alert When Product Price Changes**: **No**
    - **Allow Alert When Product Comes Back in Stock**: **No**
    - The rest of the fields are not in use as we set the product alert as **No**. Alternately, you can choose to set the product alert as **Yes** and select an e-mail template to use it.
7. Let's not worry about the **Product Alerts Run Settings** as we choose not to use product alert. Leave it as it is.
8. The **Product Image Placeholders** section enables you to specify an image for each of the sizes that are used instead of the product image, if it is missing. Upload your own store branded product images for **Base**, **Small**, and **Thumbnail** images. Note that all these images will be cropped.

9. In **Recently Viewed/Compared Products**, let's fill as follows:
    - **Show for Current**: Website
    - **Default Recently Viewed Products Count**: 5
    - **Default Recently Compared Products Count**: 5
10. Enter in **Catalog Price Scope** as **Global** in **Price**.
11. I enter the **Category Top Navigation** as 3 to allow categories up to the third level. You can set it as 3 or 0 to allow unlimited levels in the category menu.
12. The **Catalog Search** configuration is as follows on my side:
    - **Minimal Query Length**: 3
    - **Maximum Query Length**: 128
    - **Maximum Query Words Count**: 10
    - **Search Type**: **Combine (Like and Fulltext)**
    - **Apply Layered Navigation if Search Results are Less Than as**: 1000
13. Now the SEO stuff:
    - **Autogenerated Site Map**: **Enable**
    - **Popular Search Terms**: **Enable**
    - **Product URL Suffix**: .html
    - **Category URL Suffix**: .html
    - **Use Categories Path for Product URLs**: Yes
    - **Create Permanent Redirect for old URLs if Url key changed**: Yes
    - **Page Title Separator**: NIL
    - **Use Canonical Link Meta Tag For Categories**: Yes
    - **Use Canonical Link Meta Tag For Products**: Yes
14. Let's keep the **Downloadable Product Options** unchanged.
15. Edit the **Date & Time Custom Options** to fit your local time zone. You can set the **Use JavaScript Calendar** to **Yes** if you feel like.
16. Save the configuration by clicking the **Save Config** button from the top-right corner.

How it works...

We configured the **Catalog System** to meet our store requirements. We placed all those values in the Magento admin panel. The mighty Magento will handle it to show it as we set in frontend.

Playing with Products

Adding a Facebook 'Like' button in product page

Facebook recently came out with a *Like plugin*, which will provide the ability to add the **Like** or **Recommend** button to pages outside of Facebook. In this recipe, we will add a Facebook **Like** button in all product details view.

Getting ready

Open up your Magento project in your favorite IDE. Now fire up your web browser to see the Facebook **Like** button in action.

How to do it...

1. Open `view.phtml` file from `app/design/frontend/YOUR_PACKAGE/YOUR_THEME/template/catalog/product/view.html`. In most cases, it's `app/design/frontend/default/default/template/catalog/product/view.html`.

2. Go to line number 80 and add the following code snippet:

   ```
   <!---code for facebook like button starts here --->
   <?php $src = urlencode($this->helper("core/url")-
   >getCurrentUrl()); ?>
     <iframe src="http://www.facebook.com/plugins/like.
     php?href=<?php echo $src; ?>&amp;layout=button_count&amp;show_
     faces=true&amp;width=450&amp;action=like&amp;font=arial&amp;
     colorscheme=light&amp;height=21" scrolling="no"
     frameborder="0" style="border:none; overflow:hidden;
     width:450px; height:21px;" allowTransparency="true"></iframe>
   <!---//code for facebook like button ends here --->
   ```

3. Save it.

4. Now reload any product details page. You should see something like this with a Facebook **Like** button with count:

Chapter 5

How it works...

The Facebook **Like** button enables users to make connections to your pages and share content back to their friends on Facebook with one click. As the content is hosted by Facebook, the button can display personalized content whether or not the user has logged into your site. For logged-in Facebook users, the button is personalized to highlight friends who have also liked the page.

There's more...

You can learn more about the Facebook 'Like' plugin from here: `http://developers.facebook.com/docs/reference/plugins/like`.

Setting up Table Rates shipping

Shipping plays a vital role in any eCommerce shop. In Magento shops, sometimes people mess up while trying to add Table Rates for the shipping method. In this recipe, we will add some Table Rates for our Magento shop.

Getting ready

Fire up your web browser and log in to your Magento shop's admin panel.

Playing with Products

How to do it...

1. Log in to your Magento admin panel and point your browser to **System | Configuration**.
2. From the top-left corner of the Magento admin panel look for the label **Current Configuration Scope:** and select **Default Config**.
3. You will see a link at the left sidebar to navigate to the page **Shipping Methods Under Sales** tab. Click this link.
4. Expand the tab **Table Rates** and fill it up as follows:

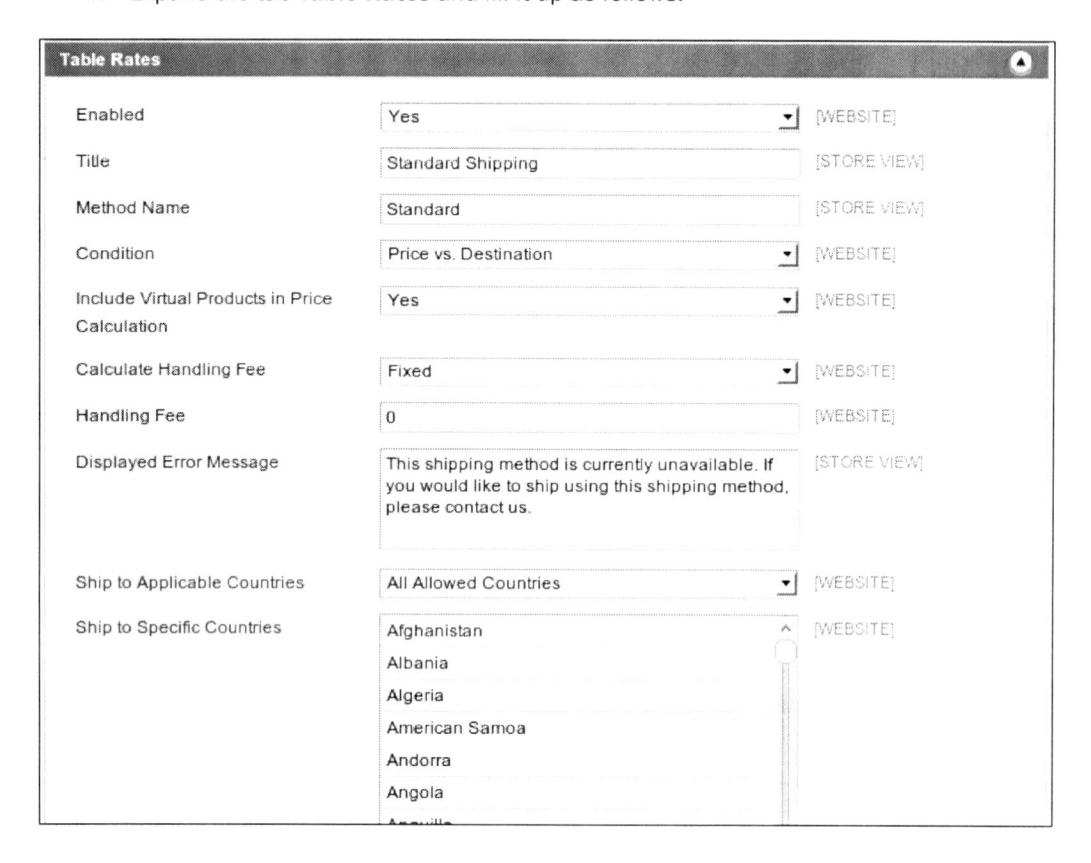

Table Rates		
Enabled	Yes	[WEBSITE]
Title	Standard Shipping	[STORE VIEW]
Method Name	Standard	[STORE VIEW]
Condition	Price vs. Destination	[WEBSITE]
Include Virtual Products in Price Calculation	Yes	[WEBSITE]
Calculate Handling Fee	Fixed	[WEBSITE]
Handling Fee	0	[WEBSITE]
Displayed Error Message	This shipping method is currently unavailable. If you would like to ship using this shipping method, please contact us.	[STORE VIEW]
Ship to Applicable Countries	All Allowed Countries	[WEBSITE]
Ship to Specific Countries	Afghanistan Albania Algeria American Samoa Andorra Angola	[WEBSITE]

5. Save this configuration.
6. We got to change the **Current Configuration Scope:** again to the website where we want to apply the Table Rates now. Let's say we will set it under the main website. Select **Main Website** from the **Current Configuration Scope:** the page will be reloaded.

7. Click on the **Export CSV** button and save the CSV file to your desired location. If you are doing this for the first time, you should see the `tablerate.csv` file content as:

   `"Country","Region/State","Zip/Postal Code","Order Subtotal (and above)","Shipping Price"`

8. Open this file with MS Excel or Open Office Spreadsheet. While opening you should select the options exactly as follows (notice that I set the **Separated by** as **Comma** only):

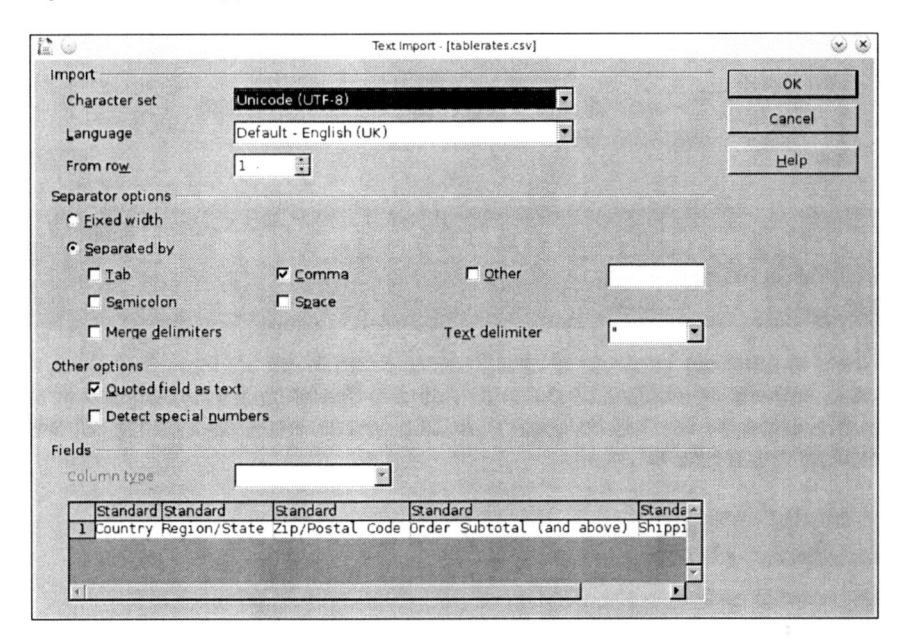

9. Let's add our table rates in this spreadsheet now. I added some rates as follows:

Country	Region/State	Zip/Postal Code	Order subtotal (and above)	Shipping price
USA	*	*	100	5
USA	*	*	50	10
USA	*	*	0	15
USA	AK	*	100	10
USA	AK	*	50	15
USA	AK	*	0	20
USA	HI	*	100	10
USA	HI	*	50	15
USA	HI	*	0	20

10. Save this file and import it from the Magento admin panel to see it in action.

Playing with Products

How it works...

A **CSV** (**Comma Separated Values**) file is used to maintain the table rates for shipping rates in Magento. The shipping Table Rates could be applied in three different ways, all of which are almost identical. In this recipe, we used **Price vs. Destination** as the condition. Alternately, you can apply any one of the other two from the select box. Magento parses the CSV file in this purpose with the delimiter Comma (,) so anything other than a comma will result in an error. Keep this in mind while working with Table Rates for shipping in Magento.

> The asterisk sign * in the table acts as a wildcard character, which denotes `All`.

Adding a product to the cart through Querystring

We often need to integrate Magento store with some external applications: therefore, we might need to add one or multiple products through the Querystring with Magento product ID or SKU. In this recipe, we will add different types of products with a Querystring. We will also add the product by the SKU externally.

Getting ready

Fire up your browser and open the Magento store's frontend and admin panel.

How to do it...

Adding a product by the Magento product ID:

1. Log in to your Magento store admin panel.
2. Navigate to **Catalog | Manage products** page.
3. In this page, you will see a listing of all the products. Locate the product that you want to add through Querystring and copy the product ID from the second column.
4. Let's say, we choose the **HTC Touch Diamond** for which the product ID is **166** (as in my Magento admin; this might be different in yours).
5. It's time to build the URL; for a simple product, the URL should be as follows:

    `http://yourstoreurl/checkout/cart/add?product=[id]&qty=[qty]`

    or

    `http://yourstoreurl/checkout/cart/add/product/[id]/qty/[qty]`

6. In my case, the URL of the product ID `166` and quantity `2` is:

   `http://magento.local.com/checkout/cart/add/product/166/qty/2`

7. Try this URL in your browser now! You should see a page similar to this:

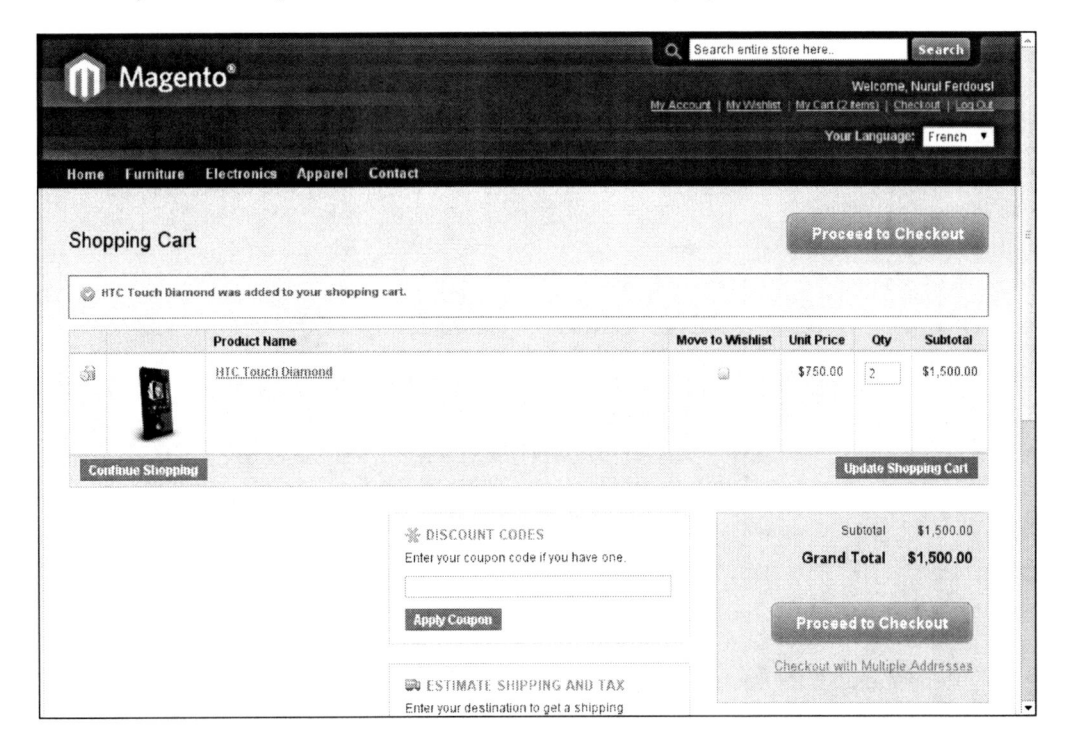

Adding a Bundle Product:

1. We have just successfully added a simple product through URL, Querystring. What if you want to add a bundle product in the same way? You might know that a bundle product has some more options unlike a simple one. We got to pass those options in Querystring. Let's do it now.

2. Grab the Magento product ID in the same way as we did in case of a simple product in the previous task. Let's say we will do it for the product `My Computer`, whose Magento product ID is `165`.

3. We will need the options ID and selected value for the various bundle options. We will collect these from the product details page. We can view this product through this URL: `http://magento.local.com/catalog/product/view/id/165`.

4. Navigate to the product details page of the product to be added on the cart through the Querystring by visiting the previously mentioned URL.

Playing with Products

5. Now collect the bundle option ID and value for each option. You can view them with a tool like Firebug. The following screenshot is taken with Firefox and Firebug to help make it easy for you for the first option:

6. I chose `47` for the bundle option `17`, but you may choose what fits best for you.
7. Repeat step 6 for each bundle option and collect the option ID and value.
8. Finally, make the URL with those ID and values, which should be something like this:

   `http://magento.local.com/checkout/cart/add/product/165/qty/2/?bundle_option[17]=47&bundle_option[22]=59&bundle_option[16]=43&bundle_option[15]=40&bundle_option[14]=36`

9. Visit the URL mentioned previously; it should redirect you to the checkout page and then add two bundle products as we specified.
10. There is no such step as step 10. Bingo!

How it works...

Magento parses the current URL and shows the appropriate page to the customer by using its MVC architecture. Somehow, if we can pass the parameters as Magento expects while adding a product to the cart, then we are done! We made the trick as we finished this recipe.

Adding a product by SKU

If you want to add a product through the unique product identifier SKU from an external application, then we must first instantiate an instance of the `Mage::app()` outside of the present application. We can do this as:

```
<?php
include_once 'app/Mage.php';
Mage::app();
Mage::getSingleton('core/session', array('name' => 'frontend'));
```

By adding a `$_GET` variable, we can get the SKU and use an instance of the Product model to get the Magento ID in this way:

```
$cProd = Mage::getModel('catalog/product');
$id = $cProd->getIdBySku("$sku");
```

Now that we have our Magento Product ID, we can add the product to the cart with the default of `1` product as the quantity. You can use other `$_GET` variables and conditions to simulate the adding of the quantity to the Querystring using the PHP header redirect:

```
header('Location: '. Mage::getUrl('checkout/cart/add', array('product' => $id)));
```

Creating a configurable product

Configurable products let customers select the variant they wish by choosing various options as specified in backend. For example, you sell hoodies in three sizes. You'd create the three variants as individual products (with their own SKUs) and then add these three to a configurable product from where customers can choose their size, then add to the cart.

In this recipe, we will learn how to create a configurable product.

Getting ready

Login to your Magento store's `backend/admin` panel. You can do so by visiting the `http://yourstoreurl/admin` or if you renamed it to something else such as `backend` then it would be `http://yourstoreurl/backend`.

Playing with Products

How to do it...

We can create multiple variants, which could be chosen from the frontend by a customer; but we will create one in this recipe. Let's start building it. Here are the few steps involved:

1. Log in to the Magento store backend and navigate to **Catalog | Attributes | Manage Attributes** page.
2. Click on the **Add New Attribute** button from the top-right corner.
3. Fill up the form as shown in the following screenshot:

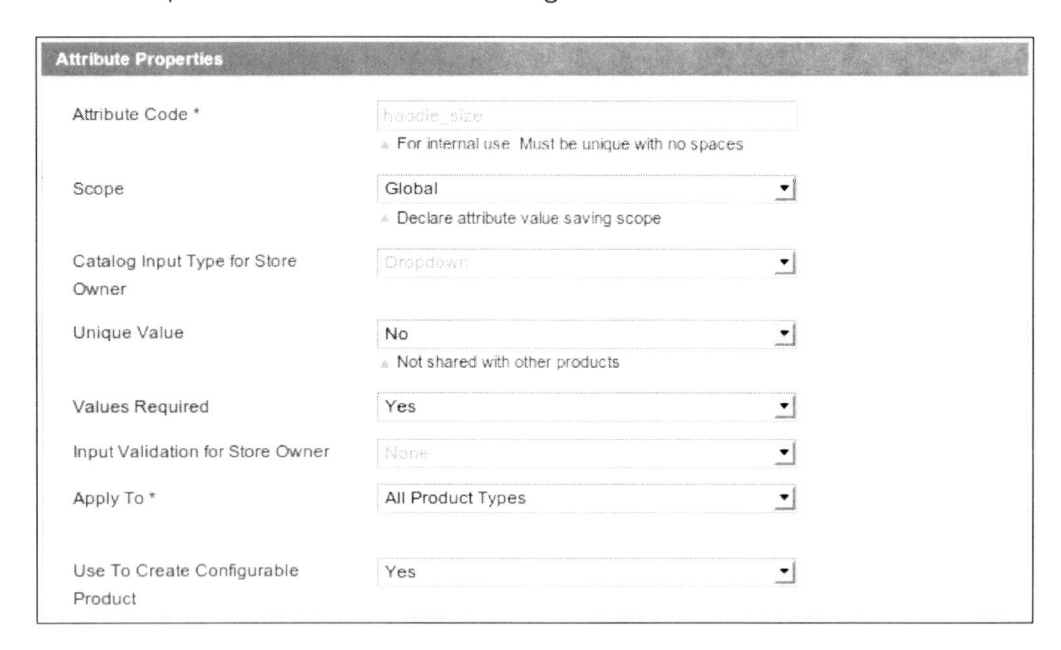

Attribute Properties	
Attribute Code *	hoodie_size
	For internal use. Must be unique with no spaces
Scope	Global
	Declare attribute value saving scope
Catalog Input Type for Store Owner	Dropdown
Unique Value	No
	Not shared with other products
Values Required	Yes
Input Validation for Store Owner	None
Apply To *	All Product Types
Use To Create Configurable Product	Yes

4. The **Label** goes as follows:

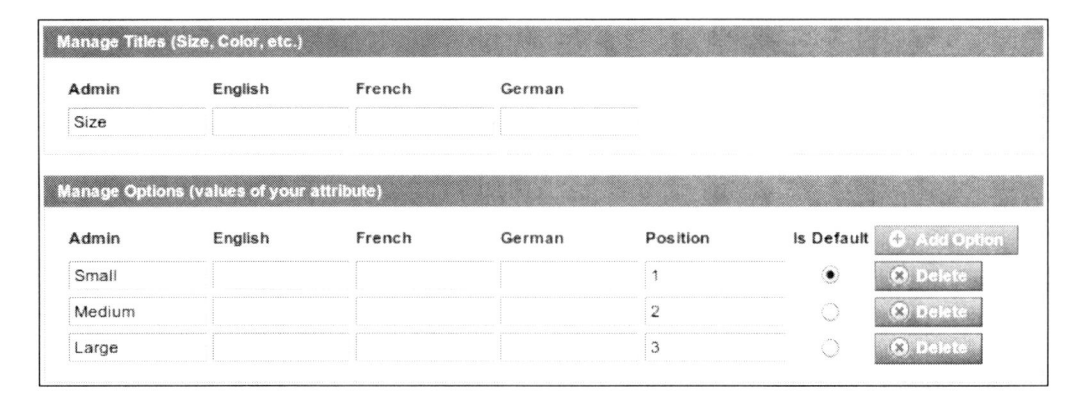

Manage Titles (Size, Color, etc.)

Admin	English	French	German
Size			

Manage Options (values of your attribute)

Admin	English	French	German	Position	Is Default	
Small				1	●	Delete
Medium				2	○	Delete
Large				3	○	Delete

5. Choose the options in the frontend options as you want, that won't block us from creating a configurable product.
6. Save this attribute by clicking on the **Save Attribute** button.
7. Navigate to **Catalog | Attributes | Manage Attribute Sets**.
8. Click on the **Add New Set** button to create a new attribute set.
9. Let's set the name as `Universal Hoodies` and base it as **Shirts General**.
10. Drag in the attribute named **hoodie_size** that we had created a while ago from the **Unassigned attributes to Groups | General**.
11. Get rid of the gender from **General** as we won't use it here. You can do it from the **Groups to Unassigned** area.
12. Okay, time to create some products now. Let's head to the page **Catalog | Manage Products**.
13. Let's create three simple products by duplicating from the first one. This is almost the same as with other standard simple products, which is **Visibility**. We will set it as **Not Visible Individually**.
14. It's time to create the Configurable Product itself! Navigate to **Catalog | Manage Products**. Click on the **Add product** button and select **Universal Hoodies** as **Attribute set** and **Configurable Product** as **Product Type**.
15. You should see a form now. Enter details as stated in the following screenshot:

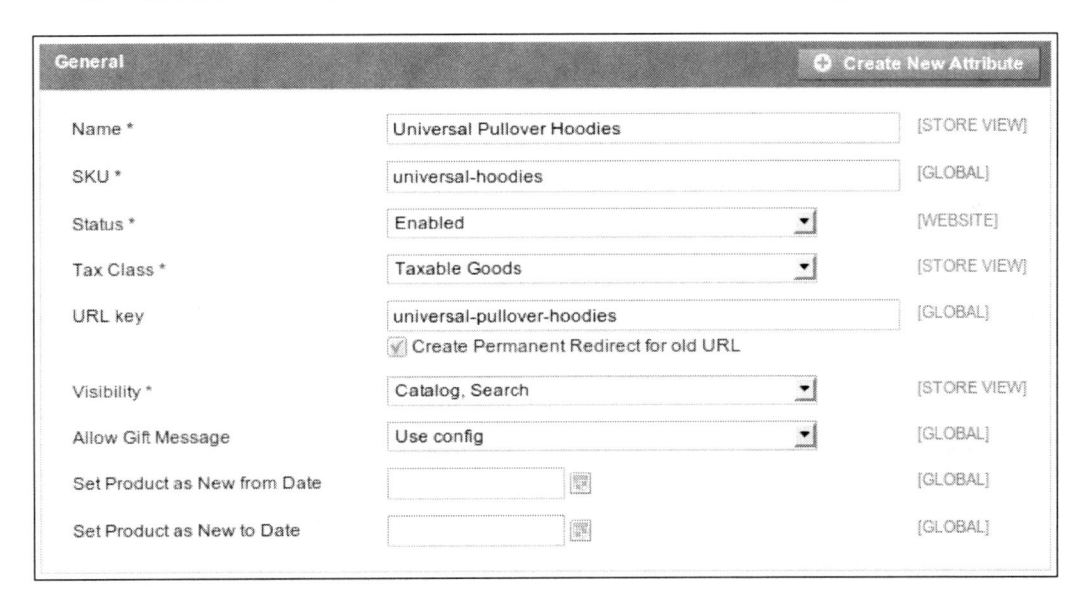

General		
Name *	Universal Pullover Hoodies	[STORE VIEW]
SKU *	universal-hoodies	[GLOBAL]
Status *	Enabled	[WEBSITE]
Tax Class *	Taxable Goods	[STORE VIEW]
URL key	universal-pullover-hoodies	[GLOBAL]
	☑ Create Permanent Redirect for old URL	
Visibility *	Catalog, Search	[STORE VIEW]
Allow Gift Message	Use config	[GLOBAL]
Set Product as New from Date		[GLOBAL]
Set Product as New to Date		[GLOBAL]

16. Click on **Associated Products** from the left menu and select the products, which we had created previously as simple products.

Playing with Products

17. Fill up the other required information, which are identical with any other product types. Save the product and look for it in frontend. Good Luck! Here is a screenshot:

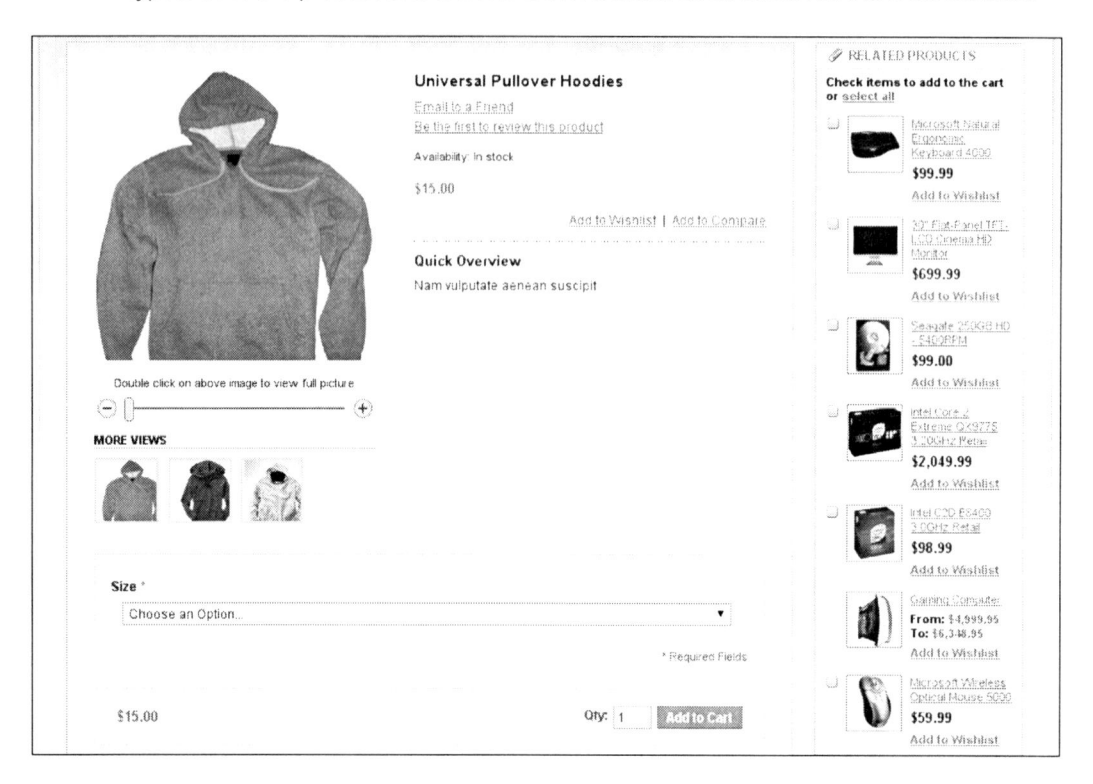

How it works...

A configurable product is a combination of some individual simple products. In this recipe, we created a new attribute for our configurable product and named it as `hoodie_size`. Then we created a new attribute set named `Universal Hoodies` and dragged in the previously created attribute `hoodie_size`. We set the individual product's visibility to `no`, you can set it to `yes` if you feel like. Then we added some individual products with the size attribute and finally added them in configurable product along with some associated products.

There's more...

Configurable product is a Magento system feature, which is very handy if you want to show some variants to a customer to choose. In Magento 1.4.x, it's much more matured than that of previous versions. Now a configurable product can be built with a visible simple product and it can be found in the search engine, layered navigation, product comparison, and so on. All we need to do is to choose as configurable product while adding it and follow the onscreen instructions; there's no jail break required!

There are six types of products in Magento 1.4.x, namely:

- Simple product
- Grouped product
- Configurable product
- Virtual product
- Bundle product
- Downloadable product

Configurable product is the one that's used most frequently. Now what's really meant by a configurable product?

Embedding a YouTube video in product details

Magento 1.4 has come up with a nice **WYSIWYG** editor. This will save us time when we embed a video in product details. In this recipe, we will add a YouTube video in the product details page.

How to do it...

We need the YouTube embedding code to add it in our product details. Visit the page in YouTube where your video is. Let's assume that we will embed the video from the URL `http://www.youtube.com/watch?v=LKV6gLi7eRA`.

1. Visit the following page: `http://www.youtube.com/watch?v=LKV6gLi7eRA`.
2. Find and click the embed button.

Playing with Products

3. You should see a form. Fill it up as you please. Here is a screenshot from me:

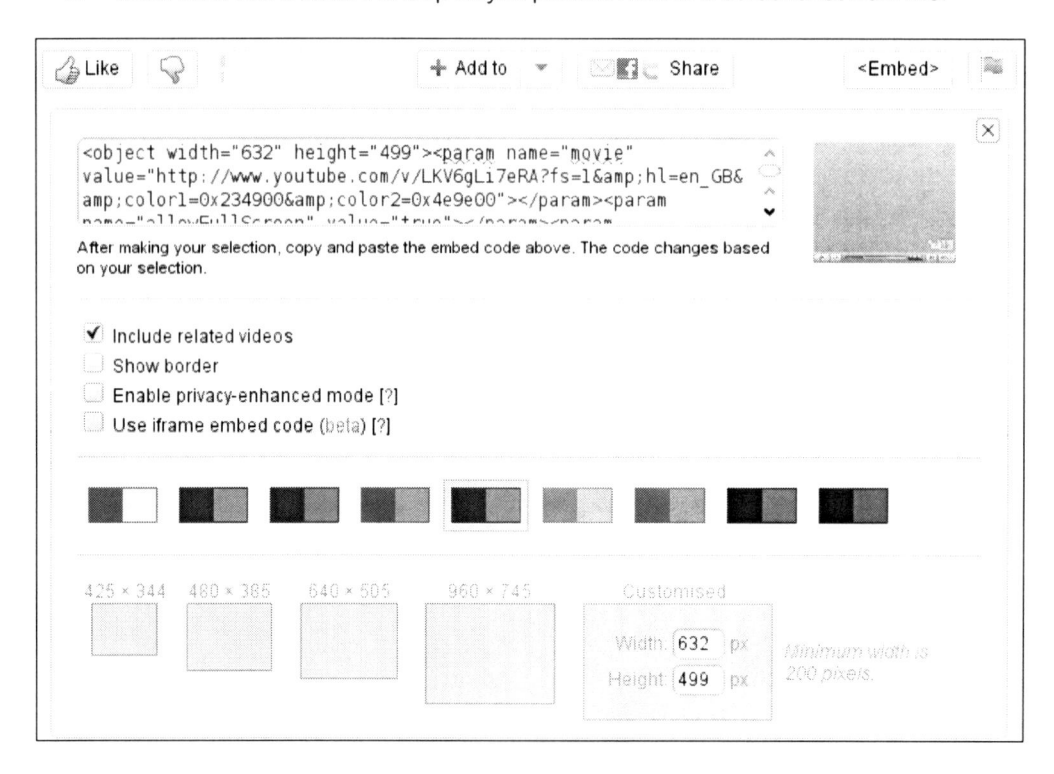

4. Note that I set the width and height as **Customised** to fit it in the product description section. You can set your own configuration and copy the embed code.
5. Now copy the embed code from the textarea. We will use it shortly in the Magento admin panel.
6. Log in to Magento admin panel.
7. Point your browser to **Catalog | Manage Products** pages.
8. Click on the product where you want to add the YouTube video.
9. On the **product edit** form, click on the **Description** link from the left-side bar.
10. Now paste the YouTube embed code in the description textarea.
11. Edit other fields as you please. Here is a screenshot of my product description with some dummy data:

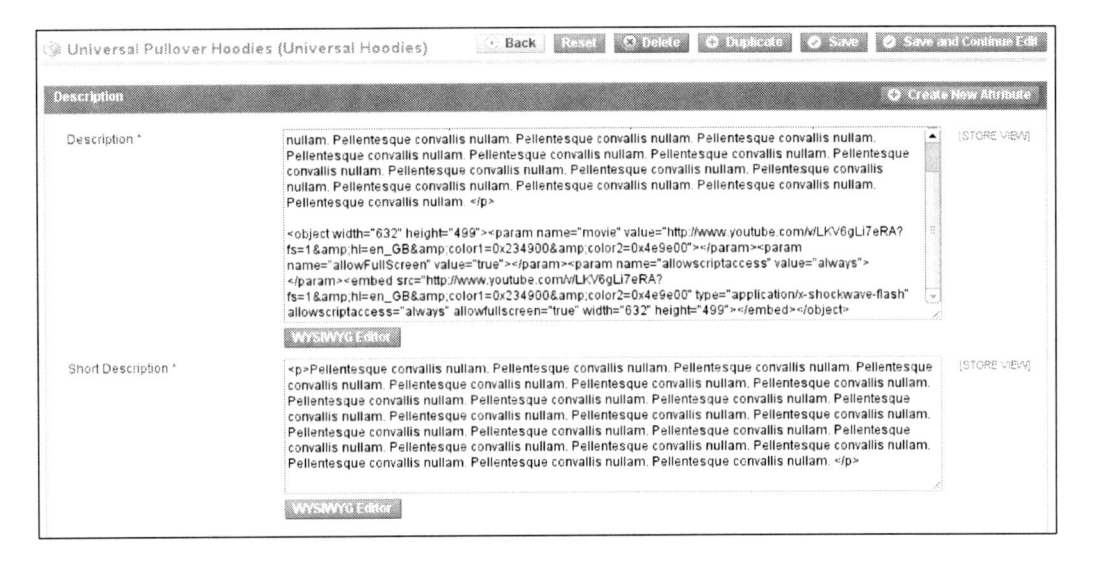

12. Save this page and see it in the frontend.
13. I got the following page with the preceding steps described as:

Playing with Products

How it works...

Magento has added TinyMCE as its default WYSIWYG editor. Through the Magento admin panel, we added the YouTube video embed code in the description textarea and saved it.

6
Adding a Professional Touch to Your Site

In this chapter, we will cover:

- Installing Magento 1.4 in PHP 5.3.2 (without mcrypt)
- Optimizing Magento store for search engines
- Implementing PayPal Website Payments Pro and Express Checkout into Magento
- Preventing a CSRF attack in Magento

Introduction

In this chapter, we will bake some cool recipes on various important topics, which relate to cutting edge trend and tech hypes. You will find it useful while you will be working on a commercial project on Magento for serious business.

Adding a Professional Touch to Your Site

Installing Magento 1.4 in PHP 5.3.2 (without mcrypt)

Magento handles the cryptography with mcrypt module. Unfortunately, in PHP 5.3.x, the mcrypt modules are not bundled with it due to some licensing issue in the U.S. If you try to install Magento without mcrypt installed in your box it won't let you do that. This is a blocking issue indeed. Without mcrypt if you try to install Magento you should see a page like this:

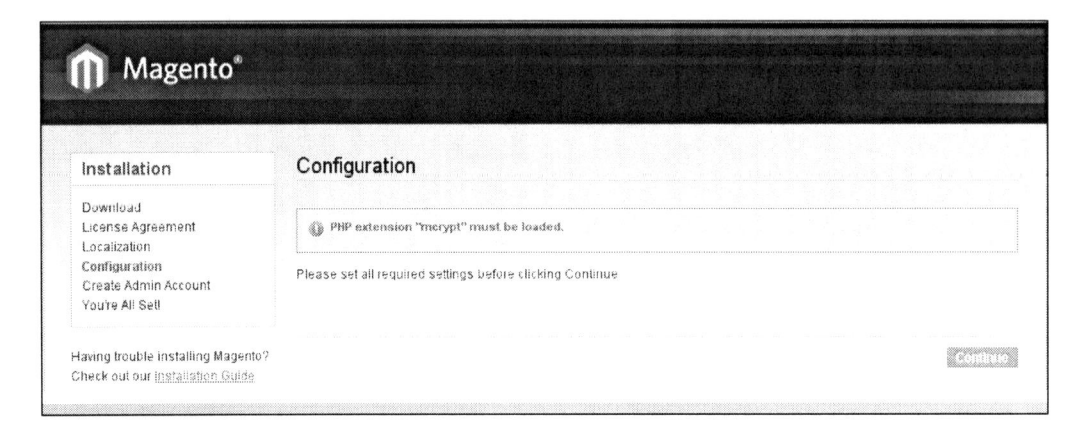

In this recipe, we will write a new plugin for Magento to handle the cryptography instead of mcrypt. We will use Base64 for that.

Getting ready

Fire up your favorite PHP IDE (in my case, it's NetBeans) and open the Magento project.

How to do it...

Let's list the steps required to complete the task:

1. Open the `Object.php` file from `/lib/Varien/` directory, and find the following:

   ```
   public function __toString(array $arrAttributes = array(), $valueSeparator=',')
   ```

2. Unfortunately, on PHP 5.3.x and onwards, the `__toString` method does not take or allow any parameter. This is why we need to replace the previous line with:

   ```
   public function __invoke(array $arrAttributes = array(), $valueSeparator=',')
   ```

> If your Magento version's code has already commented out the __toString method, you may skip step 1 and step 2.

3. Now, open the `index.php` file and set the error reporting level as:

   `error_reporting(E_ALL ^ E_DEPRECATED);`

4. We will now modify the checking of the mcrypt requirement for installing Magento. Open `app/code/core/Mage/Install/etc/install.xml` and find **check | php | extensions** in the XML navigator. The PHP block should read like this:

```xml
<php>
  <extensions>
    <spl/>
    <dom/>
    <simplexml/>
    <pdo_mysql/>
    <mcrypt/>
    <hash/>
    <curl/>
    <iconv/>
    <ctype/>
    <gd/>
  </extensions>
</php>
```

5. Modify the preceding code and make changes as follows. We need to comment out the line where mcrypt resides. We actually commented out line number 84:

```xml
<php>
  <extensions>
    <spl/>
    <dom/>
    <simplexml/>
    <pdo_mysql/>
    <!--<mcrypt/>-->
    <hash/>
    <curl/>
    <iconv/>
    <ctype/>
    <gd/>
  </extensions>
</php>
```

6. Save this file as `install.xml`.
7. Let's create a new plugin for using Base64 instead of mcrypt. Create a new file in `lib/Varien/Crypt/` directory, as `Base64.php` and put the following code into it:

```php
<?php

/**
 * Base64 plugin
 *
 * @category   Varien
 * @package    Varien_Crypt
 * @author     Nurul Ferdous <nurul.ferdous@gmail.com>
 */
class Varien_Crypt_Base64 extends Varien_Crypt_Abstract
{

    /**
     * constructor
     *
     * @param array $data
     */
    public function __construct(array $data=array())
    {
        parent::__construct($data);
    }

    /**
     * Initialize base64 module
     *
     * @param string $key cipher private key
     * @return Varien_Crypt_Mcrypt
     */
    public function init($key)
    {
        return $this;
    }

    /**
     * Encrypt data
     *
     * @param string $data source string
     * @return string
     */
    public function encrypt($data)
```

```
    {
      if (!strlen($data)) {
        return $data;
      }

        return base64_encode($data);
    }

    /**
      * Decrypt data
      *
      * @param string $data encrypted string
      * @return string
      */
    public function decrypt($data)
    {
      if (!strlen($data)) {
        return $data;
      }

        return base64_decode($data);
    }

}
```

8. We are at the last step now. Find the `Crypt.php` file from the `/lib/Varien/` directory and replace:

    `static public function factory($method='mcrypt')`
    With:
    `static public function factory($method='base64')`

9. Now, run the installation of Magento, and you should be good to go! Nobody will ask you for the mcrypt anymore.

How it works...

We already know that Magento uses mcrypt extension to handle its cryptography. We wrote a new plugin named `Base64.php` and pointed it in the Magento environment to use in lieu of mcrypt.

In some cases, the PHP version 5.3 does not have the mcrypt extension installed. If we need to install without mcrypt then we are stuck, as Magento has a dependency on it. Magento defined this dependency in an xml file located in `app/code/core/Mage/Install/etc/` directory as `install.xml`. At line number 84, we commented the line. This would let you bypass the dependency checking.

Adding a Professional Touch to Your Site

Who will handle the cryptography then? This is why we created a new plugin called `Base64.php` in the `lib/Varien/Crypt/` directory. Finally, we told Magento that the Crypt factory method is Base64 (not mcrypt any more). We did this in the `lib/Varien/Crypt.php` file, line number 43.

There's more...

There are some other available cryptography extensions available in PHP such as Crack, Hash, Mhash, and OpenSSL. You can create your very own plugin for handling cryptography in Magento. We just tried to show you a simple path to make your own plugin. The steps will be pretty similar to this recipe for creating a plugin with Crack, Hash, Mhash, or OpenSSL. For more information on cryptography in PHP you should read this: http://php.net/manual/en/refs.crypto.php

Further security

For a live application, I would suggest you to build the PHP from source with mcrypt extension. If you insist to use Base64, then you should add your own security measure to ensure the security.

Optimizing Magento store for search engines

Magento is one of the most search engine friendly eCommerce platforms. We can get most out of it if we could properly optimize our Magento store for SEO. In this recipe, we will follow some baby steps and optimize our Magento store.

How to do it...

Magento has segmented the SEO settings in its different sections. We will configure those settings from the following steps:

1. The very first step is to log in to your Magento backend and navigate to **System | Configuration | Web | Search Engines Optimization**, and set **Use Web Server Rewrites** to **Yes**.

2. In **Url Options** section, set **Add Store Code to Urls** as **No** and **Redirect to Base URL if requested URL doesn't match it** to **Yes**.

Chapter 6

3. In this step, we will set up Magento header settings. Let's navigate to the page **System | Configuration | Design | HTML Head** and enter text as follows:

Label	Value
Default Title	Packt Publishing Technical & IT Book Store
Title Prefix	Keep it empty
Title Suffix	Keep it empty
Default Description	Packt is a modern publishing company, producing cutting-edge books, eBooks, and articles for communities of developers, administrators, and newbies alike.
Default Keywords	We can leave it blank as we are using **Default Description**.
Default Robots	INDEX, FOLLOW
Miscellaneous Scripts	Keep it empty
Display Demo Store Notice	No
Logo Image Alt (in header section)	Packt Publishing Technical & IT Book Store
Welcome Text	Welcome to PACKT Demo store

> Don't enter text exactly as put in the preceding table. This is good for Packt only. Modify it to reflect your store's brand.

- **Catalog Optimization**: Okay, it's time to optimize the store catalog. Magento gives you the ability to add the name of categories to the path for product URLs. Because Magento doesn't support this functionality very well; it creates duplicate content issues. It is a very good idea to disable this. To do this navigate to the page **System | Configuration | Catalog | Search Engine Optimizations** and set it as follows:

Search Engine Optimizations		
Autogenerated Site Map	Enable	[STORE VIEW]
Popular Search Terms	Enable	[STORE VIEW]
Product URL Suffix	.html	[STORE VIEW]
	⚠ Cache refresh needed.	
Category URL Suffix	.html	[STORE VIEW]
	⚠ Cache refresh needed.	
Use Categories Path for Product URLs	No	[STORE VIEW]
Create Permanent Redirect for old URLs if Url key changed	Yes	[STORE VIEW]
Page Title Separator	-	[STORE VIEW]
Use Canonical Link Meta Tag For Categories	No	[STORE VIEW]
Use Canonical Link Meta Tag For Products	No	[STORE VIEW]

- **Category Optimization**: Let's set the details for each category in our Magento backend. Navigate to **Catalog | Manage Categories**. Edit existing categories and check the following fields:
    - **Meta Description**: Write an attractive description here; keep in mind that people will see the description in the result listings of search engines.
    - **Page Title**: Keep this empty to use the category name including parent categories. When you customize it, the title will be exactly like your input, without the parent category.
    - **URL Key**: Always try to keep a short but keyword-rich URL. It's highly discouraged to use words like "the", "and", "for", and so on. Keep in mind that you can only set this for all store views; for a multi-language store you should keep it language independent.

- **Product Optimizations**: Navigate to **Catalog | Manage Products** page to edit the product meta information for better SEO. Open each product and in **Meta Information** section, enter information that enables search engines to more easily find, and index this product.
- **CMS Page Optimization**: From the Magento backend, we can set several options for a page, which are seldom found on any other CMS. We will concentrate on the page title, URL key, and meta data for now.

> Again, you can keep the **Keywords** empty. The description has one very important function, which is enticing people to click, so make sure it states what's in the page they're clicking towards, and that it gets their attention.

- **Template Optimization**: Magento set the site logo as `h1` so it must be kept in mind that inside the content div, you have to get rid of the title of the content in an `<h1>` tag. For example, for a category page it should be the category name and for a product the product name. Clean up the over usage of headings. It's a good idea to get rid of the header usage in the side columns, or make the text relevant to the shop (such as to include keywords). There is no reason to add "static" and keyword-less titles with an `<h4>`. It is, for instance, better to change all the `<h4>` tags in `<div class="head">` to `<strong>` tags. Now it is time to optimize your content, at the category pages put the product names in a `<h3>` and the category names in a `<h1>`. On product pages, you should put the product name in an `<h1>`.

> An SEO friendly blank template could be a head start to all this stuff. You can grab one from the Magento site and create your own template by modifying it.

1. Google Sitemap Settings: These settings control how often Magento automatically regenerates its Google Sitemaps to ensure that they are current.
2. To activate Google Sitemap generation, navigate to **System | Configuration | Google Sitemap** page.
3. Set the **Enabled** setting to **Yes** to activate automatic regeneration of sitemaps. Use the **Start Time** and **Frequency** to specify how often you want the sitemaps to be regenerated. Use the **Error Email** settings to define an e-mail recipient for error messages from the automatic sitemap regeneration process.

> To use Magento's automatic generation of Google Sitemaps, you must activate the Magento Cron service.

Adding a Professional Touch to Your Site

4. This is the last of our baby steps. Copy and paste the following code into a `robots.txt` and upload it to the root directory of the Magento install:

```
User-agent: *
Disallow: /index.php/
Disallow: /*?
Disallow: /*.js$
Disallow: /*.css$
Disallow: /checkout/
Disallow: /tag/
Disallow: /catalogsearch/advanced/
Disallow: /review/
Disallow: /app/
Disallow: /downloader/
Disallow: /js/
Disallow: /lib/
Disallow: /media/
Disallow: /*.php$
Disallow: /pkginfo/
Disallow: /report/
Disallow: /skin/
Disallow: /var/
Disallow: /customer/
Disallow: /catalog/
Allow: /catalogsearch/result/?q
```

How it works...

Search Engine Optimization is a vast area. We have to read a lot to adopt it completely. The steps we described in this recipe are a small workaround to meet our primary needs. We entered some texts on Magento backend to handle the dirty job of SEO by Magento itself. Finally, we added a `robots.txt` file to the site root directory to help prevent unwanted URLs to be indexed by search engine robots.

Implementing PayPal Website Payments Pro and Express Checkout into Magento

This is what Magento says regarding **PayPal**. PayPal is a global leader in online payments, and a fast and secure way for your customers to pay online.

With PayPal and Magento, you can accept payments from all major debit and credit cards, receive online bank transfers, and customer payments from PayPal account holders. As customers don't even need a PayPal account to pay with PayPal, both you and your customers can get extra convenience without extra effort.

- It's free to open an account and to qualify for anti-fraud protection. With no set-up or cancellation fees, adding PayPal to your Magento store makes getting paid affordable and simple.
- It's also fast and easy to set up, and with over 140 million accounts worldwide, PayPal is an extremely popular payment method among millions of online shoppers. Customers who are uncomfortable sharing their financial information online can still shop at your store, and you get the added benefit of a 14 percent sales increase.
- Magento currently supports PayPal's versatile Website Payments Pro, an all-in-one payments solution that enables you to accept debit and credit card payments directly on your website, over the phone, or using fax and mail orders. This solution also allows your customers to pay with PayPal using PayPal Express. Coupled with Magento, it's a smart, scalable way to grow your business.

Getting ready

We can set up our PayPal in Magento both for staging and live right from the backend. Before setting it up, we need to have a merchant account in PayPal. If you are a developer, I would suggest you have a free developer account from PayPal staging. You can sign up for PayPal from here as we are going to need it in the next step:

- Sandbox/Developer: `https://developer.paypal.com/`
- Real account: `https://paypal.com/`

How to do it...

I assume that you already have a merchant account in PayPal. Let's get it hooked in our Magento store by following a few easy steps in the backend:

1. Head to your store backend, and navigate to the page **System | Configuration | PayPal**.
2. Open another tab in your browser and log in to your PayPal. Keep it open to collect necessary information as you need to fill up the Magento PayPal configurations.
3. Go back to the Magento store backend. In the first step for PayPal configuration, let's select our country. In my case, it's `United States`.
4. Enter your e-mail associated with your PayPal merchant account. In my case, it's (this is a test account for staging only): `nurul__1227501321_biz@yahoo.com`.

> Select the country and e-mail associated with your PayPal merchant account. This might be different from your current location.

Adding a Professional Touch to Your Site

5. The following screenshot shows the next few settings as I set them here:

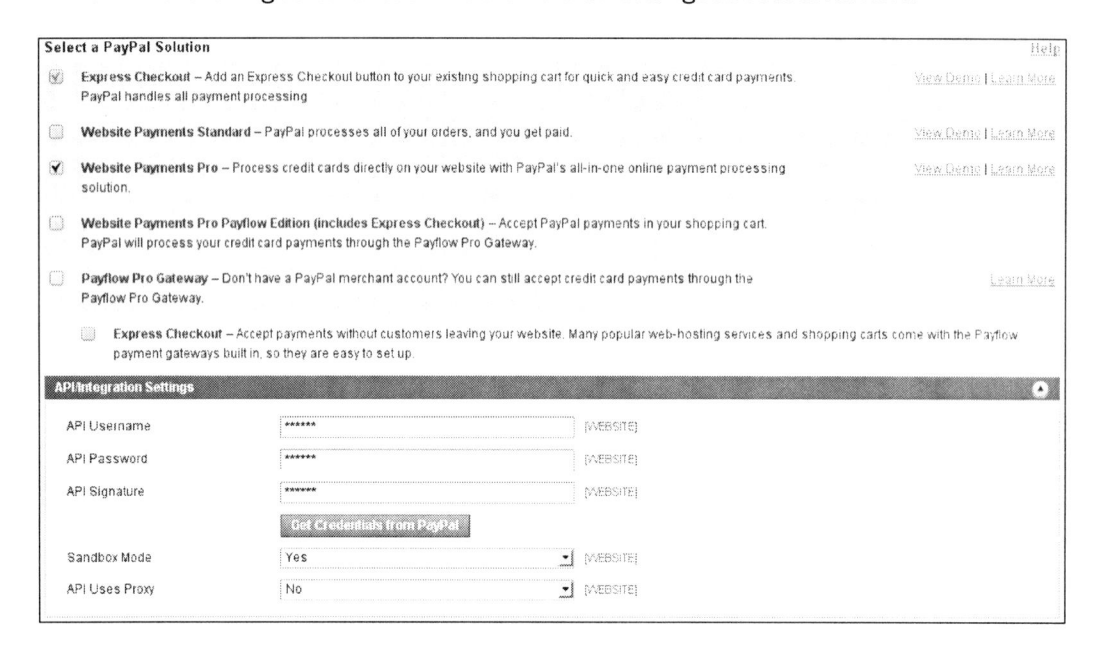

6. The rest fields are pretty self-descriptive. Anyone could set it, thus, we will skip all of these except the last one, **Frontend Experience Settings**.
7. You can choose any one logo for a better user experience where I chose **We Prefer PayPal**. For the **PayPal Merchant Pages Style**, I kept all those fields empty.
8. Save this configuration and check it in your store frontend. You should see a cool **Express Checkout** button in your product and cart page.

How it works...

PayPal is tightly coupled in Magento 1.4.x. Anyone could set it up in Magento without any hassle. All we did here is fill up some nicely labeled forms. Nothing special!

> If you are using Sandbox mode to Yes then keep your sandbox merchant account logged in, or else you would not be able to place an order. PayPal sandbox is a bit slow, so be prepared to keep your patience while working with sandbox. Don't forget to set it live while you are done with testing.

Preventing a CSRF attack in Magento

A **Cross-Site Request Forgery** (**CSRF**) is an attack that attempts to cause a victim to unknowingly send arbitrary HTTP requests, usually to URLs requiring privileged access and using the existing session of the victim to determine access. The HTTP request then causes the victim to execute a particular action based on his or her level of privilege, such as making a purchase or modifying or removing information.

How Magento is related to that, you ask? Well, the problem starts with an attack called a CSRF attack noticed by **Artisan System** in the Magento admin panel. The brilliance with this attack is that the person executing it is generally unaware and an authorized user of the website, and thus, the web software has no way to stop the actual actions from occurring.

The Magento guys later proposed a simple solution by changing the admin path URL and added some extra programmed checking, validating URLs in vulnerable points. In this recipe, we will secure our store from these types of attacks.

How to do it...

1. Locate and open the `local.xml` file from `/app/etc/` directory.
2. Now find the code block and change the admin path as I did. I changed it from admin to backend. You can set another string. Try to choose a path as difficult as you can so that bad guys cannot guess it!

```xml
<admin>
  <routers>
    <adminhtml>
      <args>
        <!---in my case I changed it from to backend--->
        <frontName><![CDATA[backend]]></frontName>
      </args>
    </adminhtml>
  </routers>
</admin>
```

> If you are stuck after changing the admin path, then here is a simple workaround. In phpmyadmin or something like this tool, try to find `core_config_data` and on its last page delete the entire fields, not just the data in them: `admin/url/use_custom` `admin/url/custom` `web/secure/base_url` `web/unsecure/base_url` and in `var/cache/` delete all the files: `mage--1` through `mage--f`.

3. The next step is in the **System | Configuration | Admin | Security** section. Open it and modify it as shown in the following table:

Label	Value
Add Secret Key to URLs	Yes
Login is Case Sensitive	Yes
Session Lifetime (seconds)	360

4. Let us modify the Web configuration to secure the cookie and session properly. Navigate to the page **System | Configuration | Web | Session Cookie Management** and save the form as shown in the following screenshot:

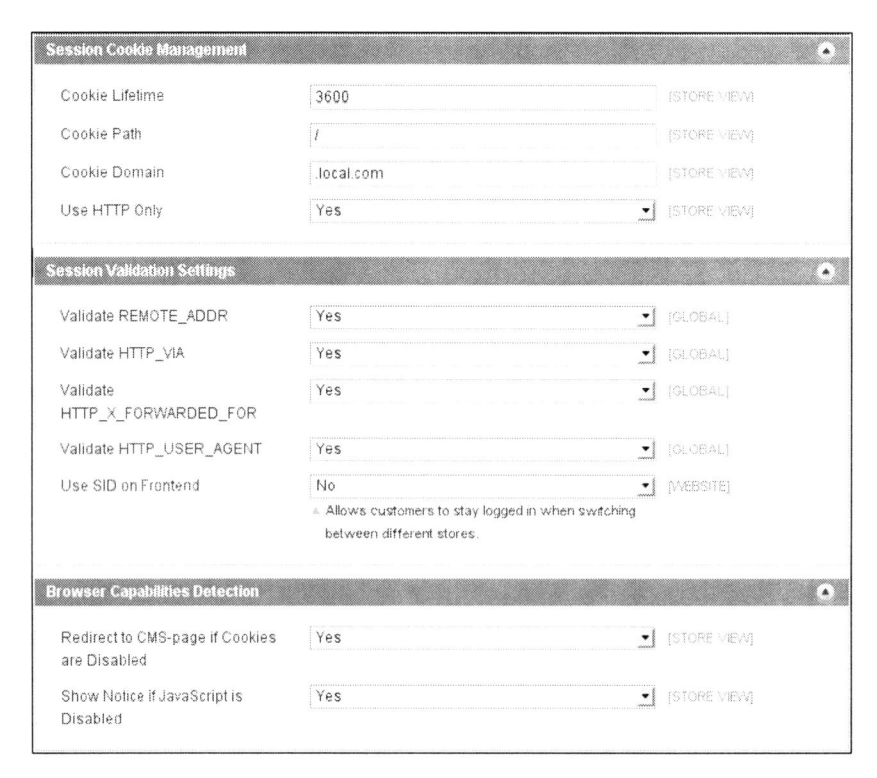

Session Cookie Management		
Cookie Lifetime	3600	[STORE VIEW]
Cookie Path	/	[STORE VIEW]
Cookie Domain	.local.com	[STORE VIEW]
Use HTTP Only	Yes	[STORE VIEW]

Session Validation Settings		
Validate REMOTE_ADDR	Yes	[GLOBAL]
Validate HTTP_VIA	Yes	[GLOBAL]
Validate HTTP_X_FORWARDED_FOR	Yes	[GLOBAL]
Validate HTTP_USER_AGENT	Yes	[GLOBAL]
Use SID on Frontend	No	[WEBSITE]
	▲ Allows customers to stay logged in when switching between different stores.	

Browser Capabilities Detection		
Redirect to CMS-page if Cookies are Disabled	Yes	[STORE VIEW]
Show Notice if JavaScript is Disabled	Yes	[STORE VIEW]

5. If we can get this far, Magento 1.4 will be capable of keeping the bad guys off the scene.

How it works...

Thankfully, Magento already employs some of these techniques to prevent CSRF attacks, which we just used from the admin panel. In the near-term, the developers will be enhancing security to include these techniques in all places. Right now though, you will have to make do with a simple workaround. By changing the URL of your admin interface, you can avoid malicious attacks because the attacker won't know what URL to send the fake requests to. Unless, of course, they pick it up from your referrer header!

> Protecting /admin/ by .htaccess would also be a solution except that some updates from Varien will change it back to some non-protective setup.

7
Database Design

In this chapter, we will cover:

- Resources and database connections
- Magento database replication using Master Slave setup
- Using the Magento's Singleton method
- Repairing the Magento database
- Working with Magento's EAV design

Introduction

Magento uses MySQL for its database and uses an advanced data modeling tool named **EAV** (**Entity-Attribute-Value**). The MySQL database has become the world's most popular open source database because of its consistently fast performance, high reliability, and ease of use. MySQL Cluster has been widely adopted for a range of telecommunications, web, and enterprise workloads demanding carrier-grade availability, with high transaction throughput, and low latency.

In this chapter, we will look into some exciting recipes that deal with the best practices for ensuring the following points:

- High-availability
- Uptime/Downtime
- Level of availability
- Single point of failure (SPOF)
- Recovery/failover
- Cluster

Database Design

Resources and database connections

A resource in Magento is used to manage database connections. Resources are defined under the global XML tag of any `config.xml` file. To make a new database connection, we have to add an XML file, such as the `app/etc/config.xml` file. Each resource has a name. Connection names are generally of the pattern `module_read`, `module_write`, or `module_setup`. In this recipe, we will play with the resource and create a new database connection, which would work on any database that we specify.

Getting ready

Open your Magento project in your code editor.

How to do it...

1. We will print the data in the product view page for development purpose. Let us open the `view.phtml` file from `app/design/frontend/YOUR_INTERFACE/YOUR_THEME/template/catalog/product/` folder.

2. Append the following code snippet at the top of `view.phtml`:

   ```
   <?php
   $singleton = Mage::getSingleton('catalog/session');
   echo '<pre>';
   var_export($singleton->debug());
   echo '</pre>';
   ?>
   ```

3. Visit any product details page to see the results in your browser.

4. Let's test the Singleton method in this code snippet:

   ```
   <?php
   $resource = Mage::getSingleton('core/resource');
   $conn     = $resource->getConnection('core_read');
   $results  = $conn->query('SELECT * FROM admin_user')->fetchAll();
   echo '<pre>';
   var_export($results);
   echo '</pre>';
   ?>
   ```

5. Run this code by visiting any product details page. You should see a page similar to this:

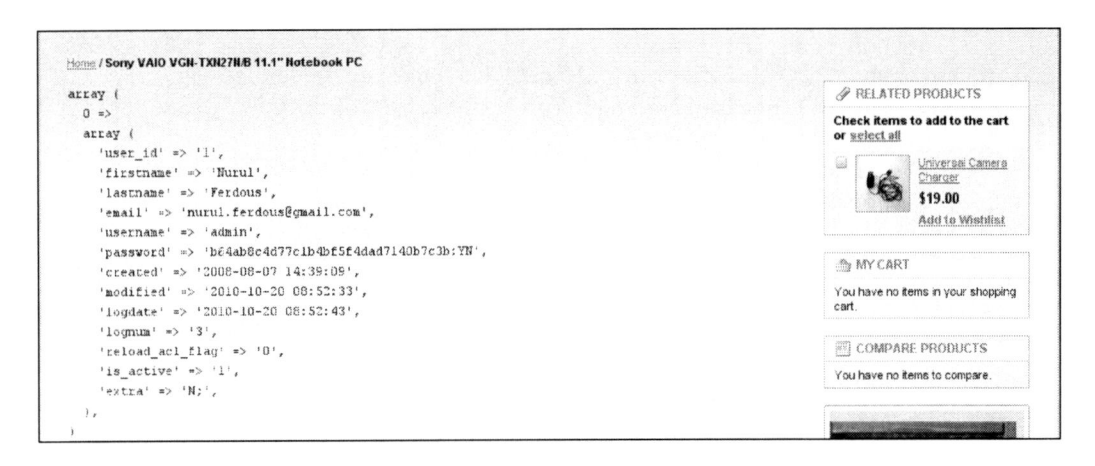

```
Home / Sony VAIO VGN-TXN27N/B 11.1" Notebook PC
array (
    0 =>
    array (
        'user_id' => '1',
        'firstname' => 'Nurul',
        'lastname' => 'Ferdous',
        'email' => 'nurul.ferdous@gmail.com',
        'username' => 'admin',
        'password' => 'be4ab8c4d77c1b4bf5f4dad7140b7c3b:YN',
        'created' => '2008-08-07 14:39:09',
        'modified' => '2010-10-20 08:52:33',
        'logdate' => '2010-10-20 08:52:43',
        'lognum' => '3',
        'reload_acl_flag' => '0',
        'is_active' => '1',
        'extra' => 'N;',
    ),
)
```

6. Let's create a new resource and use it for connecting to any database. Replace the previous code snippet with the following code block:

```php
<?php
  $conf = array(
  'host' => 'localhost',
  'username' => 'root',
  'password' => 'Owy! My password!!',
  'dbname' => 'wordpress' // you can any database name here
  );

  $_resource = Mage::getSingleton('core/resource');
  //Creating new connection to new server and new database
  $_conn = $_resource->createConnection('customConnection',
  'pdo_mysql', $conf);
  $results  = $_conn->query('SELECT * FROM wp_posts')->fetchAll();
  echo '<pre>';
  print_r($results);
  echo '</pre>';
?>
```

7. This way we can connect an external database and run the query using Magento's resource. We have connected an external WordPress database and fetched the `wp_posts` table. To see it in action, visit a product details page, such as: http://magento.local.com/index.php/sony-vaio-vgn-txn27n-b-11-1-notebook-pc.html.

Database Design

8. Here is another implementation with a filter for SKU:

   ```
   $collection_of_products = Mage::getModel('catalog/product')-
   >getCollection();
   //another neat thing about collections is you can pass them into
   the count     //function.  More PHP5 powered goodness
   echo "Our collection now has " . count($collection_of_products) .
   ' item(s)';
   $collection_of_products->addFieldToFilter('sku', 'mycomputer');
   echo '<pre>';
   var_export($collection_of_products->getFirstItem()->getData());
   echo '</pre>';
   ```

9. Hope that helps!

How it works...

Magento extensively uses **Singleton** design pattern for handling database connection. Singleton is a useful design pattern for allowing only one instance of your class. The Singleton's purpose is to control object creation, limiting the number to one but allowing the flexibility to create more objects if the situation changes. As there is only one Singleton instance, any instance fields of a Singleton will occur only once per class, just like static fields.

Magento database replication using Master Slave setup

Magento has got a cool feature for coping with a database replicating facility. Replication can be used in many cases to build effective and scalable, highly available solutions. There are a number of different methods for setting up replication, and the exact method to use depends on how you are setting up replication, and whether you already have data within your master database.

In this recipe, we will use some generic tasks that are common to all replication setups to accomplish the Master Slave setup for our Magento store. The advantage of this setup is that Magento can issue *read* queries to any of the Slave servers, saving all the *write* queries for the Master database. A database is traditionally a difficult component to scale horizontally, so replication is a happy compromise.

Getting ready

Let's decide and get two MySQL servers ready to do the replication successfully. Collect the information such as hostname, IP address, username, and password.

How to do it...

Configuring the Master:

1. Open your `my.cnf` file form `/etc/mysql` directory (if you are on a debian-based distro such as Ubuntu). If you are using a third party tool like XAMPP, then it would be `my.ini` file located in the `xampp/bin` directory.

2. Look for the following code and comment it out by adding a # before it. We need to see it as follows. This will let other networks to access MYSQL server. We will be using it from the slave.

   ```
   #bind-address           = 127.0.0.1
   ```

3. Paste the following code snippet under the `[mysqld]` section; you can modify the parameters as you fit it:

   ```
   server-id              = 1
   log_bin                = /var/log/mysql/mysql-bin.log
   expire_logs_days       = 10
   max_binlog_size        = 100M
   binlog_do_db           = magentodb
   ```

4. Restart your MYSQL server. If it's a debian-based distro then the command is:

   sudo /etc/init.d/mysql restart

5. Log in to your MYSQL console with root user:

   sudo mysql -u root -p

6. When you are in, issue the following commands in MYSQL shell:

   GRANT ALL PRIVILEGES ON `magentodb` . * TO 'slave_user'@'%' WITH GRANT OPTION IDENTIFIED BY 'slave_password';

   FLUSH PRIVILEGES;

   QUIT;

7. Log in to your MYSQL shell again with root privilege. Issue these commands and check the status of our Master:

   USE magentodb;

   FLUSH TABLES WITH READ LOCK;

   SHOW MASTER STATUS;

Database Design

8. You should see a result something like this:

```
mysql> SHOW MASTER STATUS;
+------------------+----------+--------------+------------------+
| File             | Position | Binlog_Do_DB | Binlog_Ignore_DB |
+------------------+----------+--------------+------------------+
| mysql-bin.000007 |      757 | replica      |                  |
+------------------+----------+--------------+------------------+
1 row in set (0.00 sec)

mysql>
```

9. Keep this information in a safe place as we will use it in our Slave setup.
10. Issue the following command in MYSQL shell to release the lock on tables as we have applied in the previous step:

    `UNLOCK TABLES;`

    `quit;`

11. There is no such step for Master setup. You are done!

Configuring the Slave:

1. Log in to your Slave server with root privilege as:

   `mysql -u root -p`

2. Create a new database named `magentodb` and import the exact schema exported from Master database.

3. Open `my.cnf` or `my.ini` file from `/etc/mysql` or `xampp/mysql/bin` folder. Put the following code under the `[mysqld]` section. Change it with your own server information:

   ```
   [mysqld]
   server-id = 2
   master-host = 192.168.3.12
   master-user = slave_user
   master-password = slave_password
   master-connect-retry = 60
   replicate-do-db = magentodb
   ```

4. Restart your MYSQL server now:

   `/etc/init.d/mysql restart`

5. Log in to your Slave MYSQL server shell:

   `mysql -u root -p`

6. Now issue the following command in your MySQL shell. Use the master log file and master log pos as you must have seen it while configuring the Master server.

   `CHANGE MASTER TO MASTER_HOST='192.168.3.12', MASTER_USER='slave_user', MASTER_PASSWORD='slave_password', MASTER_LOG_FILE='mysql-bin.000001', MASTER_LOG_POS=88;`

7. Now start the Slave server:

   `START SLAVE;`

8. Check the Slave status:

   `SHOW SLAVE STATUS \G`

9. It should look like this:

```
mysql> SHOW SLAVE STATUS \G
*************************** 1. row ***************************
               Slave_IO_State: Waiting for master to send event
                  Master_Host: 74.208.106.127
                  Master_User: replicator
                  Master_Port: 3306
                Connect_Retry: 60
              Master_Log_File: mysql-bin.000007
          Read_Master_Log_Pos: 757
               Relay_Log_File: mysqld-relay-bin.000012
                Relay_Log_Pos: 243
        Relay_Master_Log_File: mysql-bin.000007
             Slave_IO_Running: Yes
            Slave_SQL_Running: Yes
              Replicate_Do_DB: replica
          Replicate_Ignore_DB:
           Replicate_Do_Table:
       Replicate_Ignore_Table:
      Replicate_Wild_Do_Table:
  Replicate_Wild_Ignore_Table:
                   Last_Errno: 0
                   Last_Error:
                 Skip_Counter: 0
          Exec_Master_Log_Pos: 757
              Relay_Log_Space: 536
              Until_Condition: None
               Until_Log_File:
                Until_Log_Pos: 0
           Master_SSL_Allowed: No
           Master_SSL_CA_File:
           Master_SSL_CA_Path:
              Master_SSL_Cert:
            Master_SSL_Cipher:
               Master_SSL_Key:
        Seconds_Behind_Master: 0
Master_SSL_Verify_Server_Cert: No
                Last_IO_Errno: 0
                Last_IO_Error:
               Last_SQL_Errno: 0
               Last_SQL_Error:
1 row in set (0.00 sec)

mysql>
```

Database Design

> At this point, you can change your MySQL replication by modifying the Master database and seeing whether it changes automatically in the Slave database or not. Any change in the Master database should also apply the changes in the Slave database in (almost) real time!

10. Once you have MySQL replication functioning, configuring Magento to use multiple database servers is a relatively simple task. The only file you will have to edit is `app/etc/local.xml`. As you can see, there are two database connections configured, one called `default_setup` and one called `default_read`. The `default_setup` connection will be used for all write-based queries, and the `default_read` connection will be used for all read-based queries.

11. Here is my `app/etc/local.xml`, DIY (Do It Yourself):

    ```xml
    <resources>
      <db>
        <table_prefix><![CDATA[]]></table_prefix>
      </db>
      <default_setup>
        <connection>
          <host><![CDATA[master.localhost.com]]></host>
          <username><![CDATA[master_user]]></username>
          <password><![CDATA[owey!mypassword!!]]></password>
          <dbname><![CDATA[magentodb]]></dbname>
          <active>1</active>
        </connection>
      </default_setup>
      <default_read>
        <connection>
          <host><![CDATA[slave.localhost.com]]></host>
          <username><![CDATA[slave_user]]></username>
          <password><![CDATA[slave_password]]></password>
          <dbname><![CDATA[magentodb]]></dbname>
          <active>1</active>
        </connection>
      </default_read>
    </resources>
    ```

12. That's all for this recipe. You can test it now!

How it works...

On a replication master, you must enable binary logging and establish a unique server ID. If this has not already been done, this part of Master setup requires a server restart.

Binary logging must be enabled on the Master because the binary log is the basis for sending data changes from the Master to its Slaves. If binary logging is not enabled, replication will not be possible.

To configure replication on the Slave, you must determine the Master's current coordinates within its binary log. You will need this information so that when the Slave starts the replication process, it is able to start processing events from the binary log at the correct point.

If you can get this far, then Magento will do the rest. You don't need to worry about how it is happening there!

Using the Magento's Singleton method

Magento uses the popular Singleton design pattern to handle database connection with its resource models. It uses the PDO Adapter (`Varien_Db_Adapter_Pdo_Mysql`) object, which is just a sub-class of `Zend_Db_Adapter_Pdo_Mysql` from Zend Framework. In this recipe, we will run a custom SQL query against the Magento database by using the Singleton method.

Getting ready

Fire up your IDE and open the Magento project that we will be working on. Now open the `Mage.php` file from `app/` directory. Look for the method `getSingleton` in the `Mage.php` file. In my case, it's on line number 435. I am showing you the method here for your convenience.

```
    /**
    * Retrieve model object singleton
    *
    * @param    string $modelClass
    * @param    array $arguments
    * @return   Mage_Core_Model_Abstract
    */
       public static function getSingleton($modelClass='', array $arguments=array())
       {
          $registryKey = '_singleton/'.$modelClass;
          if (!self::registry($registryKey)) {
             self::register($registryKey, self::getModel($modelClass, $arguments));
          }
          return self::registry($registryKey);
       }
```

Look at the function header (`phpdoc`) carefully and note the function parameters within the bracket. This is the method we will be calling for running custom SQL query.

Database Design

How to do it...

1. We will print the data in the product view page for development purposes. Let us open the `view.phtml` file from the `app/design/frontend/YOUR_INTERFACE/YOUR_THEME/template/catalog/product/` folder.

2. Append the following code snippet at the top of `view.phtml`:

```
$w = Mage::getSingleton('core/resource')->getConnection('core_write');
$result = $w->query('select `entity_id` from `catalog_product_entity`');
if (!$result) {
    return false;
}
$row = $result->fetch(PDO::FETCH_ASSOC);
if (!$row) {
    return false;
}
echo '<pre>';
var_export($row);
echo '</pre>';
```

3. Visit any product details page to see the results in your browser.

How it works...

We used Magento's native database connection resource, which is core/resource with `core_write` privilege. We could use our own resources or other privileges such as `default_read`, and so on.

Repairing the Magento database

In some cases, we might face a problem with the database while working with Magento CMS. There is a pretty simple solution to revert the Magento database in its fresh version, if we have a backup of our Magento database. In this recipe, we will repair a corrupted database from a fresh backup by using the Magento database repair tool.

Getting ready

The Magento database repair tool is available in the Magento download section for free. You can download it from here: http://www.magentocommerce.com/download.

Look for the word **Database Repair Tool**, select your format, and download your copy.

How to do it...

1. Download the Magento database repair tool archive from the download page `http://www.magentocommerce.com/download`.
2. Uncompress the archive.
3. Put the `magento-db-repair-tool-1.0.php` into your `webroot` folder on your server. You don't have to put it in Magento.
4. Back up your existing database to have the ability to restore it if anything goes wrong.
5. Let's say we have two databases. One is named `magento_fresh` and another is `magento_corrupted`.
6. Point your browser to the location where you pasted the `magento-db-repair-tool-1.0.php`. You should see a page something like the following screenshot. Enter credentials as I did:

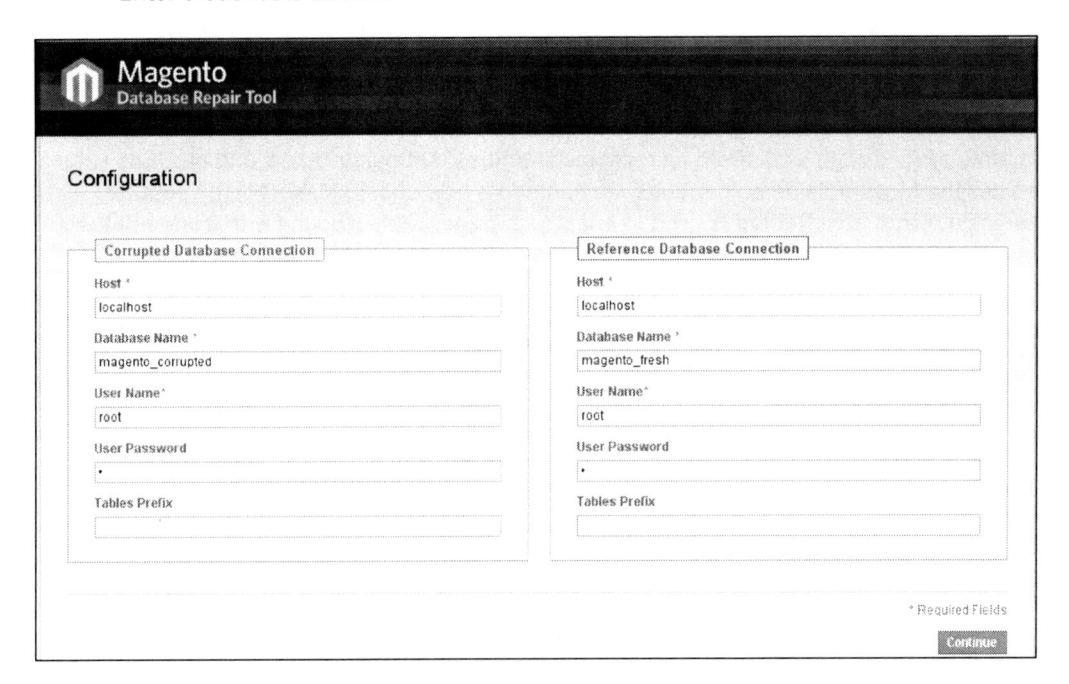

7. Upon submitting this form you will see the detailed report on the repair process.
8. Check your corrupted Magento site now.

Database Design

How it works...

The Database Repair Tool compares two databases (reference and target), and updates the target database, so it has the same structure as the reference database by doing the following:

- Adds missing tables, or repairs them to have the same engine type and charset
- Adds missing fields or repairs them
- Removes inconsistent data from tables that have broken foreign key references
- Adds missing foreign keys and indexes

Working with Magento's EAV design

Magento uses EAV to allow vertical data modeling rather than the traditional horizontal modeling. In an EAV design, we can add unlimited columns, that's the best part of it. But at the cost of deteriorating the query performance and losing your business logic, which was kept in the relational database schema.

Magento's EAV design works with its resources, entities, entity-attributes, and attribute values. Besides the Magento's default entities, we can add a new one. In Magento, the popular design pattern **Active Record** is used to ensure efficiency while working with a large dataset for serious business applications.

Entities allow you to load and save complex relationships to and from the database. But most of the time when we think of database queries, we want to write a SELECT statement that gives us a result with multiple rows. The entity models will not be able to do that. Entities are designed to load one item, or record at a time.

Only being able to deal with one record at a time means that we must know the record's primary ID value to load it. But what happens when we want to select all records from the database matching some criteria? Normally, a simple SELECT statement with a WHERE clause would work. But things are not that simple when dealing with entities. Not all of the data that makes up an entity lives in one table, so we need to JOIN more tables. To solve this problem, we will use Magento model's `getCollection()` and `addAttributeToFilter()` here.

How to do it...

1. We will print the data in the product view page for development purposes. Let us open the `view.phtml` file from the `app/design/frontend/YOUR_INTERFACE/YOUR_THEME/template/catalog/product/` folder.

2. Append the following code snippet at the top of `view.phtml`:

```
$products = Mage::getModel('catalog/product')->getCollection();
$products->addAttributeToFilter('entity_id', array('in'=>
```

```
    array(163,164,165) ));
$products->load();
echo '<pre>';
foreach($products as $product) {
    var_export($product->getData());
}
echo '</pre>';
?>
```

3. Visit any product details page to see the results in your browser. Here is a screenshot:

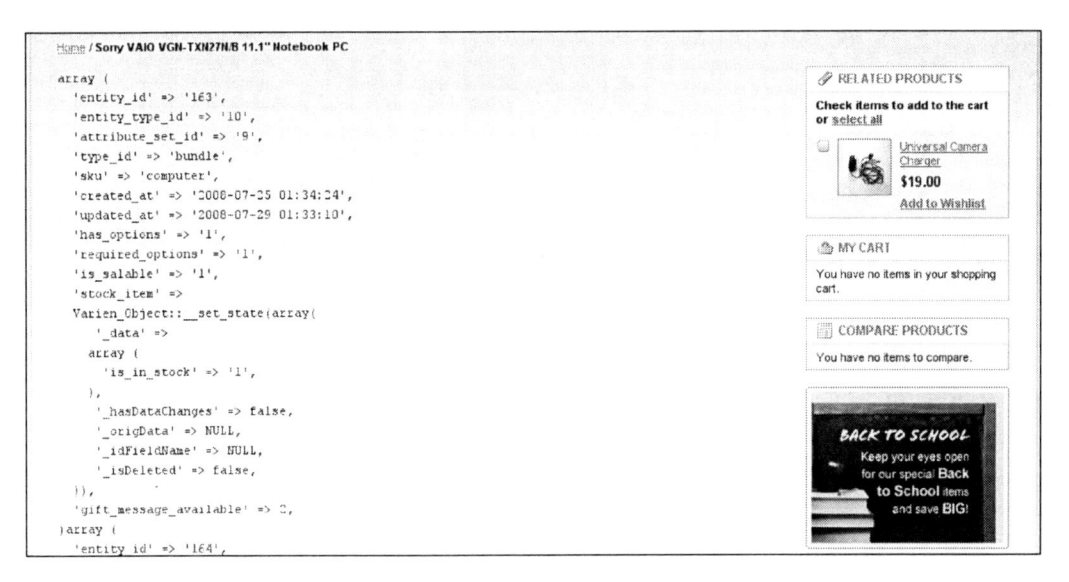

4. Here is another example for your better understanding:
```
<?php
$products = Mage::getModel('catalog/product')->getCollection();
$products->addAttributeToFilter('sku', 'uni-hoodie-medium');
$products->load();
echo '<pre>';
foreach($products as $product) {
    var_export($product->getData());
}
echo '</pre>';
?>
```

5. Hope that helps!

How it works...

We used the product model from catalog and for grabbing product collection by chaining the `getCollection()` method. Then we added a filter for a specific product listing. We can use some other types of attributes and parameters. Here is the `phpdoc` that handles the parameters of the `addFilterAtributes` routine:

```
/**
 * Build SQL statement for condition
 *
 * If $condition integer or string - exact value will be filtered
 *
 * If $condition is array is - one of the following structures is expected:
 * - array("from"=>$fromValue, "to"=>$toValue)
 * - array("like"=>$likeValue)
 * - array("neq"=>$notEqualValue)
 * - array("in"=>array($inValues))
 * - array("nin"=>array($notInValues))
 *
 * If non matched - sequential array is expected and OR conditions
 * will be built using above mentioned structure
 *
 * @param string $fieldName
 * @param integer|string|array $condition
 * @return string
 */
```

8
Creating a Module

In this chapter, we will cover:

- Creating an empty module with a Module Creator
- Creating the required directories
- Activating a module
- Creating a controller for the module
- Creating a configuration XML file for the module
- Creating a helper for the News module
- Creating models for the module
- Setting up SQL for the News module
- Designing a template for the News module
- Adding required blocks for the News module

Introduction

Modules are the building blocks of Magento CMS. Every action on the site, frontend or backend, goes through a module. Modules act as containers for one or more of the following:

- Settings
- Database schemas
- Rendering objects
- Utility helpers
- Data models
- Action controllers

Creating a Module

A module can comprise all the six items mentioned earlier, or just one (as many as required). Modules are defined as being ON or OFF through an XML configuration file located in the `app/etc/modules/` directory. Each module can specify its own settings in an XML file as well, located under the module's `etc/` directory. As everything in Magento is a module, and modules have self-contained configuration and database settings, this allows you to extend Magento exactly as the core system is built.

In this chapter, we will create a custom News module with a custom database table. This module involves both the frontend and backend related tasks. Let's start!

> Throughout this chapter we have used `Packt` as the Namespace and `News` as the module name.

Creating an empty module with a Module Creator

Before we start, I would like to thank *Daniel Nitz* who has written a nice extension named Module Creator to build the necessary directories and files in an appropriate location. In this recipe, we will create an empty module with this extension.

Getting ready

We have some preliminary work to do. We need to install the Module creator extension via Magento Connect.

1. Log in to your Magento backend.
2. Navigate to the page **System | Magento Connect | Magento Connect Manager** page.
3. Log in with your admin username and password.
4. Navigate to the **settings** tab and set **Preferred State** as: **beta**. Save this setting.
5. Navigate back to the **extensions** tab and enter the extension key for the module creator in the textbox as: `magento-community/Netz98_ModuleCreator`.
6. Click **install**.
7. After the completion of the installation process, a new directory will be created in your Magento root directory, which is `moduleCreator`.

> moduleCreator extension won't be installed if you have set your **Preferred State** as **stable**. Make sure you set it as **beta** from the **settings** tab.

How to do it...

Let's assume that we have already installed the module creator extension in our Magento installation. If you haven't installed it yet, please install it from the previously mentioned steps.

1. Navigate your browser to the following URL:

    `http://magento.local.com/moduleCreator/`

2. Enter the required information, when you see a page something like this:

Magento Module Creator

Skeleton Template: (you could build your own)	Blank News Module ▼
Namespace: (e.g. your Company Name)	Packt
Module: (e.g. Blog, News, Forum)	News
Magento Root Directory: (auto detected)	/var/www/magento.local.com/public
Design: (interface, default is 'default')	default
Design: (theme, default is 'default')	default

[create] [uninstall]

To create a new module, insert Namespace and a Module name (e.g. Blog, Forum, etc.) as well as your design above. If you want it to be installed right away into your Magento, enter your Magento install path.

3. Click on the **create** button. This will create an empty module in our Magento installation.

How it works...

Module Creator is an extension, which is available in Magento Connect as a free extension. We installed it via Magento Connect. We specified the namespace, Module name, Magento root directory, interface name, and design/theme name. Upon clicking the **create** button, this extension creates a blank module in the `app/code/local` directory. You may have a look at the directories and files that have been created by the Module Creator extension.

Creating a Module

Creating the required directories

Magento maintains a strict naming convention. We will follow it while creating new directories and files for our module. We will be using the local codePool, that is, the `app/code/local` directory.

How to do it...

1. Open your Magento root directory with your file explorer. In my case, it is at the following location:

    `/var/www/magento.local.com/public/`

2. Now go to the location `app/code/local` directory. If you followed our previous recipe, you should see a folder named `Packt` here. In that case, you may skip this recipe. If you have not followed the previous recipe, then you have to perform the following steps.

3. Let us create the directories for our module now as the following tree in the `app/code/local` directory:

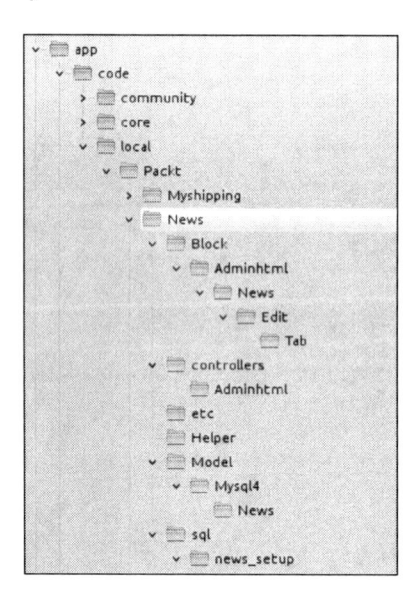

    ```
    v app
        v code
            > community
            > core
            v local
                v Packt
                    > Myshipping
                    v News
                        v Block
                            v Adminhtml
                                v News
                                    v Edit
                                        Tab
                        v controllers
                            Adminhtml
                        etc
                        Helper
                        v Model
                            v Mysql4
                                News
                        v sql
                            v news_setup
    ```

4. We are done with creating required directories for the local section. We have to create some more directories for our current Magento template.

5. Create a new directory named `News` in your active Magento theme's template directory. The template directory should reside in the `app/design/frontend/YOUR_INTERFACE/YOUR_THEME/` template. In my case, the full path of the active template is as follows:

```
/var/www/magento.local.com/public/app/design/frontend/default/
default/template/
```

6. Okay, we have created all directories for our module.
7. Let us go to the next recipe, which deals with the activation of our module.

How it works...

This is the task of our operating system while we were creating some directories on various locations. Keep in mind that we are creating these folders in `app/code/local`. Do not do it in locale directory. The `app/code` has three folders as follows:

- **Core**: The Magento core code resides here
- **Community**: This contains the code installed via Magento Connect
- **Local**: This contains the custom module's code

Activating a module

Activating or deactivating a module in Magento is handled by an XML file. In this recipe, we will activate our News module by specifying it in an XML file named `Packt_News.xml`.

How to do it...

1. Create a new XML file named INTERFACE_MODULE in the `app/etc/modules` directory. In my case, this is `Packt_News.xml`.
2. If you already have this file, there is no need to create a new one. Just replace the existing code with the following code snippet:

```xml
<?xml version="1.0"?>
<config>
  <modules>
    <Packt_News>
      <active>true</active>
      <codePool>local</codePool>
    </Packt_News>
  </modules>
</config>
```

3. Save this file and exit.

Creating a Module

How it works...

Magento depends heavily on XML file configurations. For our new module, we had to tell Magento to activate News module from the package `Packt`. And the codepool for our News module resides in the `app/code/local` directory. We wrote it in an XML file as Magento can interpret it.

Creating a controller for the module

A controller plays a vital role in mapping URL to a specific business logic. In Magento, a controller extends the Magento's front controller, which is ultimately linked with Zend Framework's front controller via Varien front action controller. In this recipe, we will create some controllers both for frontend and backend activities.

How to do it...

1. Create a new file named `IndexController.php` in the `app/code/local/Packt/News/controllers/` directory.

2. Paste the following code in the `IndexController.php` file. If it's not empty then make it empty and paste the following code:

```php
<?php
class Packt_News_IndexController extends Mage_Core_Controller_Front_Action
{
  public function indexAction()
  {
    $resource = Mage::getSingleton('core/resource');
    $read = $resource->getConnection('core_read');
    $newsTable = $resource->getTableName('news');

    $select = $read->select()
       ->from($newsTable, array('news_id', 'title', 'filename', 'content', 'status'))
       ->where('status', 1)
       ->order('created_time DESC');

    $news = $read->fetchAll($select);
    Mage::register('list', $news);

    $this->loadLayout();
    $this->renderLayout();
  }
```

```php
  public function viewAction()
  {
    $news_id = $this->getRequest()->getParam('id');

    if ($news_id != null && $news_id != '') {
      $news = Mage::getModel('news/news')->load($news_id)-
>getData();
    } else {
      $news = null;
    }

  /**
  * If no param we load a the last created item
  */
  if ($news == null) {
    $resource = Mage::getSingleton('core/resource');
    $read = $resource->getConnection('core_read');
    $newsTable = $resource->getTableName('news');

    $select = $read->select()
        ->from($newsTable, array('news_id', 'filename', 'title',
'content', 'status', 'update_time'))
        ->where('status', 1)
        ->order('created_time DESC');

      $news = $read->fetchRow($select);
  }

  Mage::register('news', $news);

    $this->loadLayout();
    $this->renderLayout();
  }

} // end of class
```

3. Save this file. We need to create another controller for the admin part of our News module.
4. Let's create another controller inside the `app/code/local/Packt/News/controllers/Adminhtml/` directory. Let us name it `NewsController.php`.
5. In my case, the full path is:

   `/var/www/magento.local.com/public/app/code/local/Packt/News/controllers/Adminhtml/`

Creating a Module

6. Our News module has two sections. One for the frontend and the other is for managing the news in the admin panel. This step will create a controller for the backend, which will be used for the **CRUD** (**Create, Read, Update, and Delete**) of a news. This controller has few methods prepended with Action, which works as their name suggests. The interaction with data is accomplished by the News model.

7. The content of News controller is dissected next for your better understanding. The full controller along with other files are bundled with this book.

8. The following code block has a method named _initAction(), which is invoked before calling any controller action. We did three tasks in _initAction():

    - Loading layout
    - Setting active menu in the backend
    - Adding breadcrumb text

```php
<?php
class Packt_News_Adminhtml_NewsController extends Mage_Adminhtml_Controller_action
{
  protected function _initAction()
  {
    $this->loadLayout()
        ->_setActiveMenu('news/items')
        ->_addBreadcrumb(Mage::helper('adminhtml')->__('Items Manager'), Mage::helper('adminhtml')->__('Item Manager'));

    return $this;
  }
```

9. This section deals with the index action of News controller in the admin area. When a user clicks on **Manage Items** from the **News** menu in the admin panel, this is the action that is invoked via the front controller:

```php
  public function indexAction()
  {
    $this->_initAction();
    $this->_addContent($this->getLayout()-
       >createBlock('news/adminhtml_news'));
    $this->renderLayout();
  }
```

10. The edit action is invoked when a user clicks on the **edit** link in the news listing under the **News item management** section. The related news ID is grabbed from the ID parameter and passed to the news model to fetch the specific news. If the given news ID yields a result, it passes the data to the news form to populate the form with the given data. Upon submission of the news edit form, the data is passed to the save

Chapter 8

action with the news ID for updating it. There are some other tasks, which have been achieved in this method such as loading layout, setting up the active menu, adding breadcrumb text, and so on.

```
public function editAction()
{
   $id = $this->getRequest()->getParam('id');
   $model = Mage::getModel('news/news')->load($id);

   if ($model->getId() || $id == 0) {
      $data = Mage::getSingleton('adminhtml/session')->getFormData(true);
       if (!empty($data)) {
         $model->setData($data);
       }
      Mage::register('news_data', $model);
        $this->loadLayout();
        $this->_setActiveMenu('news/items');
        $this->_addBreadcrumb(Mage::helper('adminhtml')->__('Item Manager'), Mage::helper('adminhtml')->__('News Item Manager'));
        $this->_addBreadcrumb(Mage::helper('adminhtml')->__('Item News'), Mage::helper('adminhtml')->__('Item News'));
        $this->getLayout()->getBlock('head')->setCanLoadExtJs(true);
        $this->_addContent($this->getLayout()->createBlock('news/adminhtml_news_edit'))
             ->_addLeft($this->getLayout()->createBlock('news/adminhtml_news_edit_tabs'));

        $this->renderLayout();
     } else {
        Mage::getSingleton('adminhtml/session')->addError(Mage::helper('news')->__('Item does not exist'));
        $this->_redirect('*/*/');
     }
}
```

11. When a user clicks on the **Add item** button the request is passed to this action, which is forwarded to the edit action without any ID. When the edit action is called without a news ID it considers the request as a new entry and loads the form as empty.

```
public function newAction()
{
   $this->_forward('edit');
}
```

Creating a Module

12. The news form's action is set to `this` method to handle the form's submitted data. If the form data is valid, it saves the data in the news table via the News model, or else it shows an appropriate error messages. This action is invoked both for a new news or editing an existing news. There is a field for photo in this form. We set the allowed extensions as 'jpg', 'jpeg', 'gif', 'png'. You can change it as you please. We set the file upload path as: `$path = Mage::getBaseDir('media') . DS . 'news' . DS`, which translates it to `media/news/`.

```php
public function saveAction()
{
   if ($data = $this->getRequest()->getPost()) {
      if (isset($_FILES['filename']['name']) && $_FILES['filename']['name'] != '') {
         try {
         /* Starting upload */
            $uploader = new Varien_File_Uploader('filename');

            // Any extention would work
            $uploader->setAllowedExtensions(array('jpg', 'jpeg', 'gif', 'png'));
            $uploader->setAllowRenameFiles(false);
            $uploader->setFilesDispersion(false);
            // We set media as the upload dir
            $path = Mage::getBaseDir('media') . DS . 'news' . DS;
            $uploader->save($path, $_FILES['filename']['name']);
         } catch (Exception $e) {
      }
      //this way the name is saved in DB
         $data['filename'] = $_FILES['filename']['name'];
      }
      $model = Mage::getModel('news/news');
      $model->setData($data)
            ->setId($this->getRequest()->getParam('id'));
      try {
         if ($model->getCreatedTime == NULL || $model->getUpdateTime() == NULL) {
            $model->setCreatedTime(now())
                  ->setUpdateTime(now());
         } else {
            $model->setUpdateTime(now());
         }
         $model->save();
         Mage::getSingleton('adminhtml/session')->addSuccess(Mage::helper('news')->__('Item was successfully saved'));
         Mage::getSingleton('adminhtml/session')->setFormData(false);
```

```
            if ($this->getRequest()->getParam('back')) {
                $this->_redirect('*/*/edit', array('id' => $model-
>getId()));
            return;
            }
            $this->_redirect('*/*/');
            return;
            } catch (Exception $e) {
                Mage::getSingleton('adminhtml/session')->addError($e-
>getMessage());
                Mage::getSingleton('adminhtml/session')-
>setFormData($data);
                $this->_redirect('*/*/edit', array('id' => $this-
>getRequest()->getParam('id')));
                return;
            }
        }
        Mage::getSingleton('adminhtml/session')->addError(Mage::help
er('news')->__('Unable to find item to save'));
        $this->_redirect('*/*/');
    }
```

13. The delete action on the news controller deals with the deletion of news specified by the ID param. In this action, we grabbed the ID parameter and checked if news exists with the given ID. If the news exists, we deleted it and redirected it to its listing page with a successful message.

```
    public function deleteAction()
    {
      if ($this->getRequest()->getParam('id') > 0) {
        try {
          $model = Mage::getModel('news/news');

          $model->setId($this->getRequest()->getParam('id'))
                ->delete();
          Mage::getSingleton('adminhtml/session')->addSuccess(Mage::
helper('adminhtml')->__('Item was successfully deleted'));
          $this->_redirect('*/*/');
        } catch (Exception $e) {
          Mage::getSingleton('adminhtml/session')->addError($e-
>getMessage());
          $this->_redirect('*/*/edit', array('id' => $this-
>getRequest()->getParam('id')));
        }
      }
      $this->_redirect('*/*/');
    }
```

Creating a Module

14. In the **News management** panel, we have provided to perform some batch processing such as mass deletion and mass status changes. This action is invoked when a user selects some news and submits the form with selecting **Delete** in the **actions** drop-down. In this action, we fetched the submitted news IDs and passed it to the news model for deletion. When the news model is done with the given news IDs, we showed appropriate status messages in the Magento admin panel and redirected it to the news index page.

    ```
    public function massDeleteAction()
    {
      $newsIds = $this->getRequest()->getParam('news');
      if (!is_array($newsIds)) {
        Mage::getSingleton('adminhtml/session')-
    >addError(Mage::helper('adminhtml')->__('Please select item(s)'));
      } else {
        try {
          foreach ($newsIds as $newsId) {
            $news = Mage::getModel('news/news')->load($newsId);
            $news->delete();
          }
          Mage::getSingleton('adminhtml/session')->addSuccess(
            Mage::helper('adminhtml')->__(
            'Total of %d record(s) were successfully deleted',
    count($newsIds)
            )
          );
        } catch (Exception $e) {
          Mage::getSingleton('adminhtml/session')->addError($e-
    >getMessage());
        }
      }
      $this->_redirect('*/*/index');
    }
    ```

15. There is another batch action in our news controller to swap the existing news status between "enabled" and "disabled". This action handles the form data when a user selects some existing news in the admin panel and submits it with a changed status. This action is helpful when a user wants to change multiple news in a single request. In this action, all news IDs are harvested from the form and iterated over it to apply the appropriate status as requested in the admin panel.

    ```
    public function massStatusAction()
    {
      $newsIds = $this->getRequest()->getParam('news');
      if (!is_array($newsIds)) {
        Mage::getSingleton('adminhtml/session')->addError($this->__
    ('Please select item(s)'));
    ```

```
      } else {
        try {
          foreach ($newsIds as $newsId) {
            $news = Mage::getSingleton('news/news')
                    ->load($newsId)
                    ->setStatus($this->getRequest()-
>getParam('status'))
                    ->setIsMassupdate(true)
                    ->save();
          }
          $this->_getSession()->addSuccess(
          $this->__('Total of %d record(s) were successfully
updated', count($newsIds))
          );
        } catch (Exception $e) {
          $this->_getSession()->addError($e->getMessage());
        }
      }
      $this->_redirect('*/*/index');
    }
```

16. The `exportCsvAction` works as its name suggests. We used Magento's CSV parsing feature to handle the export process. We set the name as `news.csv`, which could be set as you like. The exported `news.csv` file will be downloaded upon submission of the form in the admin panel. The file will contain all news in a CSV (comma separated value) with the column names as the first row.

```
    public function exportCsvAction()
    {
      $fileName = 'news.csv';
      $content = $this->getLayout()->createBlock('news/adminhtml
    ->getCsv();

      $this->_sendUploadResponse($fileName, $content);
    }
```

17. This action is similar to the previous one while this time the output formatting will be in XML. In this function, another protected function is called to send some XML-related headers.

```
    public function exportXmlAction()
    {
      $fileName = 'news.xml';
      $content = $this->getLayout()->createBlock('news/adminhtml_
    news_grid')
                  ->getXml();

      $this->_sendUploadResponse($fileName, $content);
    }
```

Creating a Module

18. This function is called in `exportXmlAction` to send some HTTP headers while exporting the news grid as XML.

    ```
    protected function _sendUploadResponse($fileName, $content, $contentType='application/octet-stream')
    {
        $response = $this->getResponse();
        $response->setHeader('HTTP/1.1 200 OK', '');
        $response->setHeader('Pragma', 'public', true);
        $response->setHeader('Cache-Control', 'must-revalidate, post-check=0, pre-check=0', true);
        $response->setHeader('Content-Disposition', 'attachment; filename=' . $fileName);
        $response->setHeader('Last-Modified', date('r'));
        $response->setHeader('Accept-Ranges', 'bytes');
        $response->setHeader('Content-Length', strlen($content));
        $response->setHeader('Content-type', $contentType);
        $response->setBody($content);
        $response->sendResponse();
        die;
    }
    ```

19. This was all about the news controller for the **News management** area in Magento admin. The file is bundled with the others along with this book.

How it works...

A controller in Magento works as any other Zend Framework-based application's controller. A controller works behind the whole MVC design pattern. It manipulates models, decides which view to display based on the user's request and other factors, passes along the data that each view will need, or hands off control to another controller entirely. It's always a good practice to keep a controller as skinny as possible.

The `IndexController` class has two actions: index and view. Index action shows the listing page for news while view renders the news details for specific news. This controller is responsible for the frontend functionalities.

The `NewsController` inside the `Adminhtml` folder deals the management of news in the admin panel. It has the following actions:

- index
- new
- edit
- delete

- exportCsv
- exportXml
- massDelete
- massStatus
- save

> Every action in Zend Framework is appended with Action, which helps in mapping the correct route for that action in a controller.

Creating a configuration XML file for the module

The `config.xml` file is the heart of any module in Magento CMS. It plays a vital role for binding all the components of a module. In this recipe, we will create the configuration file, which is `config.xml` for our News module.

How to do it...

1. Create a new file named `config.xml` in the `app/code/local/NAMESPACE/MODULE/etc` directory. In my case, it's `/var/www/magento.local.com/public/app/code/local/Packt/News/etc/config.xml`.

2. Replace the content with the following:
   ```
   <?xml version="1.0"?>
   <config>
     <modules>
       <Packt_News>
         <version>0.1.0</version>
       </Packt_News>
     </modules>
     <frontend>
       <routers>
         <news>
           <use>standard</use>
           <args>
             <module>Packt_News</module>
             <frontName>news</frontName>
           </args>
         </news>
       </routers>
   ```

Creating a Module

```xml
        <layout>
          <updates>
            <news>
              <file>news.xml</file>
            </news>
          </updates>
        </layout>
      </frontend>
      <admin>
        <routers>
          <news>
            <use>admin</use>
            <args>
              <module>Packt_News</module>
              <frontName>news</frontName>
            </args>
          </news>
        </routers>
      </admin>
      <adminhtml>
        <menu>
          <news module="news">
            <title>News</title>
            <sort_order>71</sort_order>
            <children>
              <items module="news">
                <title>Manage Items</title>
                <sort_order>0</sort_order>
                <action>news/adminhtml_news</action>
              </items>
            </children>
          </news>
        </menu>
        <acl>
          <resources>
            <all>
              <title>Allow Everything</title>
            </all>
            <admin>
              <children>
                <Packt_News>
                  <title>News Module</title>
                  <sort_order>10</sort_order>
                </Packt_News>
```

```xml
          </children>
        </admin>
      </resources>
    </acl>
    <layout>
      <updates>
        <news>
          <file>news.xml</file>
        </news>
      </updates>
    </layout>
  </adminhtml>
  <global>
    <models>
      <news>
        <class>Packt_News_Model</class>
        <resourceModel>news_mysql4</resourceModel>
      </news>
      <news_mysql4>
        <class>Packt_News_Model_Mysql4</class>
        <entities>
          <news>
            <table>news</table>
          </news>
        </entities>
      </news_mysql4>
    </models>
    <resources>
      <news_setup>
        <setup>
          <module>Packt_News</module>
        </setup>
        <connection>
          <use>core_setup</use>
        </connection>
      </news_setup>
      <news_write>
        <connection>
          <use>core_write</use>
        </connection>
      </news_write>
      <news_read>
        <connection>
            <use>core_read</use>
```

Creating a Module

```
          </connection>
        </news_read>
      </resources>
      <blocks>
        <news>
          <class>Packt_News_Block</class>
        </news>
      </blocks>
      <helpers>
        <news>
          <class>Packt_News_Helper</class>
        </news>
      </helpers>
    </global>
</config>
```

3. Save and close.
4. There is no such step as step 4!

How it works...

This file holds the information of different components of our News module both for frontend and backend. If we have a look on the structure of this `config.xml` file, we will see there are five blocks:

1. **modules**: This holds the version information
2. **frontend**: This holds router and layout information
3. **admin**: This is the router settings and arguments for the admin part
4. **adminhtml**: This is the menu, acl, and layout for the admin
5. **global**: This holds configuration for model, resources, blocks, and helpers

> Make sure that there is no line break inside **global | models | news | class** tag.

Creating a helper for the News module

In an MVC application, the model handles the business logic and returns data to the controller and the controller ultimately passes the data to views. If we need to apply a fairly complex logic that needs to be repeated or we don't want to place it in a view file, then Helper is the component that will help. In most cases a Helper helps organizing data in a presentable fashion and deals with the logic in it that would be repeated in place. In this recipe, we will create an empty Helper file for our News module. Here are some common use cases for a Helper in Magento:

- Accessing models
- Performing complex or repeatable display logic
- Manipulating and formatting model data
- Persisting data between view scripts

How to do it...

1. Create a new PHP file named `Data.php` in the `app/code/local/NAMESPACE/MODULE/Helper/` directory. In my case, the `Data.php` resides in:

   `/var/www/magento.local.com/public/app/code/local/Packt/News/Helper/Data.php`

2. The content should be as follows:

   ```php
   <?php
   class Packt_News_Helper_Data extends Mage_Core_Helper_Abstract
   {

   }
   ```

How it works...

This file is a part of our News module. We could add some methods in it if we like. We kept it empty as we didn't have any complex logic for our News module. But you got the idea why a Helper is required in Magento and what it does.

Creating models for the module

A model is the thing that manipulates the business logics of an MVC application. In Magento, a model handles fetching, updating database records, talking to web services, and so on. The model is the important part of an MVC design pattern. A Magento model uses `Zend_Db_Table_Abstract`, which is connected via Varien object while working with database. In this recipe, we will create a bunch of models to work with our custom table for News module.

Creating a Module

How to do it...

1. Create a new file named `News.php` in the `app/code/local/Packt/News/Model/` directory.

2. Replace the content with the following code:

```php
<?php
class Packt_News_Model_News extends Mage_Core_Model_Abstract
{

  public function _construct()
  {
    parent::_construct();
    $this->_init('news/news');
  }

}
```

3. Let us create another model for MySQL4 version. Create a new file named `News.php` in the `app/code/local/Packt/News/Model/Mysql4/` folder. Replace the content with the following:

```php
<?php
class Packt_News_Model_Mysql4_News extends Mage_Core_Model_Mysql4_Abstract
{

  public function _construct()
  {
     // Note that the news_id refers to the key field in your database table.
     $this->_init('news/news', 'news_id');
  }

}
```

4. Create another model class file named `Collection.php` in the `app/code/local/Packt/News/Mode/Mysql4/News/` folder and replace the content with the following code:

```php
<?php

class Packt_News_Model_Mysql4_News_Collection extends Mage_Core_Model_Mysql4_Collection_Abstract
{

  public function _construct()
```

```
    {
      parent::_construct();
      $this->_init('news/news');
    }

}
```

5. Let's create the last model for our News module. Create a new file named `Status.php` in the `app/code/local/Packt/News/Model` directory and replace the content with the following:

```
<?php
class Packt_News_Model_Status extends Varien_Object
{
  const STATUS_ENABLED = 1;
  const STATUS_DISABLED = 2;

  static public function getOptionArray()
  {
    return array(
      self::STATUS_ENABLED => Mage::helper('news')->__('Enabled'),
      self::STATUS_DISABLED => Mage::helper('news')->__('Disabled')
    );
  }

}
```

6. Save and close `Status.php`.
7. There is no task left for model creation this time.

How it works...

A model in Magento works with a database via the `Varien_Object`, which relates to `Zend_Db_Abstract`. We just extended the Varien's `Mage_Core_Model_Abstract` class, which is connected with `Zend_Db_Adapter`. We used some common methods for our needs.

The very first model we wrote is `News.php`. In this file we extended the `Mage_Core_Model_Abstract` class, which is ultimately connected to the database. Inside the constructor we called its parent constructor and the `_init()`, which is actually a protected function in the `Mage_Core_Model_Abstract` class. This initialization will let us use the methods defined in `Mage_Core_Model_Abstract`, such as: `load()`, `save()`, `delete()`, among others.

The `Status.php` file is the model that deals with the status update in Magento admin for the news module. This model is extended to `Varien_Object`, which has some common functionalities to update the status of a database record in the Magento admin panel.

Creating a Module

The models inside the `Mysql4` folder perform similar tasks as outside the Mysql4 models. They extend different classes of Magento to provide similar functionalities in MySQL 4 version.

Setting up SQL for the News module

In this recipe, we will create a new PHP file, which will create a new table in the Magento database during installation.

How to do it...

1. Create a new file named `mysql4-install-0.1.0.php` inside the `app/code/local/Packt/News/sql/news_setup/` directory.

2. Replace the current content with the following:

```php
<?php

$installer = $this;

$installer->startSetup();

$installer->run("

-- DROP TABLE IF EXISTS {$this->getTable('news')};
CREATE TABLE {$this->getTable('news')} (
  `news_id` int(11) unsigned NOT NULL auto_increment,
  `title` varchar(255) NOT NULL default '',
  `filename` varchar(255) NOT NULL default '',
  `content` text NOT NULL default '',
  `status` smallint(6) NOT NULL default '0',
  `created_time` datetime NULL,
  `update_time` datetime NULL,
  PRIMARY KEY (`news_id`)
) ENGINE=InnoDB DEFAULT CHARSET=utf8;

    ");

$installer->endSetup();
```

3. Save and close this file.

How it works...

During installation this file will be invoked as we specified it in the configuration file. It drops any existing table named `news` in our Magento database and creates a new one with the previously mentioned schema.

You are encouraged to modify the SQL file to fit your needs.

Designing a template for the News module

We have already set up the required business logics in our previous recipes in this chapter. In this recipe, we will render the data via Magento's presentation layer that is `View`. We will create some view files in our current interface's active theme directory. Let's do it now!

How to do it...

1. Create a new file named `News.phtml` in the `app/design/frontend/YOUR_INTERFACE/YOUR_THEME/template/news/` directory. In my case, the full path is `/var/www/magento.local.com/public/app/design/frontend/default/default/template/news/news.phtml`.

2. Replace the existing content with the following code:

```
<h3><?php echo $this->__('Latest news from Packt') ?></h3>

<table>
<?php foreach($this->getNewsList() as $item): ?>
<tr>
  <td><img src="<?php echo Mage::getBaseUrl('media') . 'news' . DS . $item['filename'] ?>" alt="<?php echo $item['title'] ?>" width="64" height="64" style="border: 1px solid #d5d5d5;padding:3px;margin-right: 10px;" /></td>
  <td>
    <h5><?php echo $item['title'] ?></h5>
    <p><?php echo $this->limitCharacter($item['content'], 180, "<a href='/news/index/view/id/".$item['news_id']."'>read more</a>") ?></p>
  </td>
</tr>
<?php endforeach; ?>
</table>
```

Creating a Module

3. Create another file named `view.phtml` in the same location and replace the existing code with the following:

```
<?php $item = $this->getNews(); ?>
<h3><?php echo $item['title']; ?></h3>
<p style="font-size: small;color: #777">published on: <?php echo date('M jS, Y', strtotime($item['update_time'])); ?> <a href="/news">Back to all news</a></p>
<div>
  <span style="float: left">
      <img src="<?php echo Mage::getBaseUrl('media') . 'news' . DS . $item['filename'] ?>" alt="<?php echo $item['title'] ?>" width="128" height="128" style="border: 1px solid #d5d5d5;padding:3px;margin-right: 10px;" />
  </span>
  <span>
    <p><?php echo $item['content']; ?></p>
  </span>
  <p style="clear: both"></p>
</div>
<a href="/news">Back to all news</a>
```

4. Save and close this file.

5. We have to create the layout file for our template. Create a new XML file named `News.xml` in the `app/design/frontend/YOUR_INTERFACE/YOUR_THEME/layout/` directory.

6. Replace existing content with the following:

```
<?xml version="1.0"?>
<layout version="0.1.0">
  <default>
  </default>
  <news_index_index>
     <reference name="content">
        <block type="news/news" name="news" template="news/news.phtml" />
     </reference>
  </news_index_index>

  <news_index_view>
     <reference name="content">
        <block type="news/news" name="news" template="news/view.phtml" />
     </reference>
  </news_index_view>
</layout>
```

7. Save this file.

Chapter 8

How it works...

Magento maintains its view file as `*.phtml` file. We wrote two view files for the frontend—one for news listing and another one for the news details page.

Adding required blocks for the News module

Blocks are Magento's important parts, which is a defined part of the screen. The full page is divided into several blocks to allow the granularity in Magento CMS. In every module, blocks are an inevitable part. In this recipe, we will create some blocks that will help present data for our News module.

How to do it...

1. Open your PHP IDE and create a new PHP file in `app/code/local/Packt/News/Block/News.php`.
2. Replace the existing code with the following code:

```php
<?php
class Packt_News_Block_News extends Mage_Core_Block_Template
{
  public function _prepareLayout()
  {
    return parent::_prepareLayout();
  }

  public function getNews()
  {
    if (!$this->hasData('news')) {
      $this->setData('news', Mage::registry('news'));
    }
    return $this->getData('news');
  }

  public function getNewsList()
  {
    if (!$this->hasData('list')) {
      $this->setData('list', Mage::registry('list'));
    }
    return $this->getData('list');
  }

  function limitCharacter($string, $limit = 20, $suffix = '...')
```

Creating a Module

```php
{
  $string = strip_tags($string);

  if (strlen($string) < $limit) {
    return $string;
  }

  for ($i = $limit; $i >= 0; $i--) {
    $c = $string[$i];
    if ($c == ' ' OR $c == "\n") {
      return substr($string, 0, $i) . $suffix;
    }
  }

  return substr($string, 0, $limit) . $suffix;
}

}
```

3. We need another helper for the admin part. Create a new file called `News.php` in the `app/code/local/Packt/News/Block/Adminhtml/` directory and replace the content with the following code:

```php
<?php

class Packt_News_Block_Adminhtml_News extends Mage_Adminhtml_Block_Widget_Grid_Container
{

  public function __construct()
  {
    $this->_controller = 'adminhtml_news';
    $this->_blockGroup = 'news';
    $this->_headerText = Mage::helper('news')->__('Item Manager');
    $this->_addButtonLabel = Mage::helper('news')->__('Add Item');
    parent::__construct();
  }

}
```

4. Create another block file named `Edit.php` in the `app/code/local/Packt/News/Block/Adminhtml/News/` folder and replace the content with the following:

```php
<?php
class Packt_News_Block_Adminhtml_News_Edit extends Mage_Adminhtml_Block_Widget_Form_Container
{
```

```php
    public function __construct()
    {
      parent::__construct();

      $this->_objectId = 'id';
      $this->_blockGroup = 'news';
      $this->_controller = 'adminhtml_news';

      $this->_updateButton('save', 'label', Mage::helper('news')->__
('Save Item'));
      $this->_updateButton('delete', 'label',
Mage::helper('news')->__('Delete Item'));

      $this->_addButton('saveandcontinue', array(
      'label' => Mage::helper('adminhtml')->__('Save And Continue
Edit'),
      'onclick' => 'saveAndContinueEdit()',
       'class' => 'save',
      ), -100);
      $this->_formScripts[] = "
        function toggleEditor() {
           if (tinyMCE.getInstanceById('news_content') == null) {
              tinyMCE.execCommand('mceAddControl', false, 'news_
content');
           } else {
              tinyMCE.execCommand('mceRemoveControl', false, 'news_
content');
           }
        }

        function saveAndContinueEdit(){
           editForm.submit($('edit_form').action+'back/edit/');
        }
      ";
    }

    public function getHeaderText()
    {
       if (Mage::registry('news_data') && Mage::registry('news_
data')->getId()) {
          return Mage::helper('news')->__("Edit Item '%s'", $this->htm
lEscape(Mage::registry('news_data')->getTitle()));
       } else {
          return Mage::helper('news')->__('Add Item');
       }
```

Creating a Module

```
    }
}
```

Next block is to create Grid.php in app/code/local/Packt/News/Block/Adminhtml/News/Gr<?php

```php
class Packt_News_Block_Adminhtml_News_Grid extends Mage_Adminhtml_Block_Widget_Grid
{
  public function __construct()
  {
    parent::__construct();
    $this->setId('newsGrid');
    $this->setDefaultSort('news_id');
    $this->setDefaultDir('ASC');
    $this->setSaveParametersInSession(true);
  }

  protected function _prepareCollection()
  {
    $collection = Mage::getModel('news/news')->getCollection();
    $this->setCollection($collection);
    return parent::_prepareCollection();
  }

  protected function _prepareColumns()
  {
    $this->addColumn('news_id', array(
       'header' => Mage::helper('news')->__('ID'),
       'align' => 'right',
       'width' => '50px',
       'index' => 'news_id',
    ));
    $this->addColumn('title', array(
       'header' => Mage::helper('news')->__('Title'),
       'align' => 'left',
       'index' => 'title',
    ));
    $this->addColumn('status', array(
       'header' => Mage::helper('news')->__('Status'),
       'align' => 'left',
       'width' => '80px',
       'index' => 'status',
       'type' => 'options',
```

```php
        'options' => array(
          1 => 'Enabled',
          2 => 'Disabled',
        ),
      ));

      $this->addColumn('action',
      array(
        'header' => Mage::helper('news')->__('Action'),
        'width' => '100',
        'type' => 'action',
        'getter' => 'getId',
        'actions' => array(
          array(
            'caption' => Mage::helper('news')->__('Edit'),
            'url' => array('base' => '*/*/edit'),
            'field' => 'id'
          )
        ),
        'filter' => false,
        'sortable' => false,
        'index' => 'stores',
        'is_system' => true,
      ));

      $this->addExportType('*/*/exportCsv',
Mage::helper('news')->__('CSV'));
      $this->addExportType('*/*/exportXml',
Mage::helper('news')->__('XML'));

      return parent::_prepareColumns();
    }

    protected function _prepareMassaction()
    {
      $this->setMassactionIdField('news_id');
      $this->getMassactionBlock()->setFormFieldName('news');

      $this->getMassactionBlock()->addItem('delete', array(
        'label' => Mage::helper('news')->__('Delete'),
        'url' => $this->getUrl('*/*/massDelete'),
        'confirm' => Mage::helper('news')->__('Are you sure?')
```

Creating a Module

```
   ));
   $statuses = Mage::getSingleton('news/status')-
>getOptionArray();
   array_unshift($statuses, array('label' => '', 'value' =>
''));
   $this->getMassactionBlock()->addItem('status', array(
      'label' => Mage::helper('news')->__('Change status'),
      'url' => $this->getUrl('*/*/massStatus', array('_current'
=> true)),
      'additional' => array(
         'visibility' => array(
            'name' => 'status',
            'type' => 'select',
            'class' => 'required-entry',
            'label' => Mage::helper('news')->__('Status'),
            'values' => $statuses
         )
      )
   ));
   return $this;
   }
   public function getRowUrl($row)
   {
      return $this->getUrl('*/*/edit', array('id' => $row-
>getId()));
   }
}
```

5. Create `Tabs.php` in the `app/code/local/Packt/News/Block/Adminhtml/News/Edit/` folder. Here is the content:

```
<?php
class Packt_News_Block_Adminhtml_News_Edit_Tabs extends Mage_
Adminhtml_Block_Widget_Tabs
{
   public function __construct()
   {
      parent::__construct();
      $this->setId('news_tabs');
      $this->setDestElementId('edit_form');
      $this->setTitle(Mage::helper('news')->__('Item
Information'));
   }
   protected function _beforeToHtml()
```

```
        {
           $this->addTab('form_section', array(
              'label' => Mage::helper('news')->__('Item Information'),
              'title' => Mage::helper('news')->__('Item Information'),
              'content' => $this->getLayout()->createBlock('news/
        adminhtml_news_edit_tab_form')->toHtml(),
           ));
           return parent::_beforeToHtml();
        }
}
```

6. Time to create another helper named Form.php in the app/code/local/Packt/News/Block/Adminhtml/News/Edit/ folder. Replace the content with the following code:

```
<?php

class Packt_News_Block_Adminhtml_News_Edit_Form extends Mage_Adminhtml_Block_Widget_Form
{
   protected function _prepareForm()
   {
      $form = new Varien_Data_Form(array(
         'id' => 'edit_form',
         'action' => $this->getUrl('*/*/save', array('id' => $this->getRequest()->getParam('id'))),
         'method' => 'post',
         'enctype' => 'multipart/form-data'
         )
      );
      $form->setUseContainer(true);
      $this->setForm($form);
      return parent::_prepareForm();
   }
}
```

7. We came at the last block, Form.php in the app/code/local/Packt/News/Block/Adminhtml/Edit/Tab folder. Replace the content with the following code:

```
<?php
class Packt_News_Block_Adminhtml_News_Edit_Tab_Form extends Mage_Adminhtml_Block_Widget_Form
{
   protected function _prepareForm()
   {
```

Creating a Module

```php
        $form = new Varien_Data_Form();
        $this->setForm($form);
        $fieldset = $form->addFieldset('news_form', array('legend'
=> Mage::helper('news')->__('Item information')));

        $fieldset->addField('title', 'text', array(
          'label' => Mage::helper('news')->__('Title'),
          'class' => 'required-entry',
          'required' => true,
          'name' => 'title',
        ));
        $fieldset->addField('filename', 'file', array(
          'label' => Mage::helper('news')->__('File'),
          'required' => false,
          'name' => 'filename',
        ));
        $fieldset->addField('status', 'select', array(
          'label' => Mage::helper('news')->__('Status'),
          'name' => 'status',
          'values' => array(
            array(
              'value' => 1,
              'label' => Mage::helper('news')->__('Enabled'),
            ),
            array(
              'value' => 2,
              'label' => Mage::helper('news')->__('Disabled'),
            ),
          ),
        ));

        $fieldset->addField('content', 'editor', array(
          'name' => 'content',
          'label' => Mage::helper('news')->__('Content'),
          'title' => Mage::helper('news')->__('Content'),
          'style' => 'width:700px; height:500px;',
          'wysiwyg' => false,
          'required' => true,
        ));
        if (Mage::getSingleton('adminhtml/session')->getNewsData())
    {
            $form->setValues(Mage::getSingleton('adminhtml/session')-
```

```
>getNewsData());
    Mage::getSingleton('adminhtml/session')-
>setNewsData(null);
    } elseif (Mage::registry('news_data')) {
        $form->setValues(Mage::registry('news_data')->getData());
    }
    return parent::_prepareForm();
  }
}
```

8. We are done with creating blocks!

How it works...

Blocks are an important part of Magento. In this recipe, we created seven blocks for making the news module functional. We wrote some methods in every block to pass the data to layout. The very first block, `News.php`, is responsible for the frontend while the others inside the `Adminhtml` are for the admin panel. The `News.php` has four methods:

- `_prepareLayout()`: We just called its parent `_prepareLayout()`. This method is used to change layout.
- `GetNews()`: This function is used to set news data in registry and retrieve it.
- `GetNewsList()`: This function is same as the previous method but in this case, it retrieves a list of news.
- `LimitCharacter()`: This is a utility method which truncates text to a given length.

Magento back office (admin panel) is pretty organized. We followed their conventions to give the user similar UI while managing news in the admin panel. This is why we had to create six blocks for rendering and handling the actions in the admin panel. The `Packt/News/Block/Adminhtml/News.php` file has the configuration for specifying the controller file, groups, label and texts for header, button, and so on. Inside the `Edit` folder there are some blocks which deal with the edit form, tab, and grid for the News admin panel.

Creating a Module

There are no more steps left for making our Packt News module! Let's give it a go in the browser! Let's visit the admin panel first. Log in to your Magento backend. You should see a new menu named **News**, go for it! I found it, as shown in the following screenshot (after adding some dummy news):

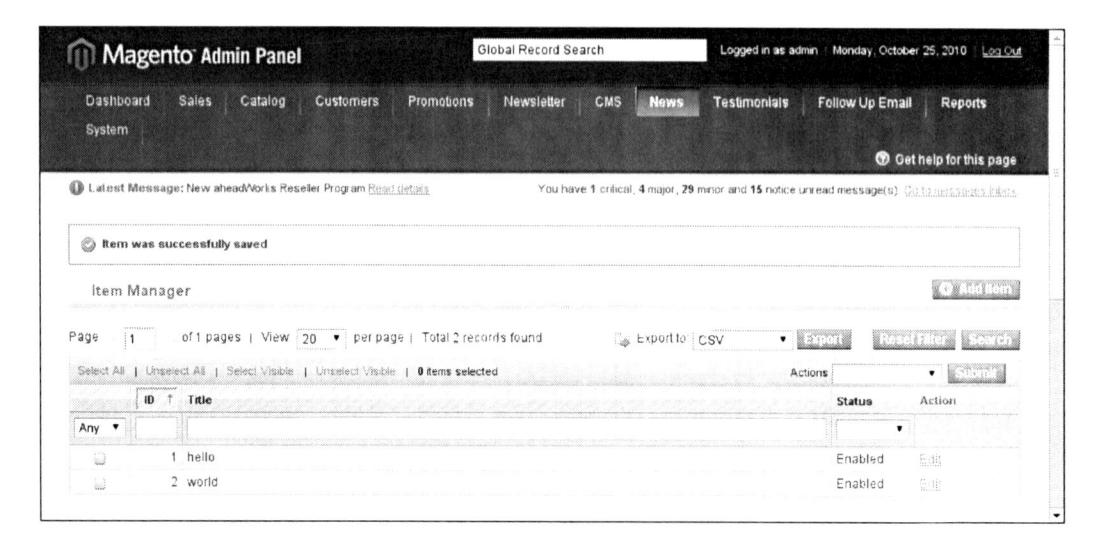

If you point your browser to `http://magento.local.com/news` as in my local box, you should see a page something like the following screenshot:

Here is another screenshot for the admin panel:

	ID	Title	Status	Action
	1	Quisque dictum viverra lorem, ut malesuada.	Enabled	Edit
	2	Quisque mollis tristique tellus. Vivamus sit.	Enabled	Edit
	3	where can I get some	Enabled	Edit
	4	where does it come from?	Enabled	Edit
	5	1994 translation by Rockham	Enabled	Edit
	6	Section 1.10.33 of "de Finibus Bonorum et Malorum", written by Cicero in 45 BC	Enabled	Edit

9
Creating a Shipping Module

In this chapter, we will cover:

- Initializing module configuration
- Writing an adapter model
- Adding a module in backend
- Adding a module in frontend

Introduction

Shipping a product to the customer's destination is one of the vital parts of an eCommerce transaction. By default, Magento provides the following carriers:

- UPS
- USPS
- FedEx
- DHL

If we need to add an additional carrier, then all we need is to create a new shipping module. This chapter will guide you through creating a custom shipping module of your own that will add an additional settings in Magento admin area for specifying Canada Post as shipping career.

Initializing module configuration

During creation of a new module in Magento, the very first task is to write the configuration files like any other module. This recipe will describe the steps on how to create the configuration file for our new shipping module.

Creating a Shipping Module

Getting ready

Fire up your PHP editor and open the Magento project.

How to do it...

1. Create a new folder named `Packt` in the `app/code/local` directory.
2. Create a new folder named "`Myshipping`" (of course without quotes) in `app/code/local/Packt/`.
3. Create two more directories inside the `Myshipping` directory and name them as `Model` and `etc` respectively. The final outcome should be as follows:

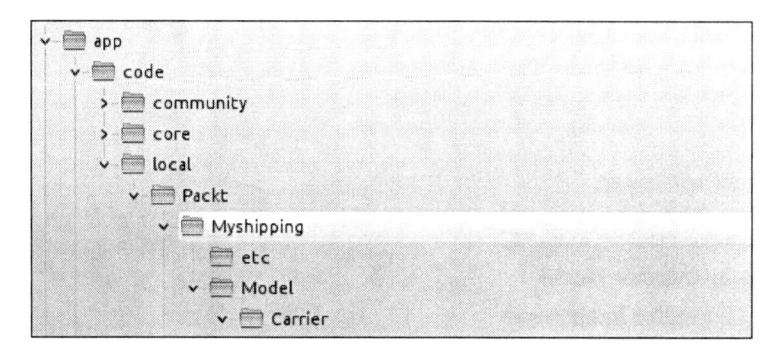

```
v app
  v code
    > community
    > core
    v local
      v Packt
        v Myshipping
          etc
          v Model
            v Carrier
```

4. Let's create the `config.xml` file in the `app/code/local/Packt/Myshipping/etc` directory and paste the following code in it:

```xml
<?xml version="1.0"?>
<config>
  <modules>
    <Packt_Myshipping>
      <version>1.0.0</version>
      <depends>
        <Mage_Shipping />
      </depends>
    </Packt_Myshipping>
  </modules>

  <global>
    <models>
      <myshipping>
        <class>Packt_Myshipping_Model</class>
      </myshipping>
    </models>
```

Chapter 9

```xml
      <resources>
        <myshipping_setup>
          <setup>
            <module>Packt_Myshipping</module>
          </setup>
          <connection>
            <use>core_setup</use>
          </connection>
        </myshipping_setup>
      </resources>
    </global>

    <default>
      <carriers>
        <myshipping>
          <active>1</active>
          <model>myshipping/carrier</model>
        </myshipping>
      </carriers>
    </default>
</config>
```

5. Save and close the `config.xml` file.
6. We need another XML file named as `system.xml` in the `app/code/local/Packt/Myshipping/etc/` folder. Create it!
7. The `System.xml` file has got long snippets of code. For our better understanding we shall split the code blocks to describe it while the full module is bundled with this book. You can download it from `www.packtpub.com`.
8. The following code block deals with the `Myshipping` module configurations such as the label in admin panel, sort order and visibility in different stores and sites.

```xml
<?xml version="1.0"?>
<config>
  <sections>
    <carriers>
      <groups>
        <myshipping translate="label" module="shipping">

          <label>Canada Post</label>
          <frontend_type>text</frontend_type>
          <sort_order>13</sort_order>
          <show_in_default>1</show_in_default>
          <show_in_website>1</show_in_website>
          <show_in_store>1</show_in_store>
```

Creating a Shipping Module

9. The `fields` block holds the configurations of all fields, which are displayed in admin panel. All fields hold some similar information such as label, frontend type, sort order, visibility in default, visibility in website, and visibility in store.

```xml
<fields>
  <account translate="label">
    <label>Account number</label>
    <frontend_type>text</frontend_type>
    <sort_order>7</sort_order>
    <show_in_default>1</show_in_default>
    <show_in_website>1</show_in_website>
    <show_in_store>1</show_in_store>
  </account>

  <active translate="label">
    <label>Enabled</label>
    <frontend_type>select</frontend_type>
    <source_model>adminhtml/system_config_source_yesno
    </source_model>
    <sort_order>1</sort_order>
    <show_in_default>1</show_in_default>
    <show_in_website>1</show_in_website>
    <show_in_store>1</show_in_store>
  </active>

  <contentdesc translate="label">
    <label>Package Description</label>
    <frontend_type>text</frontend_type>
    <sort_order>12</sort_order>
    <show_in_default>1</show_in_default>
    <show_in_website>1</show_in_website>
    <show_in_store>1</show_in_store>
  </contentdesc>
```

10. If the `free_shipping_enable` flag is enabled, then the system will check `free_shipping_subtotal` to give free shipping details or else it will use Shopping Cart Price Rule behaviour.

```xml
<free_shipping_enable translate="label">
  <label>Free shipping with minimum order amount</label>
  <frontend_type>select</frontend_type>
  <source_model>adminhtml/system_config_source_
  enabledisable</source_model>
  <sort_order>21</sort_order>
  <show_in_default>1</show_in_default>
```

```xml
      <show_in_website>1</show_in_website>
      <show_in_store>1</show_in_store>
</free_shipping_enable>

<free_shipping_subtotal translate="label">
  <label>Minimum order amount for free
  shipping</label>
  <frontend_type>text</frontend_type>
  <sort_order>22</sort_order>
  <show_in_default>1</show_in_default>
  <show_in_website>1</show_in_website>
  <show_in_store>1</show_in_store>
</free_shipping_subtotal>

<dutiable translate="label">
  <label>Shipment Dutiable</label>
  <frontend_type>select</frontend_type>
  <source_model>adminhtml/system_config_source_yesno
  </source_model>
  <sort_order>13</sort_order>
  <show_in_default>1</show_in_default>
  <show_in_website>1</show_in_website>
  <show_in_store>1</show_in_store>
</dutiable>

<gateway_url translate="label">
  <label>Gateway URL</label>
  <frontend_type>text</frontend_type>
  <sort_order>2</sort_order>
  <show_in_default>1</show_in_default>
  <show_in_website>1</show_in_website>
  <show_in_store>1</show_in_store>
</gateway_url>

<handling_type translate="label">
  <label>Calculate Handling Fee</label>
  <frontend_type>select</frontend_type>
  <source_model>shipping/source_handlingType
  </source_model>
  <sort_order>10</sort_order>
  <show_in_default>1</show_in_default>
  <show_in_website>1</show_in_website>
  <show_in_store>0</show_in_store>
</handling_type>
```

```xml
<handling_action translate="label">
  <label>Handling Applied</label>
  <frontend_type>select</frontend_type>
  <source_model>shipping/source_handlingAction
  </source_model>
  <sort_order>11</sort_order>
  <show_in_default>1</show_in_default>
  <show_in_website>1</show_in_website>
  <show_in_store>0</show_in_store>
</handling_action>

<handling_fee translate="label">
  <label>Handling fee</label>
  <frontend_type>text</frontend_type>
  <sort_order>12</sort_order>
  <show_in_default>1</show_in_default>
  <show_in_website>1</show_in_website>
  <show_in_store>1</show_in_store>
</handling_fee>

<max_package_weight translate="label">
  <label>Maximum Package Weight (Please consult your
  shipping carrier for maximum supported shipping
  weight)</label>
  <frontend_type>text</frontend_type>
  <sort_order>13</sort_order>
  <show_in_default>1</show_in_default>
  <show_in_website>1</show_in_website>
  <show_in_store>1</show_in_store>
</max_package_weight>

<id translate="label">
  <label>Access ID</label>
  <frontend_type>text</frontend_type>
  <backend_model>adminhtml/system_config_backend_
  encrypted</backend_model>
  <sort_order>5</sort_order>
  <show_in_default>1</show_in_default>
  <show_in_website>1</show_in_website>
  <show_in_store>1</show_in_store>
</id>

<password translate="label">
  <label>Password</label>
```

```xml
    <frontend_type>text</frontend_type>
    <backend_model>adminhtml/system_config_backend_
    encrypted</backend_model>
    <sort_order>6</sort_order>
    <show_in_default>1</show_in_default>
    <show_in_website>1</show_in_website>
    <show_in_store>1</show_in_store>
</password>

<shipping_intlkey translate="label">
    <label>Shipping key (International)</label>
    <frontend_type>text</frontend_type>
    <backend_model>adminhtml/system_config_backend_
    encrypted</backend_model>
    <sort_order>8</sort_order>
    <show_in_default>1</show_in_default>
    <show_in_website>1</show_in_website>
    <show_in_store>1</show_in_store>
</shipping_intlkey>

<shipping_key translate="label">
    <label>Shipping key</label>
    <frontend_type>text</frontend_type>
    <backend_model>adminhtml/system_config_
    backend_encrypted</backend_model>
    <sort_order>8</sort_order>
    <show_in_default>1</show_in_default>
    <show_in_website>1</show_in_website>
    <show_in_store>1</show_in_store>
</shipping_key>

<sort_order translate="label">
    <label>Sort order</label>
    <frontend_type>text</frontend_type>
    <sort_order>100</sort_order>
    <show_in_default>1</show_in_default>
    <show_in_website>1</show_in_website>
    <show_in_store>1</show_in_store>
</sort_order>

<title translate="label">
    <label>Title</label>
    <frontend_type>text</frontend_type>
    <sort_order>2</sort_order>
```

Creating a Shipping Module

```xml
        <show_in_default>1</show_in_default>
        <show_in_website>1</show_in_website>
        <show_in_store>1</show_in_store>
    </title>

    <sallowspecific translate="label">
        <label>Ship to applicable countries</label>
        <frontend_type>select</frontend_type>
        <sort_order>90</sort_order>
        <frontend_class>shipping-applicable-
        country</frontend_class>
        <source_model>adminhtml/system_config_source_
        shipping_allspecificcountries</source_model>
        <show_in_default>1</show_in_default>
        <show_in_website>1</show_in_website>
        <show_in_store>1</show_in_store>
    </sallowspecific>

    <specificcountry translate="label">
        <label>Ship to Specific countries</label>
        <frontend_type>multiselect</frontend_type>
        <sort_order>91</sort_order>
        <source_model>adminhtml/system_config_source_country
        </source_model>
        <show_in_default>1</show_in_default>
        <show_in_website>1</show_in_website>
        <show_in_store>1</show_in_store>
    </specificcountry>

    <showmethod translate="label">
        <label>Show method if not applicable</label>
        <frontend_type>select</frontend_type>
        <sort_order>92</sort_order>
        <source_model>adminhtml/system_config_source_yesno
        </source_model>
        <show_in_default>1</show_in_default>
        <show_in_website>1</show_in_website>
        <show_in_store>1</show_in_store>
    </showmethod>

    <specificerrmsg translate="label">
        <label>Displayed Error Message</label>
        <frontend_type>textarea</frontend_type>
        <sort_order>80</sort_order>
        <show_in_default>1</show_in_default>
```

```xml
            <show_in_website>1</show_in_website>
            <show_in_store>1</show_in_store>
          </specificerrmsg>
        </fields>
      </myshipping>
    </groups>
  </carriers>
</sections>
</config>
```

11. We are at the last step in creating configuration for our new shipping module. Let's create a new file `app/etc/modules/Packt_Myshipping.xml` and write the following code in it:

```xml
<?xml version="1.0"?>
<config>
  <modules>
    <Packt_Myshipping>
      <active>true</active>
        <codePool>local</codePool>
    </Packt_Myshipping>
  </modules>
</config>
```

12. There is no such step as step 12.

How it works...

We already know that XML files are the building blocks of Magento CMS. For any Magento module, XML configuration files are mandatory. Thus, we wrote two configuration files. One is `config.xml` and the other is `system.xml`.

The XML files are pretty self-descriptive. We just followed the conventions from Magento to make our shipping module work.

In this recipe, we laid out the necessary files and folders for the configuration of our shipping module. We created two XML files, `config.xml` and `system.xml`. The `config.xml` file holds the information about the module such as version, dependency on the `Mage_Shipping` module, and model association for this module.

The `system.xml` file holds the information about the the carrier, necessary fields, and rendering configuration for admin UI while visiting **System | Configuration | Shipping Methods** page. The fields in the **Canada post** accordion are also defined in the `system.xml` file. Keep in mind that the field's name will be fetched from the adapter model by its name as: `$this->getConfigData('handling_fee')` in `Carrier.php`.

Creating a Shipping Module

The last file we created, `Packt_Myshipping.xml`, is responsible for making this module active in Magento. This file has two important tags one is `active` and another is `codePool`. The active tag has value `true` and `local` for the tag codePool as this is our own module.

Writing an adapter model

Models handle all the business logic in Magento like any other MVC application. In this recipe, we will write a model adapter class for our shipping module, which will extend the `Mage_Shipping_Model_Carrier_Abstract` class. The purpose of this class is to collect rates for the shipping method based on the information in the request.

How to do it...

1. Create a new file named `Carrier.php` in the `app/code/local/Packt/Myshipping/Model/` directory.

2. Paste the following code:

```php
<?php

class Packt_Myshipping_Model_Carrier extends Mage_Shipping_Model_Carrier_Abstract
{

  /**
   * unique identifier for our shipping module
   * @var string $_code
   */
  protected $_code = 'myshipping';

  /**
   * Collect rates for this shipping method based on information
   * in $request
   *
   * @param Mage_Shipping_Model_Rate_Request $data
   * @return Mage_Shipping_Model_Rate_Result
   */
  public function collectRates(Mage_Shipping_Model_Rate_Request $request)
  {
    if (!$this->getConfigData('active')) {
      Mage::log('The ' . $this->_code . 'my shipping module is not active.');
        return false;
    }

    $handling = $this->getConfigData('handling_fee');
    $result = Mage::getModel('shipping/rate_result');
```

```php
            foreach ($request as $method) {
              $method = Mage::getModel('shipping/rate_result_method');

              $method->setCarrier($this->_code);
              $method->setCarrierTitle($this->getConfigData('title'));

              $method->setMethod($method['code']);
              $method->setMethodTitle($method['title']);

              $method->setCost($method['amount']);

              $method->setPrice($method['amount'] + $handling);

              $result->append($method);
            }
        return $result;
      }

    }
```

3. Save and close this file.

How it works...

This model class applies the business rules for shipping method. There is a method in this class named `collectRates()`, which takes the `Mage_Shipping_Model_Rate_Request` object as a parameter and passes it along the method.

We grabbed the configuration and called the `shipping/rate_result_method` model to fetch required data and process it. Finally, we returned it.

This file is important for calculating the handling fee and returning it to the shipping form. The `collectRates()` method is responsible for that. We just showed you how it works. The shipping handling fee differs on various aspects; set your own fields as we did in `system.xml` and apply the business logic in `Carrier.php`, this is how it should work.

Adding a module in backend

In this recipe, we will enable our newly created shipping module.

How to do it...

1. Log in to your Magento store backend.
2. Point your browser to **System| Configuration Advanced| Advanced page**.

Creating a Shipping Module

3. Look for our newly created module named `Packt_Myshipping` and make sure this is enabled.
4. Now navigate to the page **System | Configuration | Sales | Shipping methods** page. Look for the label **Canada Post** as we entered it in our previous recipe.
5. Enter the required data in the form as it suggests.
6. The following is a sample screenshot:

7. Make sure you set it as enabled.
8. Please consult your shipping provider to make sure the configurations are correct. Save the configuration.

How it works...

We made this module as any other standard shipping module such as UPS, USPS, FedEx, and others. Any standard shipping method parameters could be passed here and Magento's core shipping method will take care of it.

Adding a module in frontend

This recipe involves adding our newly created shipping module in Magento frontend. Let's describe the steps to be followed to attain this goal.

How to do it...

We have to do it in Magento backend actually. In our previous recipe, we described it though. Here is a simple example of how to do it:

1. Log in to your Magento backend/admin panel.
2. Navigate to **System** | **Configuration** | **Sales** | **Shipping Methods** pages.
3. Enter relevant information in the **Canada Post** section.
4. Save this configuration.
5. Go back to the frontend and see it in action while you visit the **Checkout** page!

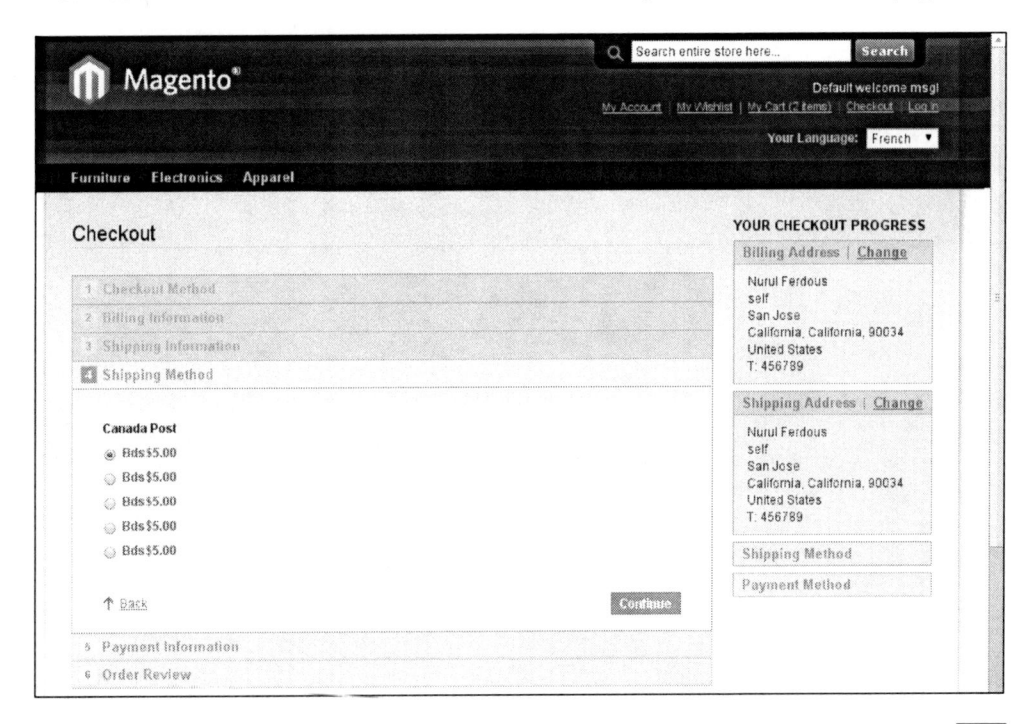

Creating a Shipping Module

How it works...

We added the relevant information in `system.xml` and applied the logics in `Carrier.php` in the earlier recipe; this will handle the workflow for frontend.

See also...

You may also refer to the *Adding a module in backend* recipe of this chapter.

10
Writing a Social Widget

In this chapter, we will cover:

- Creating an empty module and an enabler file
- Creating a config file and declaring the widgets
- Writing the default module helper `Data.php`
- Creating a source model for services multi select in widget configuration
- Creating frontend block for our widget
- Creating templates

Introduction

Magento widgets is a new feature that came out recently (from version 1.4 or higher) to cope with a cool frontend modification from the CMS page admin panel that can be achieved without any programming knowledge for a store owner. This is a frontend block with some predefined configurations. The ability to easily set widget configuration options allows for the full control of widget placement on a page for store owners.

Writing a Social Widget

After completion of this chapter, we will be done with making our own widget and also sharing this widget with various social network links. The following is a screenshot of what we will achieve after completing this chapter:

> We added five links for letting you know how it works. You are highly encouraged to add some more links.

A widget can have one or more other widgets in it. In this chapter, we will create one widget that will hold multiple widgets in it.

Creating an empty module and an enabler file

A widget is pretty similar to any module but has some different configuration directives. It requires a `config.xml` file and some other files as any other module does. In this recipe, we will create the necessary file structure and configuration files, which will enable a new widget. Okay let's start with it, what are we waiting for!

How to do it...

1. Create `Packt` folder in the `app/code/local` folder if it does not exist already.
2. Create a folder named `Socialwidget` in the `app/code/local/Packt` folder.
3. Create **Block**, **etc**, **Helper**, and **Model** folders in the `app/code/local/Socialwidget` folder, as the following screenshot depicts:

Chapter 10

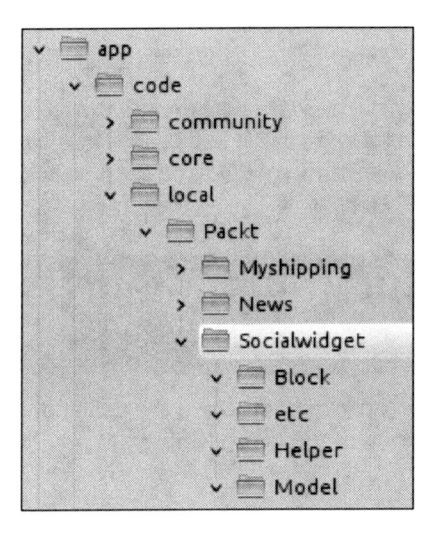

```
v 📁 app
  v 📁 code
    > 📁 community
    > 📁 core
    v 📁 local
      v 📁 Packt
        > 📁 Myshipping
        > 📁 News
        v 📁 Socialwidget
          v 📁 Block
          v 📁 etc
          v 📁 Helper
          v 📁 Model
```

4. Now create an XML file named `Packt_Socialwidget.xml` in the `app/etc/modules` folder and put the following code block in it:

   ```xml
   <?xml version="1.0"?>
   <!--
   /**
    * @category   Packt
    * @package    Packt_Socialwidget
    * @license    http://opensource.org/licenses/osl-3.0.php  Open Software License (OSL 3.0)
    */
   -->
   <config>
     <modules>
       <Packt_Socialwidget>
         <active>true</active>
         <codePool>local</codePool>
         <depends>
           <Mage_Cms />
         </depends>
       </Packt_Socialwidget>
     </modules>
   </config>
   ```

5. Save and close this file. This will enable our new widget named `Packt_Socialwidget` in the **System | Configuration | Advanced** section of the Magento admin panel.

Writing a Social Widget

How it works...

This is very similar as any other standard module creation process. We added the required directory structure and created an enabler file in the `app/etc/modules` folder. We used local codepool as this is our own custom module and set it as active. There is one dependency for this module, which is `Mage_Cms`.

Creating a config file and declaring the widgets

`config.xml` and `widget.xml` are the files where the definitions of a widget resides. This recipe deals with the creation of these two files.

How to do it...

1. Let's create a new XML file in the `app/code/local/Socialwidget/etc` folder and name it as `config.xml`.
2. Replace the existing content with the following:

```xml
<?xml version="1.0"?>
<!--
/**
 * @category   Packt
 * @package    Packt_Socialwidget
 * @license    http://opensource.org/licenses/osl-3.0.php  Open Software License (OSL 3.0)
 */
-->
<config>
  <modules>
    <Packt_Socialwidget>
      <version>0.0.1</version>
    </Packt_Socialwidget>
  </modules>
  <global>
    <helpers>
      <socialwidget>
        <class>Packt_Socialwidget_Helper</class>
      </socialwidget>
    </helpers>
    <blocks>
      <socialwidget>
        <class>Packt_Socialwidget_Block</class>
```

```xml
          </socialwidget>
       </blocks>
       <models>
          <socialwidget>
             <class>Packt_Socialwidget_Model</class>
          </socialwidget>
       </models>
    </global>
</config>
```

3. Save it.
4. We have to create another XML file as this is a widget. Create another XML file in the same folder and name it as `widget.xml`.
5. Replace the existing content with the following:

```xml
<?xml version="1.0"?>
<!--
/**
 * @category   Packt
 * @package    Packt_Socialwidget
 * @license    http://opensource.org/licenses/osl-3.0.php  Open Software License (OSL 3.0)
 */
-->
<widgets>
   <socialwidget_list type="socialwidget/list" translate="name description" module="socialwidget">
      <name>Packt Share this</name>
      <description>Adds a list of share links</description>
      <parameters>
        <enabled_services>
           <label>Enabled Services</label>
           <visible>1</visible>
           <required>1</required>
           <type>multiselect</type>
           <source_model>socialwidget/services</source_model>
        </enabled_services>
        <template translate="label">
           <label>Frontend Template</label>
           <visible>1</visible>
           <required>1</required>
           <type>select</type>
           <values>
              <text translate="label">
                 <value>socialwidget/text.phtml</value>
```

Writing a Social Widget

```xml
            <label>Text Links</label>
          </text>
          <icons translate="label">
            <value>socialwidget/icons.phtml</value>
            <label>Icon Links</label>
          </icons>
        </values>
      </template>
    </parameters>
  </socialwidget_list>
</widgets>
```

6. Save this file.

How it works...

In the `config.xml` file, we declared the necessary block, helper, and models. We named our module's company as `Packt` and the widget name as `Socialwidget`, which could be named as your choice.

The `widget.xml` file has configuration options those will be visible in the Magento store admin panel in the CMS page in the widget form while the store owner initiates the insert widget and chooses this widget.

Writing the default module helper Data.php

This is the easiest recipe of this chapter! We need to create an empty class for our module.

How to do it...

1. Create a new PHP file in the `app/code/local/Packt/Socialwidget/Helper` folder and name it as `Data.php`.
2. Enter the following content and save this file:

```php
<?php

/**
 * Packt Socialwidget Helper class
 *
 * @category    Packt
 * @package     Packt_Socialwidget
 * @license     http://opensource.org/licenses/osl-3.0.php  Open Software License (OSL 3.0)
 */
```

Chapter 10

```
class Packt_Socialwidget_Helper_Data extends Mage_Core_Helper_
Abstract
{

}
```

How it works...

Usually a helper class formats the data before rendering it to the screen. In this case, we just created an empty helper named as `Packt_Socialwidget_Helper_Data` and extended it with `Mage_Core_Helper_Abstract` to access some core functionalities.

Creating a source model for services multi select in widget configuration

We will write a model, which will return the services that would be used in our social widget as links either in text or in an icon as the store owner chooses. This is no other than a simple PHP class.

How to do it...

1. Create a new PHP file in the `app/code/local/Packt/Socialwidget/Model` folder and name it as `Services.php`.

2. Replace the existing content with the following:

   ```
   <?php
   
   /**
    * Packt Socialwidget Services model
    *
    * @category    Packt
    * @package     Packt_Socialwidget
    * @subpackage  Model
    * @license     http://opensource.org/licenses/osl-3.0.php  Open Software License (OSL 3.0)
    */
   class Packt_Socialwidget_Model_Services
   {
   
     /**
      * Generate available services as array
      *
      * you can add a new value to the array if you wish to add yet another link
      * to this widget. keep in mind that you have to add the details
   ```

191

Writing a Social Widget

```
      in the
      * List Block as well.
      *
      * @return array
      */
      public function toOptionArray()
      {
        return array(
          array('value' => 'buzz', 'label' => 'Buzz'),
          array('value' => 'facebook', 'label' => 'Facebook'),
          array('value' => 'twitter', 'label' => 'Twitter'),
          array('value' => 'digg', 'label' => 'Digg'),
          array('value' => 'delicious', 'label' => 'Delicious')
        );
      }

}
```

3. Save and close this file.

How it works...

There is only one function in our model, which has some values in an array and returns it.

Creating frontend block for our widget

This recipe is the important part of this chapter, where we will generate HTML for the links and return it. The template files will render it later. This is the Magento way!

How to do it...

1. Create a new PHP file in the `app/code/local/Packt/Socialwidget/Block` folder and name it as `List.php`.
2. This file has got some good amount of code. We will discuss it in parts while the full file itself along with others is bundled with this book.
3. The very first of `List.php` is the class declaration and the constructor and a protected property named `$_serializer`. Inside the constructor, we assigned an instance of the `Varien_Object()` to the `$_serializer` and called its parent constructor.

```
<?php

class Packt_Socialwidget_Block_List extends Mage_Core_Block_
Template implements Mage_Widget_Block_Interface
{
```

```
protected $_serializer = null;

protected function _construct()
{
  $this->_serializer = new Varien_Object();
  parent::_construct();
}
```

4. `_toHtml()` is a Magento template function, which renders HTML markups. In this method, we have iterated in the specified services and assigned it to lists.

   ```
   protected function _toHtml()
   {
     $html = '';
     $config = $this->getData('enabled_services');
     if (empty($config)) {
       return $html;
     }
     $services = explode(',', $config);
     $list = array();
     foreach ($services as $service) {
       $item = $this->_generateServiceLink($service);
       if ($item) {
         $list[] = $item;
       }
     }
     $this->assign('list', $list);
     return parent::_toHtml();
   }
   ```

5. This is the function where all social links are created from a given service. There is a switch case block in this function, which determines the service and generates the appropriate link. If you have added more links, then you ought to add a case block and generate the correct link as the service suggests.

   ```
   protected function _generateServiceLink($service)
   {
     $pageTitle = '';

     $headBlock = $this->getLayout()->getBlock('head');
       if ($headBlock) {
         $pageTitle = $headBlock->getTitle();
       }

       $currentUrl = $this->getUrl('*/*/*', array('_current' =>
   ```

Writing a Social Widget

```
            true, '_use_rewrite' => true));

        $attributes = array();

        $icon = '';

        switch ($service) {
          case 'buzz':
            $attributes = array(
              'href' => 'http://www.google.com/buzz/post?message='
                . $pageTitle
                .'&url='.rawurlencode($currentUrl),
              'title' => ucfirst($service),
              'target' => '_blank'
            );
            $icon = 'buzz.png';
            break;
          case 'facebook':
            $attributes = array(
              'href' => 'http://www.facebook.com/sharer.php?u='
                . rawurlencode($currentUrl)
                .'&t='.$pageTitle.'%26s+website',
              'title' => ucfirst($service),
              'target' => '_blank'
            );
            $icon = 'facebook.png';
            break;
          case 'twitter':
            $attributes = array(
              'href' => 'http://twitter.com/home?status='
                . rawurlencode('Check it out ' . $pageTitle . ' at ' .
$currentUrl),
              'title' => ucfirst($service),
              'target' => '_blank'
            );
            $icon = 'twitter.png';
            break;
          case 'digg':
            $attributes = array(
              'href' => 'http://www.digg.com/submit?url=' .
rawurlencode($currentUrl) . '&amp;phase=2',
              'title' => ucfirst($service),
              'target' => '_blank'
            );
            $icon = 'digg.png';
            break;
          case 'delicious':
            $attributes = array(
              'href' => 'http://del.icio.us/post?url=' .
rawurlencode($currentUrl),
```

Chapter 10

```
            'title' => ucfirst($service),
            'onclick' => 'window.open(\'http://del.icio.us/post?v=4&amp;noui&amp;jump=close&amp;url='
. rawurlencode($currentUrl) . "&amp;title=" . rawurlencode($pageTitle)
                . "','delicious','toolbar=no,width=700,height=400');
return false;",
        );
        $icon = 'delicious.png';
        break;
        default:
        return array();
        break;
    }

    $item = array(
       'text' => $attributes['title'],
       'attributes' => $this->_serializer->setData($attributes)->serialize(),
       'image' => $this->getSkinUrl("images/socialwidget/" . $icon),
     );

    return $item;
  }

}
```

6. Save and close this file.

How it works...

This is where we created the required attributes for each link as an array. Each element of this array has some common attributes, which are rendered in template files. We invoked the services and converted it as an array, then passed it as a parameter to the `_generateServiceLink()` method.

The `_generateServiceLink()` method populates an array and assigns it to Magento, so that it could be rendered in templates.

Writing a Social Widget

Creating templates

This widget could be shown in two formats either in text or icons. This recipe will let you write two templates—one for text and the other for icons.

How to do it...

1. Create a new folder in the `app/design/frontend/YOUR_PACKAGE/YOUR_THEME/template` folder and name it as `socialwidget`. In my case, this is `app/design/frontend/default/default/template/socialwidget/`.

2. Create a new empty file and name it `text.phtml`.

   > Magento uses `*.phtml` file as template files.

3. Paste the following code in `text.phtml`:

   ```
   <div style="border-top: 1px dotted #777;border-bottom: 1px dotted #777;padding: 5px 10px;margin: 20px 0;">

     <?php foreach ($list as $item) : ?>

       <a style="margin-right: 5px;" <?php echo $item['attributes']; ?>><?php echo $this->escapeHtml($item['text']); ?></a>

     <?php endforeach; ?>

   </div>
   ```

4. Save and close it.

5. Let's create another template for showing links in icons. Create another file as `icons.phtml`, same as `text.phtml`.

6. Put the following content:

   ```
   <div style="border-top: 1px dotted #777;border-bottom: 1px dotted #777;padding: 5px 10px;margin: 20px 0;">

     <?php foreach ($list as $item) : ?>
       <a style="margin-right: 5px;" <?php echo $item['attributes']; ?>><img src="<?php echo $item['image']; ?>" title="<?php echo $this->escapeHtml($item['text']); ?>" border="0" /></a>
     <?php endforeach; ?>

   </div>
   ```

7. Save and close this file.
8. The last step for this chapter is to create/collect some social icons for using in our template file and put it in a proper place. Create a new folder in the `skin/frontend/YOUR_PACKAGE/YOUR_THEME/images` folder and name it as `socialwidget`. In my case, it is `/skin/frontend/default/default/images/socialwidget/`.
9. Paste the icons here. Make sure that your icon's filenames are same as we wrote in the `List.php` block.
10. Hey! You are moving, check it out in Magento backend now. Edit any page (such as home page) and insert our new widget. If you click on the **Insert Widget** button and choose our new widget, your screen should read something like the following screenshot:

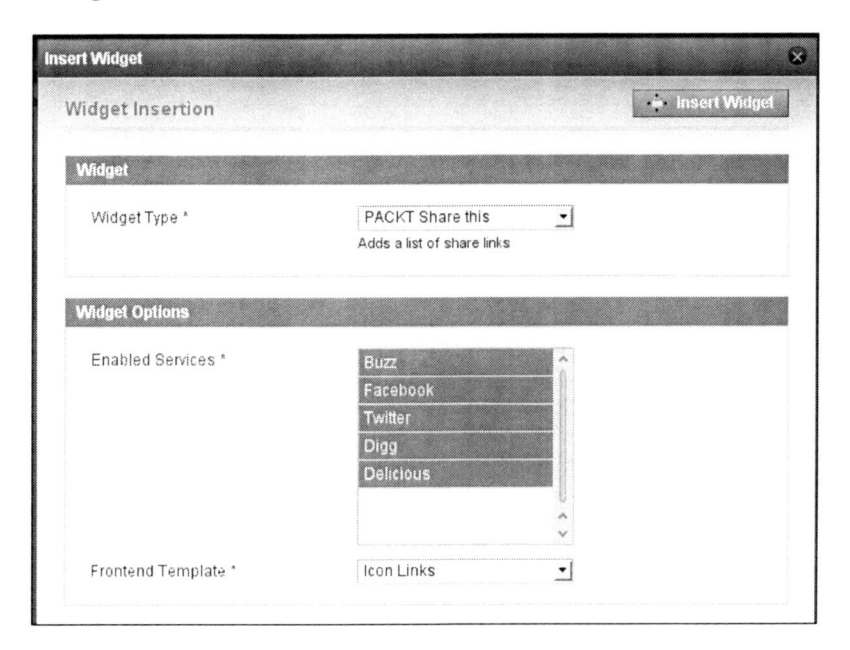

11. Save the page.

Writing a Social Widget

12. Give it a go in frontend! You should see the following screenshot as it is shown in the introduction of this chapter:

How it works...

Templates are pretty simple. We just iterated an array and printed it as an anchor. No rocket science!

The entire widget is added, you can download it from `www.packtpub.com`.

11
Performance Optimization

In this chapter, we will cover:

- Measuring/benchmarking your Magento with Siege, ab, Magento profiler, YSlow, Page Speed, GTmetrix, and WebPagetest
- Optimizing Magento database and MySQL configuration
- Optimizing web server configuration (Apache)
- Tuning Magento configurations
- Using APC/Memcached as the cache backend
- Accelerating PHP: php.ini configuration
- Applying YSlow and Page Speed rules

Introduction

Users really respond to speed.—Marissa Mayer, Google vice president of the research section and user experience.

We will explain why this quote is true throughout this chapter. Her key insight for the crowd at the Web 2.0 Summit is that "slow and steady doesn't win the race". Today people want fast and furious. Not convinced? Okay, let's have a look at some arguments:

- 500ms lost is to lose 20 percent of traffic for Google (this might be why there are only ten results per page in the research).
- Increased latency of 100ms costs 1 percent of sales for Amazon.

Performance Optimization

- Reducing by 25 percent the weight of a page is to win 25 percent of users in the medium term for Google.
- Losing 400ms is to have a 5-9 percent drop in addition to Yahoo!, an editorial site.

As we can see, this is the era of milliseconds and terabytes, so we have to pay a big price if we can't keep up. This chapter will ensure the optimum performance of your Magento store and overcome some of the most common pitfalls that people encounter. For example, in Magento, backoffice is slow, frontend tends to die while loading, accessibility is far from perfect, an AJAX request is not successful due to expiration of the session, nothing happens, no error message, just nothing, the nightmare of XML layout, and so on.

This chapter will be very helpful whether you are a novice or a pro on performance optimization. Follow every single chapter and your Magento store should get a notable performance raise.

By applying the techniques described in different recipes in this chapter, you can achieve a tremendous performance boost (approximately 300 percent) on any LAMP application.

Measuring/benchmarking your Magento with Siege, ab, Magento profiler, YSlow, Page Speed, GTmetrix, and WebPagetest

The very first task of any website's performance optimization is to know its pitfalls. In other words, know why it is taking too much time. Who are the culprits? Fortunately, we have some amicable friends who will guide us through. Let's list them:

- **ab (ApacheBench)**: This is bundled with every Apache as a benchmarking utility.
- **Siege**: This is an open source stress/regression test and benchmark utility by Joe Dog.
- **Magento profiler**: This is a built-in Magento profiler.
- **YSlow**: This is a tool from Yahoo! We have been using it for years. This is in fact a firebug add-on.
- **Page Speed**: This is yet another firebug add-on from Google to analyze page performance on some common rules.
- **GTmetrix**: This is a cool online web application from which you can get both YSlow and Page Speed in the same place. Opera fanboys who don't like Firefox or Chrome might use it for YSlow and Page Speed here.
- **WebPagetest**: This is another online tool for benchmarking as GTmetrix. It also collects and shows screenshots with the reports.

Okay, we are introduced to our new friends. In this recipe, we will work with them and find the pitfalls of our Magento store, which will be addressed throughout the whole chapter. Let's play!

Getting ready

Before starting the work, we have to make sure that every required tool is in place. Let's check it.

ab: This Apache benchmarking tool is bundled with every Apache installation. If you are on a Linux-based distribution, you can give it a go by issuing the following command in the terminal:

```
ab -h
```

Siege: We will use this tool in the same box as our server. So make sure you have it installed. You can see it by typing this command (note that the option is capital V):

```
siege -V
```

If it's installed, you should see the installed version information of Siege. If it's not, you can install it with the following command in any Debian-based Distro:

```
sudo apt-get install siege
```

You can also install it from source. To do so, grab the latest source from here: `ftp://ftp.joedog.org/pub/siege/siege-latest.tar.gz`, then issue the following steps sequentially:

```
# go the location where you downloaded siege
tar xvzf siege-latest.tar.gz
# go to the siege folder. You should read it with something like siege-2.70
./configure
make
make install
```

If you are on a Windows-based box, you would find it as:

`apache/bin/ab.exe`

Magento Profile: This is also a built-in tool with Magento.

YSlow: This firebug add-on from Firefox could be installed via the Internet from here: `http://developer.yahoo.com/yslow/`. Firebug add-on is a dependency for YSlow.

Page Speed: This is also a firebug add-on that can be downloaded and installed from: `http://code.google.com/speed/page-speed/download.html`.

For using GTmetrix and WebPagetest, we will need an active Internet connection. Make sure you have these.

Performance Optimization

How to do it...

Using the simple tool ab:

1. If you are on a Windows environment, go to the `apache/bin/` folder and if you are on Unix, fire up your terminal and issue the following command:

    ```
    ab -c 10 -n 50 -g mage.tsv http://magento.local.com/
    ```

2. In the previous command, the params denote the following:

    - **-c**: This is the concurrency number of multiple requests to perform at a time. The default is one request at a time.
    - **-n**: This requests the number of requests to perform for the benchmarking session. The default is to just perform a single request, which usually leads to non-representative benchmarking results.
    - **-g (gnuplot-file)**: This writes all measured values out as a gnuplot or **TSV** (**tab separate values**) file. This file can easily be imported into packages like Gnuplot, IDL, Mathematica, Igor, or even Excel. The labels are on the first line of the file.

3. The preceding command generates some benchmarking report in the terminal and a file named `mage.tsv` in the current location, as we specified in the command.

4. If we open the `mage.tsv` file in a spreadsheet editor such as Open Office or MS Excel, it should read as follows:

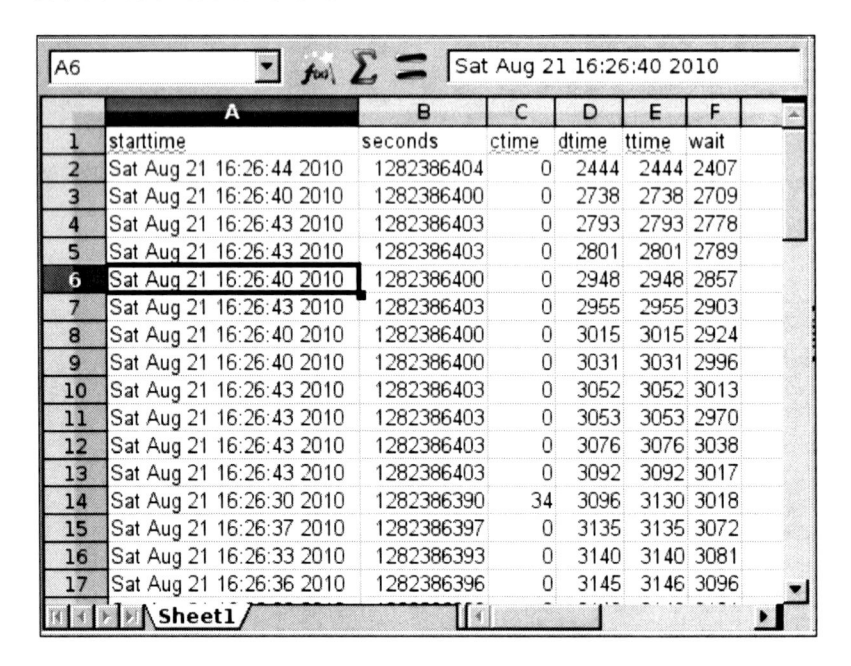

	A	B	C	D	E	F
1	starttime	seconds	ctime	dtime	ttime	wait
2	Sat Aug 21 16:26:44 2010	1282386404	0	2444	2444	2407
3	Sat Aug 21 16:26:40 2010	1282386400	0	2738	2738	2709
4	Sat Aug 21 16:26:43 2010	1282386403	0	2793	2793	2778
5	Sat Aug 21 16:26:43 2010	1282386403	0	2801	2801	2789
6	Sat Aug 21 16:26:40 2010	1282386400	0	2948	2948	2857
7	Sat Aug 21 16:26:43 2010	1282386403	0	2955	2955	2903
8	Sat Aug 21 16:26:40 2010	1282386400	0	3015	3015	2924
9	Sat Aug 21 16:26:40 2010	1282386400	0	3031	3031	2996
10	Sat Aug 21 16:26:43 2010	1282386403	0	3052	3052	3013
11	Sat Aug 21 16:26:43 2010	1282386403	0	3053	3053	2970
12	Sat Aug 21 16:26:43 2010	1282386403	0	3076	3076	3038
13	Sat Aug 21 16:26:43 2010	1282386403	0	3092	3092	3017
14	Sat Aug 21 16:26:30 2010	1282386390	34	3096	3130	3018
15	Sat Aug 21 16:26:37 2010	1282386397	0	3135	3135	3072
16	Sat Aug 21 16:26:33 2010	1282386393	0	3140	3140	3081
17	Sat Aug 21 16:26:36 2010	1282386396	0	3145	3146	3096

Chapter 11

5. You can tweak the ab params and view a full listing of params by typing `ab -h` in the terminal.

Using Siege:

1. Let's lay Siege to it! Siege is an HTTP regression testing and benchmarking utility. It was designed to let web developers measure the performance of their code under duress, to see how it will stand up to load on the Internet. Siege supports basic authentication, cookies, HTTP, and HTTPS protocols. It allows the user to hit a web server with a configurable number of concurrent simulated users. These users place the web server 'under Siege'.

2. Let's create a text file with the URLs that would be tested under Siege. We can pass a single URL in the command line as well. We will use an external text file to use more URLs through a single command. Create a new text file in the terminal's current location. Let's assume that we are in the `/Desktop/mage_benchmark/` directory. Create a file named `mage_urls.txt` here and put the following URLs in it:

```
http://magento.local.com/
http://magento.local.com/skin/frontend/default/default/favicon.ico
http://magento.local.com/js/index.php?c=auto&f=,prototype/prototype.js,prototype/validation.js,scriptaculous/builder.js,scriptaculous/effects.js,scriptaculous/dragdrop.js,scriptaculous/controls.js,scriptaculous/slider.js,varien/js.js,varien/form.js,varien/menu.js,mage/translate.js,mage/cookies.js
http://magento.local.com/skin/frontend/default/default/css/print.css
http://magento.local.com/skin/frontend/default/default/css/styles-ie.css
http://magento.local.com/skin/frontend/default/default/css/styles.css
http://magento.local.com/skin/frontend/default/default/images/np_cart_thumb.gif
http://magento.local.com/skin/frontend/default/default/images/np_product_main.gif
http://magento.local.com/skin/frontend/default/default/images/np_thumb.gif
http://magento.local.com/skin/frontend/default/default/images/slider_btn_zoom_in.gif
http://magento.local.com/skin/frontend/default/default/images/slider_btn_zoom_out.gif
http://magento.local.com/skin/frontend/default/default/images/spacer.gif
http://magento.local.com/skin/frontend/default/default/images/media/404_callout1.jpg
http://magento.local.com/electronics/cameras.html
http://magento.local.com/skin/frontend/default/default/images/
```

```
media/furniture_callout_spot.jpg
http://magento.local.com/skin/adminhtml/default/default/boxes.css
http://magento.local.com/skin/adminhtml/default/default/ie7.css
http://magento.local.com/skin/adminhtml/default/default/reset.css
http://magento.local.com/skin/adminhtml/default/default/menu.css
http://magento.local.com/skin/adminhtml/default/default/print.css
http://magento.local.com/nine-west-women-s-lucero-pump.html
```

3. These URLs will vary with yours. Modify it as it fits. You can add more URLs if you want.

4. Make sure that you are in the `/Desktop/mage_benchmark/` directory in your terminal. Now issue the following command:

   `siege -c 50 -i -t 1M -d 3 -f mage_urls.txt`

5. This will take a fair amount of time. Be patient. After completion it should return a result something like the following:

   ```
   Lifting the server siege..       done.
   Transactions:                      603 hits
   Availability:                    96.33 %
   Elapsed time:                    59.06 secs
   Data transferred:                10.59 MB
   Response time:                    1.24 secs
   Transaction rate:                10.21 trans/sec
   Throughput:                       0.18 MB/sec
   Concurrency:                     12.69
   Successful transactions:           603
   Failed transactions:                23
   Longest transaction:             29.46
   Shortest transaction:             0.00
   ```

6. Repeat the steps 1 and 3 to produce reports with some variations and save them wherever you want.

7. The option details could be found by typing the following command in the terminal:

   `siege -h`

Magento profiler:

1. Magento has a built-in profiler. You can enable it from the backend's **System | Configuration | Advanced | Developer | Debug** section.

2. Now open the `index.php` file from your Magento root directory. Uncomment line numbers 65 and 71. The lines read as follows:

   ```
   line 65: #Varien_Profiler::enable(); // delete #
   line 71: #ini_set(<display_errors>, 1); // delete #
   ```

3. Save this file and reload your Magento frontend in the browser. You should see the profiler data at the bottom of the page, similar to the following screenshot:

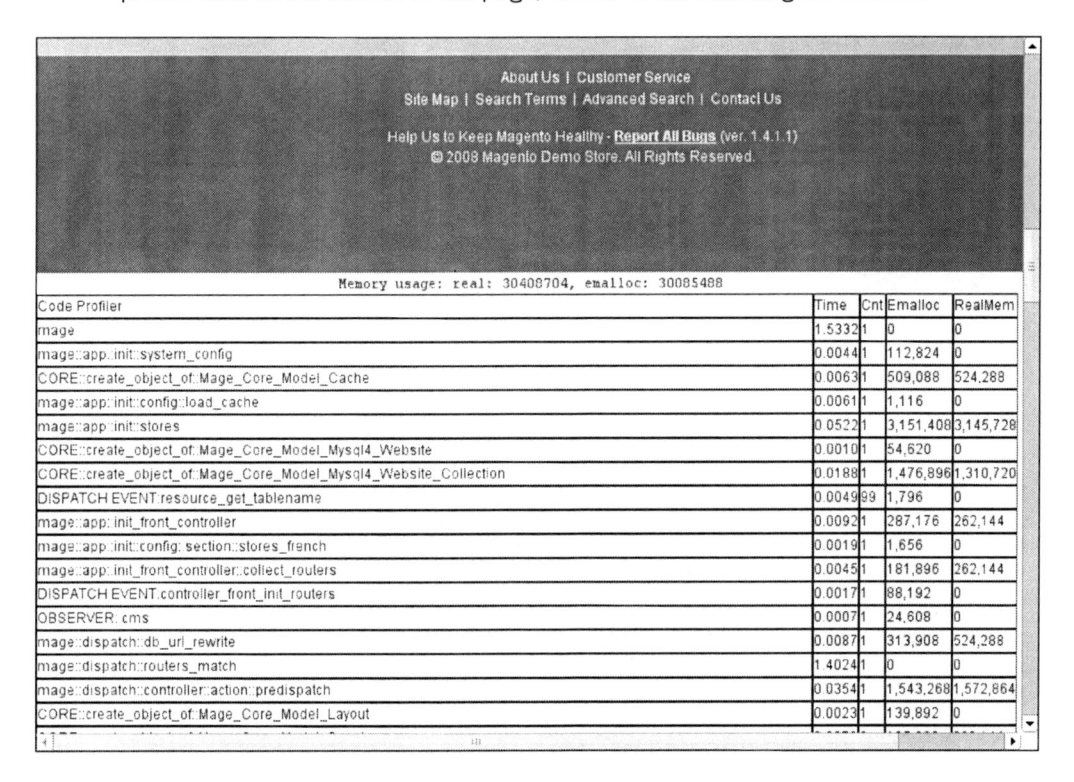

Code Profiler	Time	Cnt	Emalloc	RealMem
mage	1.5332	1	0	0
mage::app::init::system_config	0.0044	1	112,824	0
CORE::create_object_of::Mage_Core_Model_Cache	0.0063	1	509,088	524,288
mage::app::init::config::load_cache	0.0061	1	1,116	0
mage::app::init::stores	0.0522	1	3,151,408	3,145,728
CORE::create_object_of::Mage_Core_Model_Mysql4_Website	0.0010	1	54,620	0
CORE::create_object_of::Mage_Core_Model_Mysql4_Website_Collection	0.0188	1	1,476,896	1,310,720
DISPATCH EVENT:resource_get_tablename	0.0049	99	1,796	0
mage::app::init_front_controller	0.0092	1	287,176	262,144
mage::app::init::config::section::stores_french	0.0019	1	1,656	0
mage::app::init_front_controller::collect_routers	0.0045	1	181,896	262,144
DISPATCH EVENT:controller_front_init_routers	0.0017	1	88,192	0
OBSERVER: cms	0.0007	1	24,608	0
mage::dispatch::db_url_rewrite	0.0087	1	313,908	524,288
mage::dispatch::routers_match	1.4024	1	0	0
mage::dispatch::controller::action::predispatch	0.0354	1	1,543,268	1,572,864
CORE::create_object_of::Mage_Core_Model_Layout	0.0023	1	139,892	0

Memory usage: real: 30408704, emalloc: 30085488

Yslow:

1. We have already installed the YSlow firebug add-on. Open the Firefox browser and let's activate it by pressing the *F12* button or clicking the firebug icon from the bottom-right corner of Firefox.

2. Click on the **YSlow** link in firebug.

3. Select the **Rulesets**. In my case I chose **YSlow (V2)**.

4. Click on the **Run Test** button.

Performance Optimization

5. After a few seconds you will see a report page with the grade details. Here is mine:

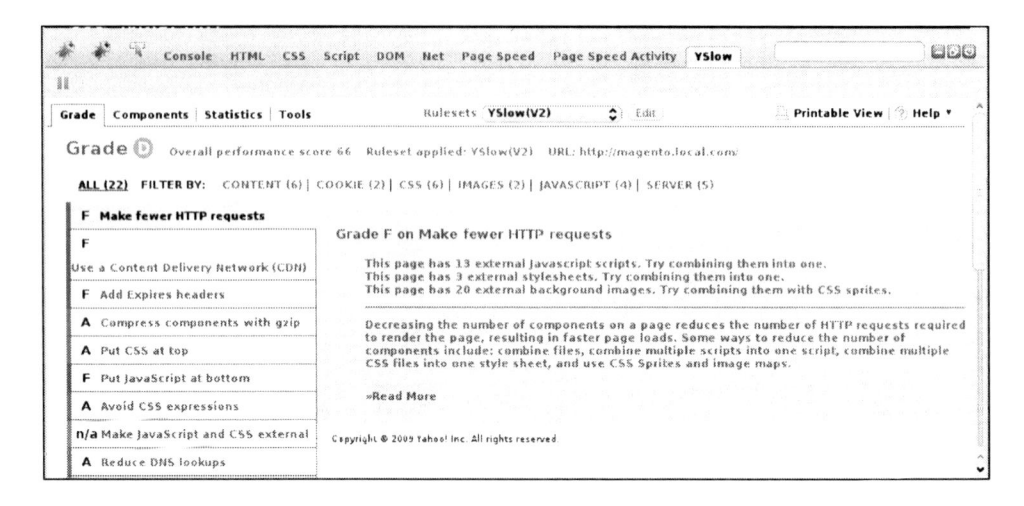

6. You can click on the links and see what it says.

Page Speed:

1. Fire up your Firefox browser.
2. Activate the firebug panel by pressing *F12*.
3. Click on the **Page Speed** link.
4. Click on the **Performance** button and see the **Page Speed Score** and details. The output should be something like the following screenshot:

Using GTmetrix:

This is an online tool to benchmark a page with a combination of YSlow and Page Speed. Visit `http://gtmetrix.com/` and DIY (Do It Yourself).

Using WebPagetest:

This is a similar tool as GTmetrix, which can be accessed from here: `http://www.webpagetest.org/`.

How it works...

ab is a tool for benchmarking your Apache Hypertext Transfer Protocol (HTTP) server. It is designed to give you an impression of how your current Apache installation performs. This especially shows you how many requests per second your Apache installation is capable of serving.

The analysis that Siege leaves you with can tell you a lot about the sustainability of your code and server under duress. Obviously, availability is the most critical factor. Anything less than 100 percent means there's a user who may not be able to access your site. So, in the above case, there's some issue to be looked at, given that availability was only 96.33 percent on a sustained 50 concurrent, one minute user Siege.

Concurrency is measured as the time of each transaction (defined as the number of server hits including any possible authentication challenges) divided by the elapsed time. It tells us the average number of simultaneous connections. High concurrency can be a leading indicator that the server is struggling. The longer it takes the server to complete a transaction while it's still opening sockets to deal with new traffic, the higher the concurrent traffic and the worse the server performance will be.

Yahoo!'s exceptional performance team has identified 34 rules that affect web page performance. YSlow's web page analysis is based on the 22 of these 34 rules that are testable. We used one of their predefined ruleset. You can modify and create your own as well.

When analyzing a web page, YSlow deducts points for each infraction of a rule and then applies a grade to each rule. An overall grade and score for the web page is computed by summing up the values of the score for each rule weighted by the rule's importance. Note that the rules are weighted for an average page. For various reasons, there may be some rules that are less important for your particular page.

In YSlow 2.0, you can create your own custom rulesets in addition to the following three predefined rulesets:

- YSlow(V2): This ruleset contains the 22 rules
- Classic(V1): This ruleset contains the first 13 rules
- Small Site or Blog: This ruleset contains 14 rules that are applicable to small websites or blogs

Performance Optimization

Page Speed generates its results based on the state of the page at the time you run the tool. To ensure the most accurate results, you should wait until the page finishes loading before running Page Speed. Otherwise, Page Speed may not be able to fully analyze resources that haven't finished downloading.

> Windows users can use Fiddler as an alternative to Siege. You can download it from http://www.fiddler2.com/fiddler2/, which is developed by Microsoft.

Optimizing Magento database and MySQL configuration

We already know the bottlenecks of our Magento store. Let us start with the Magento database and our MySQL server as it impacts drastically on the overall performance. In this recipe, we will optimize our store database as well as our MySQL server.

How to do it...

Optimizing the Magento database:

1. This is a simple task. Launch your MySQL administration tool. phpMyAdmin is fine. Select your Magento database.
2. You should see there are two pages for table structures. Click on the **check all** button from the bottom.
3. Now keeping all tables selected, click on the **Repair** table from the drop-down besides the **check all** link.
4. Do the same for the **Optimize** table from the drop-down.
5. Repeat these steps for page 2 as well.
6. At this stage, our database is good to go.
7. Replicate your MySQL server as instructed in *Chapter 7, Database Design*, the *Magento database replication using Master Slave setup* recipe
8. Split the write and read to master and slave database. Refer to *Chapter 7, Database Design*, the *Magento database replication using Master Slave setup* recipe.

Optimizing MySQL server:

1. Let us start from the system's operating system itself. To get the best use of multiple-CPU machines, you should use Linux (because 2.4 and later kernels have good SMP support). File systems such as ReiserFS and XFS do not have any size 2

GB limitation that is on ext2 though; ext2 could be patched for more than 2 GB size with the LFS patch. For running Magento, it's highly recommended to use a dedicated server or at least a VPS.

2. If you have enough RAM, you could remove all swapped devices. Some operating systems use a swap device in some contexts even if you have free memory.

3. Avoid external locking by using skip-external-locking in the `[mysqld]` section of `my.cnf`.

4. The next important task is to set the `key_buffer_size` for MyISAM engine. Log in to your MySQL server with root access in the terminal.

    `mysql> SHOW VARIABLES LIKE '%key_buffer%';`

5. You should specify the current allocation for `key_buffer_size`. It is used by MyISAM tables to cache Index only, not data. If you have got a MyISAM system only, then the `key_buffer_size` should be 30 percent of memory. Remember that there is a limit of **4 GB** per key buffer. MyISAM tables are used for temporary tables anyway. Let's set it as 512M. So, the following will be the MySQL command:

    `mysql> SET GLOBAL key_buffer_size = 536870912;`

6. We will set the rest of the configurations via the `my.cnf` file from the `/etc/mysql/` directory.

7. Open it and create the `[mysqld]` section as follows:

    ```
    [mysqld]
    key_buffer = 512M
    max_allowed_packet = 64M
    thread_stack = 192K
    thread_cache_size = 32
    table_cache = 512
    query_cache_type = 1
    query_cache_size = 52428800
    tmp_table_size = 128M
    expire_logs_days = 10
    max_binlog_size = 100M
    sort_buffer_size = 4M
    read_buffer_size = 4M
    read_rnd_buffer_size = 2M
    myisam_sort_buffer_size = 64M
    wait_timeout = 300
    max_connections = 400
    ```

8. Save and restart your MySQL server.

How it works...

The most important tuning for any MySQL server are `key_buffer`, `query_cache` and `table_cache`. Make sure that you have specified the appropriate unit and value. Skip-external-locking is also an important tuning. It helps to deny any external locking.

Performance Optimization

You can view the current MySQL server status and variables by issuing the following commands:

Command	Description
`mysql> SHOW STATUS;`	This shows the current MySQL server status. It is available since MySQL 5.0, and `SHOW STATUS` now defaults to this. Some variables are global only; they will still be shown in the `SHOW STATUS` output.
`mysql> SHOW VARIABLES;`	This shows the MySQL variables.
`mysql> SHOW INNODB STATUS;`	This shows the current `InnoDB` status.
`mysql> SHOW GLOBAL STATUS;`	This shows the global server status load. It is good for understanding the load.
`mysql> SHOW LOCAL STATUS;`	This is great for query/transaction profiling.
`mysql> mysqladmin extended -i100 -r`	This is great to sample what is happening with MySQL Server Now.

You are encouraged to benchmark your server while applying these tunings. You should get about a 50 percent performance gain after these settings are applied.

There's more

Some wrong units in MySQL server tuning:

- `table_cache=128M`

  Wrong, table cache is measured in entries

- `key_buffer_size=1024`

  Wrong again, key buffer should be specified in bytes

- `innodb_max_dirty_pages_pct=8G`

  This one is set in percents

Optimizing Apache web server configuration

Now-a-days there are some other alternatives for Apache, but still the majority of us use Apache as a web server. The ultimate performance of any web application depends on some other factors as well such as CPU, network card, disk, OS, and RAM.

The most important hardware that affects any web server's performance is RAM. The more the better. In this recipe, we will optimize the web server, preferably a DS or at least a VPS.

How to do it...

1. Update the operating system to its latest stable release. In most cases, OS suppliers have introduced significant performance improvements to their TCP stacks and thread libraries.

2. Update your sendfile(2) system call support with the latest patch if your box is Linux and its kernel is lower than 2.4. If your box has got a kernel higher than 2.4 then it's ok. This ensures Apache 2 to deliver static contents faster with lower CPU utilization.

3. Keep other background applications minimum. For example, in Unix, switch off NFS, any printing services, and even sendmail if it's not needed. Under Windows, use the system control panel to optimize the system for applications and system cache, and optimize the system for performance.

4. ReiserFS and XFS are some good filesystems to use for better disk I/O.

5. Web server should never ever have to swap, as swapping increases the latency of each request. You should control the MaxClients setting so that your server does not spawn so many children, that it starts swapping. Determine the size of your average Apache process, by looking at your process list via a tool such as top, and divide this into your total available memory, leaving some room for other processes.

6. Set **HostnameLookups** to **Off**, if your Apache is lower than 1.3. If Apache is higher than 1.3, then **HostnameLookups** is defaulted to **Off**.

7. It is highly discouraged to use `SymLinksIfOwnerMatch`, you can rather use it as `Options FollowSymLinks + SymLinksIfOwnerMatch` for specific directories. And for other locations use `Options FollowSymLinks`. This will prevent `lstat(2)` system calls. By the way, the results of `lstat()` are never cached.

8. Never use `DirectoryIndex` as a wildcard, such as the following:

   `DirectoryIndex index`

9. Rather, use a complete one such as the following:

   `DirectoryIndex index.php index.html index.cgi index.pl index.shtml`

10. Enable mod deflate and mod header with the following command:

    sudo a2enmod deflate

    sudo a2enmod header

11. Let us add some deflate settings in our `.htaccess` of our Magento store. Find and open the `.htaccess` from Magento root and modify it to show the deflate block as follows:

    ```
    <IfModule mod_deflate.c>

    ############################################
    ## enable apache served files compression
    ## http://developer.yahoo.com/performance/rules.html#gzip
    ```

Performance Optimization

```
    # Insert filter on all content
    SetOutputFilter DEFLATE
    # Insert filter on selected content types only
    AddOutputFilterByType DEFLATE text/html text/plain text/xml
text/css text/javascript

    # Netscape 4.x has some problems...
    BrowserMatch ^Mozilla/4 gzip-only-text/html

    # Netscape 4.06-4.08 have some more problems
    BrowserMatch ^Mozilla/4\.0[678] no-gzip

    # MSIE masquerades as Netscape, but it is fine
    BrowserMatch \bMSIE !no-gzip !gzip-only-text/html

    # Don›t compress images
    SetEnvIfNoCase Request_URI \.(?:gif|jpe?g|png)$ no-gzip dont-vary

    # Make sure proxies don›t deliver the wrong content
    Header append Vary User-Agent env=!dont-vary

</IfModule>
```

12. The next task is to set up mod expires. Issue the following command in your Linux terminal:

    sudo a2enmod expires

    sudo /etc/init.d/apache2 restart

13. We must add expires settings in our `.htaccess`. Find the `expires` block and make it as follows:

```
<IfModule mod_expires.c>

############################################
## Add default Expires header
## http://developer.yahoo.com/performance/rules.html#expires

    ExpiresDefault «access plus 1 year»
    ExpiresActive On
    ExpiresByType image/gif «access plus 30 days»
    ExpiresByType image/jpg «access plus 30 days»
    ExpiresByType image/jpeg «access plus 30 days»
    ExpiresByType image/png «access plus 30 days»
```

```
ExpiresByType image/x-icon «access plus 30 days»
ExpiresByType text/css «access plus 30 days»
ExpiresByType application/x-javascript «access plus 30 days»
```

```
</IfModule>
```
Apache 1.1 comes with the Keep-Alive support on by default.

14. Apache 1.1 and higher has come up with it's `KeepAlive` directive as `On` by default. Make sure that the `KeepAlive` is `On`. This is a trick where multiple HTTP requests can be funneled through a single TCP connection. You can modify it from the `/etc/apache2/apache2.conf` file.

15. Set up your MPM as best. Experiment with it. Here is my configuration, this might and should be different depending on your system's resources:

```
StartServers           50
MinSpareServers        15
MaxSpareServers        30
MaxClients             225
MaxRequestsPerChild    4000
```

16. Benchmark your Magento again and see your changes in action!

How it works...

The overall performance of a LAMP application depends on the factors described previously and obviously your application itself. If your application cannot serve 100 concurrent hits then trying to optimize it is sort of a waste of time. If you are doing it on your own application other than Magento then make sure your application's code is able to serve at least 100 concurrent hits.

Server software, hardware also has a great impact on overall performance, so make it as high as possible. For overcoming common bottlenecks of a web application, we have some predefined rulesets that are described elaborately in Yahoo! and Google for YSlow and Page Speed, respectively. Follow them and you are good to go.

Last but not least, is to host your application in a server located in the same area as your targeted customer's location.

Tuning Magento configurations

Magento configuration is defaulted to run in a wide variety of servers, which might hinder the best performance. This recipe will help you tune the Magento configurations to let it perform fast and furious!

Performance Optimization

How to do it...

1. Log in to your Magento backend as admin.
2. Cleanup (uninstall and delete) all extensions/modules that you are not using.
3. Enable all types of caching from the Magento backend | **System** | **Cache Management** page. Don't forget to flush/clear all cache storages.
4. Compile your Magento from the **System** | **Tools** | **Compilation** | **Run Compilation** process. It compiles all Magento installation files and creates a single include path. It will speed up pages 25 to 50 percent, according to the official documentation.
5. Go to the page **System** | **Configuration** | **Advanced** | **Disable Modules Output** and disable those which you are not using such as **Mage_poll**.
6. Navigate to the page **System** | **Configurations** | **Advanced** | **Developers** and make it read as follows:

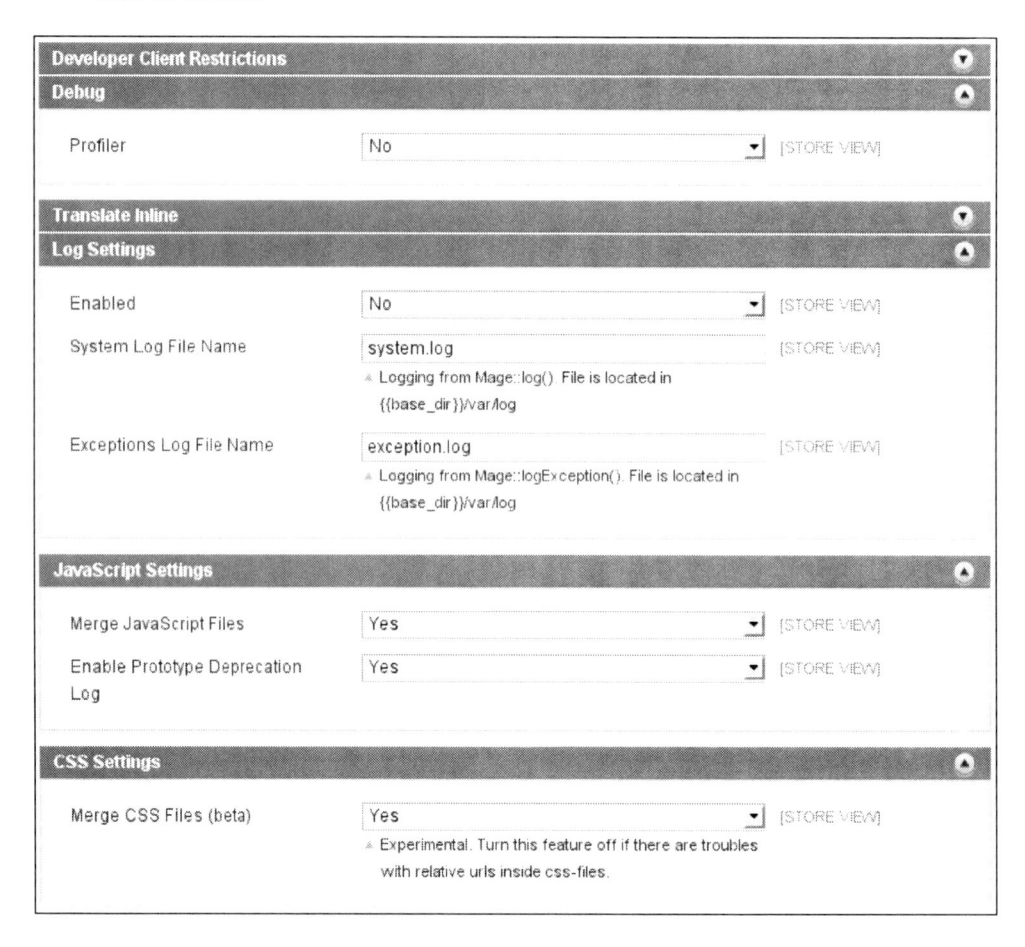

Developer Client Restrictions		
Debug		
Profiler	No	[STORE VIEW]
Translate Inline		
Log Settings		
Enabled	No	[STORE VIEW]
System Log File Name	system.log	[STORE VIEW]
	Logging from Mage::log(). File is located in {{base_dir}}/var/log	
Exceptions Log File Name	exception.log	[STORE VIEW]
	Logging from Mage::logException(). File is located in {{base_dir}}/var/log	
JavaScript Settings		
Merge JavaScript Files	Yes	[STORE VIEW]
Enable Prototype Deprecation Log	Yes	[STORE VIEW]
CSS Settings		
Merge CSS Files (beta)	Yes	[STORE VIEW]
	Experimental. Turn this feature off if there are troubles with relative urls inside css-files.	

7. Navigate to the **Catalog** | **Attributes** | **Manage Attributes** page. Set only those attribute frontend properties to **Yes** that you're actually going to use. Set all others to **No**. Don't use them in quick search, advanced search compare, and so on.

8. Use store content's mark-up as W3 valid and avoid expressions in CSS like this:
   ```
   background-color: expression( (new Date()).getHours()%2 ?
   "#B8D4FF" : "#F08A00" );
   ```

9. As shown previously, the `expression` method accepts a JavaScript expression. The CSS property is set to the result of evaluating the JavaScript expression. The expression method is ignored by other browsers, so it is useful for setting the properties in Internet Explorer that are needed to create a consistent experience across browsers.

How it works...

These are the configurations provided by the Magento administration panel. We tweaked it to get a better performance. Note that Merging JavaScript and CSS is a beta feature that is available in Magento 1.4.x version. Merging JavaScript and CSS is recommended both by YSlow and Page Speed.

Using APC/Memcached as the cache backend

Magento has got a cache system that is based on files by default. We can boost the overall performance by changing the cache handler to a better engine like APC or Memcached. This recipe will help us to set up APC or Memcached as the cache backend.

Getting ready

Installation of APC:

Alternative PHP Cache (**APC**) is a PECL extension. For any Debian-based Distro, it can be installed with an easy command from the terminal:

`sudo apt-get install php5-apc`

Or:

`sudo pecl install APC`

You can also install it from the source. The package download location for APC is: `http://pecl.php.net/package/APC`. Check whether it exists or not in `phpinfo()`. If you cannot see an APC block there, then you might not have added APC in the `php.ini` file.

Performance Optimization

Installation of Memcached:

Memcached is also available in most OS package repositories. You can install it from the command line:

`sudo apt-get install php5-memcached`

Memcached could be installed from source as well. Check whether it exists or not in `phpinfo()`. If you cannot see a Memcached block there, then you might not have added Memcached in the `php.ini` file.

You can also check it via the telnet client. Issue the following command in the terminal:

`telnet localhost 11211`

We can issue the `get` command now:

`get greeting`

Nothing happened? We have to set it first.

`set greeting 1 0 11`

`Hello World`

`STORED`

`get greeting`

`Hello World`

`END`

`quit`

How to do it...

1. Okay, we are all set to go for the APC or Memcached. Let's do it now for APC. Open `local.xml` in your favorite PHP editor. Add the cache block as follows:

   ```
   <?xml version="1.0"?>
   <config>
     <global>
       <install>
         <date><![CDATA[Sat, 26 Jun 2010 11:55:18 +0000]]></date>
       </install>
       <cache>
         <backend>apc</backend>
         <prefix>alphanumeric</prefix>
       </cache>
       <crypt>
           <key><![CDATA[870f60e1ba58fd34dbf730bfa8c9c152]]></key>
   ```

Chapter 11

```xml
        </crypt>
        <disable_local_modules>false</disable_local_modules>
        <resources>
          <db>
            <table_prefix><![CDATA[]]></table_prefix>
          </db>
          <default_setup>
            <connection>
              <host><![CDATA[localhost]]></host>
              <username><![CDATA[root]]></username>
              <password><![CDATA[f]]></password>
              <dbname><![CDATA[magento]]></dbname>
              <active>1</active>
            </connection>
          </default_setup>
        </resources>
        <session_save><![CDATA[files]]></session_save>
      </global>
      <admin>
        <routers>
          <adminhtml>
            <args>
              <frontName><![CDATA[backend]]></frontName>
            </args>
          </adminhtml>
        </routers>
      </admin>
    </config>
```

2. Delete all files from the `var/cache/` directory. Reload your Magento and benchmark it now to see the boost in performance. Run the benchmark several times to get an accurate result.

   `ab -c 5 -n 100 http://magento.local.com/`

3. You can use either APC or Memcached. Let's test it with Memcached now. Delete the cache block as we set with APC previously and add the cache block as follows:

```xml
<?xml version="1.0"?>
<config>
  <global>
    <install>
      <date><![CDATA[Sat, 26 Jun 2010 11:55:18 +0000]]></date>
    </install>
    <crypt>
      <key><![CDATA[870f60e1ba58fd34dbf730bfa8c9c152]]></key>
```

```xml
        </crypt>
        <disable_local_modules>false</disable_local_modules>
        <resources>
          <db>
            <table_prefix><![CDATA[]]></table_prefix>
          </db>
          <default_setup>
            <connection>
              <host><![CDATA[localhost]]></host>
              <username><![CDATA[root]]></username>
              <password><![CDATA[f]]></password>
              <dbname><![CDATA[magento]]></dbname>
              <active>1</active>
            </connection>
          </default_setup>
        </resources>
        <session_save><![CDATA[files]]></session_save>

    <cache>
        <backend>memcached</backend> apc / memcached / xcache /
empty=file
        <slow_backend>file</slow_backend>  database / file (default)
- used for 2 levels cache setup, necessary for all shared memory
storages
        <memcached> memcached cache backend related config
          <servers> any number of server nodes can be included
            <server>
              <host><![CDATA[127.0.0.1]]></host>
              <port><![CDATA[11211]]></port>
              <persistent><![CDATA[1]]></persistent>
              <weight><![CDATA[2]]></weight>
              <timeout><![CDATA[10]]></timeout>
              <retry_interval><![CDATA[10]]></retry_interval>
              <status><![CDATA[1]]></status>
            </server>
          </servers>
          <compression><![CDATA[0]]></compression>
          <cache_dir><![CDATA[]]></cache_dir>
          <hashed_directory_level><![CDATA[]]>
          </hashed_directory_level>
          <hashed_directory_umask><![CDATA[]]>
          </hashed_directory_umask>
          <file_name_prefix><![CDATA[]]></file_name_prefix>
        </memcached>
```

```
        </cache>

      </global>
      <admin>
        <routers>
          <adminhtml>
            <args>
              <frontName><![CDATA[backend]]></frontName>
            </args>
          </adminhtml>
        </routers>
      </admin>
    </config>
```

4. Save the `local.xml` file, clear all cache files from `/var/cache/` and reload your Magento in the frontend and check the performance.
5. Mount `var/cache` as TMPFS:

   ```
   mount tmpfs /path/to/your/magento/var/cache -t tmpfs -o size=64m
   ```

How it works...

Alternative PHP Cache (APC) is a free, open source opcode cache framework that optimizes PHP intermediate code and caches data and compiled code from the PHP bytecode compiler in shared memory, which is similar to Memcached. APC is quickly becoming the de facto standard PHP caching mechanism, as it will be included built-in to the core of PHP, starting with PHP 6. The biggest problem with APC is that you can only access the local APC cache.

Memcached's magic lies in its two-stage hash approach. It behaves as though it were a giant hash table, looking up key = value pairs. Give it a key, and set or get some arbitrary data. When doing a memcached lookup, first the client hashes the key against the whole list of servers. Once it has chosen a server, the client then sends its request, and the server does an internal hash key lookup for the actual item data. Memcached affords us endless possibilities (query caching, content caching, session storage) and great flexibility. It's an excellent option for increasing performance and scalability on any website without requiring a lot of additional resources.

Changing the var/cache to TMPFS is a very good trick to increase disk I/O. I personally found both APC's and Memcached's performance pretty similar. Both are good to go. If you want to split your cache in multiple servers go for the Memcached. Good Luck!

> The highlighted sections in code are for the APC and Memcached settings, respectively.

Performance Optimization

Accelerating PHP: php.ini configuration

If you don't use an APC-like accelerator, then it's time to use one. As, when a PHP script is requested, PHP reads the script and compiles it into what's called Zend opcode, a binary representation of the code to be executed. This opcode is then executed by the PHP engine and thrown away. An opcode cache saves this compiled opcode and reuses it the next time the page is called. This saves a considerable amount of time. In this recipe, we will learn how to optimize the `php.ini` configuration for its best performance.

Getting ready

There are many PHP accelerators out there. You can go for any of them. Such as APC, eAceelerator, XCache, Zend Accelerator (a tool in Zend server), Zend Platform, and so on. Here are some URLs for your convenience:

- APC: http://pecl.php.net/package/APC
- EAccelerator: http://eaccelerator.net/
- XCache: http://xcache.lighttpd.net/

How to do it...

1. The very first job is to use an efficient process manager such as php-fpm, which runs FastCGI with impressive speed.

2. Use `realpath_cache_size` in `php.ini`. This denotes the size of the realpath cache to be used by PHP. This value should be increased on systems where PHP opens many files, to reflect the quantity of the file operations performed. Here is mine:

   ```
   realpath_cache_size=1M
   realpath_cache_ttl=86400
   ```

3. There are some other resources as well, which can improve the overall performance:

Setting	Description	Recommended value
`max_execution_time`	How many CPU-seconds a script can consume	30
`max_input_time`	How long (seconds) a script can wait for input data	60
`memory_limit`	How much memory (bytes) a script can consume before being killed	32M
`output_buffering`	How much data (bytes) to buffer before sending out to the client	4096

4. Last but not the least is to set error reporting to off.

How it works...

These numbers depend mostly on your application. If you accept large files from users, then `max_input_time` may have to be increased, either in `php.ini` or by overriding it in code. Similarly, a CPU- or memory-heavy program may need larger settings. The purpose is to mitigate the effect of a runaway program, so disabling these settings globally isn't recommended. Another note on `max_execution_time`: This refers to the CPU time of the process, not the absolute time. Thus, a program that does lots of I/O and few calculations may run for much longer than `max_execution_time`. It's also how `max_input_time` can be greater than `max_execution_time`.

The amount of logging that PHP can do is configurable. In a production environment, disabling all but the most critical logs saves disk writes. If logs are needed to troubleshoot a problem, you can turn up logging as needed. `error_reporting = E_COMPILE_ERROR|E_ERROR|E_CORE_ERROR` turns on enough logging to spot problems but eliminates a lot of chatter from scripts.

Applying YSlow and Page Speed rules

YSlow and Page Speed both are very useful, FREE tools for optimization experts. Personally, I use both of them. Both have some defined rulesets and options to create on your own by modifying a ruleset. This recipe will let us apply those rules in our application.

Most of the rules have already been applied in our previous recipes in this chapter. We will now deal with the rest of the recipes.

Getting ready

We must have installed the Firefox browser and the following add-ons to work with this recipe. Make sure these tools are installed and regarding versions, the later the better.

Tool	Download link
Firefox	`http://www.mozilla-europe.org/en/firefox/`
Firebug	`http://getfirebug.com/`
YSlow	`http://developer.yahoo.com/yslow/`
Page Speed	`http://code.google.com/speed/page-speed/`

Performance Optimization

How to do it...

YSlow analyzes a web page on a selected ruleset, Ruleset YSlow(v2) and Ruleset YSlow(v1). v2 comprised 22 rules while v1 has 13 rules. We will be using v2, which has the following rules. Studies have shown that web page response time can be improved by 25 percent to 50 percent by following these rules:

- Minimize HTTP requests
- Use a content delivery network
- Add an expires or a cache-control header
- Gzip components
- Put StyleSheets at the top
- Put scripts at the bottom
- Avoid CSS expressions
- Make JavaScript and CSS external
- Reduce DNS lookups
- Minify JavaScript and CSS
- Avoid redirects
- Remove duplicate scripts
- Configure ETags
- Make AJAX cacheable
- Use GET for AJAX requests
- Reduce the number of DOM elements
- No 404s
- Reduce cookie size
- Use cookie-free domains for components
- Avoid filters
- Do not scale images in HTML
- Make `favicon.ico` small and cacheable

1. If you have not followed the previous recipes of this chapter, you are strongly recommended to follow those and then come back to this one. At this stage, if we run the YSlow test then we should see the overall grade is B. We failed at "use a content delivery network (CDN)". For convenience, I am attaching the full and final `.htaccess` file here:

```
##############################################
## uncomment these lines for CGI mode
## make sure to specify the correct cgi php binary file name
## it might be /cgi-bin/php-cgi
```

```
#       Action php5-cgi /cgi-bin/php5-cgi
#       AddHandler php5-cgi .php

################################################
## GoDaddy specific options

#       Options -MultiViews

## you might also need to add this line to php.ini
##      cgi.fix_pathinfo = 1
## if it still doesn›t work, rename php.ini to php5.ini

################################################
## this line is specific for 1and1 hosting

    #AddType x-mapp-php5 .php
    #AddHandler x-mapp-php5 .php

################################################
## default index file

    DirectoryIndex index.php

<IfModule mod_php5.c>

################################################
## adjust memory limit

#       php_value memory_limit 64M
    php_value memory_limit 128M
    php_value max_execution_time 18000

################################################
## disable magic quotes for php request vars

    php_flag magic_quotes_gpc off

################################################
## disable automatic session start
## before autoload was initialized

    php_flag session.auto_start off

################################################
```

Performance Optimization

```
    ## enable resulting html compression

        php_flag zlib.output_compression on

#############################################
# disable user agent verification to not break multiple image
upload

        php_flag suhosin.session.cryptua off

#############################################
# turn off compatibility with PHP4 when dealing with objects

        php_flag zend.ze1_compatibility_mode Off

</IfModule>

<IfModule mod_security.c>
#############################################
# disable POST processing to not break multiple image upload

        SecFilterEngine Off
        SecFilterScanPOST Off
</IfModule>

<IfModule mod_deflate.c>

#############################################
## enable apache served files compression
## http://developer.yahoo.com/performance/rules.html#gzip

        # Insert filter on all content
        SetOutputFilter DEFLATE
        # Insert filter on selected content types only
        AddOutputFilterByType DEFLATE text/html text/plain text/xml
text/css text/javascript

        # Netscape 4.x has some problems...
        BrowserMatch ^Mozilla/4 gzip-only-text/html

        # Netscape 4.06-4.08 have some more problems
        BrowserMatch ^Mozilla/4\.0[678] no-gzip

        # MSIE masquerades as Netscape, but it is fine
```

```
    BrowserMatch \bMSIE !no-gzip !gzip-only-text/html

    # Don›t compress images
    SetEnvIfNoCase Request_URI \.(?:gif|jpe?g|png)$ no-gzip dont-
vary

    # Make sure proxies don›t deliver the wrong content
    Header append Vary User-Agent env=!dont-vary

</IfModule>

<IfModule mod_ssl.c>

################################################
## make HTTPS env vars available for CGI mode

    SSLOptions StdEnvVars

</IfModule>

<IfModule mod_rewrite.c>

################################################
## enable rewrites

    Options +FollowSymLinks
    RewriteEngine on

################################################
## you can put here your magento root folder
## path relative to web root

    #RewriteBase /magento/

################################################
## workaround for HTTP authorization
## in CGI environment

    RewriteRule .* - [E=HTTP_AUTHORIZATION:%{HTTP:Authorization}]

################################################
## always send 404 on missing files in these folders

    RewriteCond %{REQUEST_URI} !^/(media|skin|js)/
```

Performance Optimization

```
##################################################
## never rewrite for existing files, directories and links

    RewriteCond %{REQUEST_FILENAME} !-f
    RewriteCond %{REQUEST_FILENAME} !-d
    RewriteCond %{REQUEST_FILENAME} !-l

##################################################
## rewrite everything else to index.php

    RewriteRule .* index.php [L]

</IfModule>


##################################################
## Prevent character encoding issues from server overrides
## If you still have problems, use the second line instead

    AddDefaultCharset Off
    #AddDefaultCharset UTF-8

<IfModule mod_expires.c>

##################################################
## Add default Expires header
## http://developer.yahoo.com/performance/rules.html#expires

    ExpiresDefault «access plus 1 year»
    ExpiresActive On
    ExpiresByType image/gif «access plus 30 days»
    ExpiresByType image/jpg «access plus 30 days»
    ExpiresByType image/jpeg «access plus 30 days»
    ExpiresByType image/png «access plus 30 days»
    ExpiresByType image/x-icon «access plus 30 days»
    ExpiresByType text/css «access plus 30 days»
    ExpiresByType application/x-javascript «access plus 30 days»

</IfModule>

##################################################
## By default allow all access
```

```
        Order allow,deny
        Allow from all

#################################################
## If running in cluster environment, uncomment this
## http://developer.yahoo.com/performance/rules.html#etags

        FileETag none
```

2. The `.htaccess` is optimized both as recommended by YSlow and Page Speed.
3. Let us optimize our images using a superb tool from Yahoo! named Smush It! At YSlow you will see a link for all tools. Click it and navigate to **All Smush It!**. Upon clicking you would see a page something like the following:

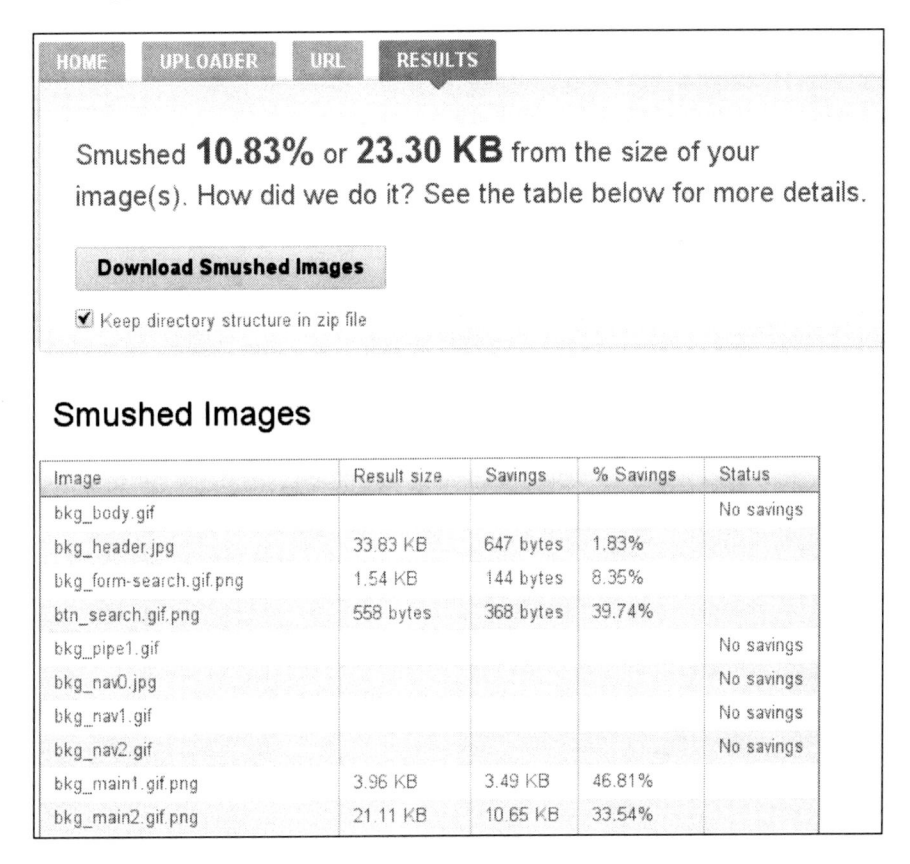

Smushed **10.83%** or **23.30 KB** from the size of your image(s). How did we do it? See the table below for more details.

Smushed Images

Image	Result size	Savings	% Savings	Status
bkg_body.gif				No savings
bkg_header.jpg	33.83 KB	647 bytes	1.83%	
bkg_form-search.gif.png	1.54 KB	144 bytes	8.35%	
btn_search.gif.png	558 bytes	368 bytes	39.74%	
bkg_pipe1.gif				No savings
bkg_nav0.jpg				No savings
bkg_nav1.gif				No savings
bkg_nav2.gif				No savings
bkg_main1.gif.png	3.96 KB	3.49 KB	46.81%	
bkg_main2.gif.png	21.11 KB	10.65 KB	33.54%	

Performance Optimization

4. Next, download the optimized images and replace your local images. If you are reading this recipe for some LAMP app other than Magento, then you can use some other tools provided by YSlow such as compression of your js and css files. Kinda cool huh!

5. For Page Speed, it's already applied most of the recommended rules except Parallelize downloads across hostnames. You can adopt it by using a CDN.

6. There are so many CDN providers out there. You can choose any one and pull the static contents from a CDN. After completion of this one, if we run YSlow and Page Speed, it should be all green!

How it works...

YSlow and Page Speed both have online documentation to apply their rulesets. You can and should read it thoroughly to make it better.

- YSlow: `http://developer.yahoo.com/performance/rules.html`.
- Page Speed: `http://code.google.com/speed/page-speed/docs/using.html`.

See also...

You may also refer to the *Measuring/benchmarking your Magento with Siege, ab, Magento profiler, YSlow, Page Speed, GTmetrix, and WebPagetest* recipe of this chapter.

12
Debugging and Unit Testing

In this chapter, we will cover:

- Installing and configuring Xdebug
- Using FirePHP with Zend Wildfire plugin
- Installing PHPUnit and necessary PHP CLI binaries
- Writing your first Magento test case

Introduction

Debugging (and Unit testing) is a very important part of a PHP developer as now-a-days a website is not just a collection of some HTML pages. We are implementing some of the most complex business logics in our applications. We can minimize the debugging time and deliver rock solid application by using some extra tools like Xdebug, Zend Wildfire plugin, PHPUnit, and so on. This chapter will guide you through to install, configure, and use Xdebug, Zend Wildfire, and PHPUnit in an easy way.

Installing and configuring Xdebug

The PHP statement echo and the functions `var_dump()`, `debug_zval_dump()`, and `print_r()` are common and popular debugging aids that can help solve a variety of issues. However, these statements and even more robust instrumentation is what is called Xdebug, which is a very popular tool for PHP developers around the world. The creator of this tool, *Derick Rethans*, called this tool as the PHP developer's swiss-army knife. Xdebug's basic functions include the display of stack traces on error conditions, maximum nesting level protection, and time tracking.

Debugging and Unit Testing

Debugging through deduction is a brute-force approach. You collect data and shift through it, trying to deduce what's happened. If you lack vital information, you must restructure your code, repeat your steps, and restart your investigation. A far more efficient strategy is to probe the application while it's running. You can catalog request parameters, shift through the procedure call stack, and query any variable or object you'd like. You can temporarily interrupt the application and be alerted when a variable changes value. In some cases, you can actually affect variables interactively to ask "What if?" questions. In this recipe, we will install and configure to debug our Magento script both in IDE or in the browser with the given breakpoints.

How to do it...

Installing Xdebug:

1. Xdebug could be installed in various ways depending on your operating system. You can download a binary Xdebug module for recent versions of PHP from the Xdebug website http://www.xdebug.org/files/. We will build Xdebug from source and install it, which is pretty common for Unix-like operating systems. We will need some basic tools to make it happen, such as: `wget`, `phpize`, and some other build-essentials.

2. To proceed, grab the latest source code in `archive/tarball` format from the Xdebug download section (`wget` command could make the job easy):

    ```
    wget http://www.xdebug.org/files/xdebug-2.1.0.tgz
    ```

3. Extract the archive and change your working directory to the extracted location:

    ```
    tar -xzvf xdebug-2.1.0.tgz
    cd xdebug-2.1.0
    ```

4. Run `phpize` to prepare the Xdebug code for your version of PHP:

    ```
    phpize

    Configuring for:
    PHP Api Version:         20090626
    Zend Module Api No:      20090626
    Zend Extension Api No:   220090626
    ```

5. Let's run the configure script now; this will check for some required headers and binaries:

    ```
    ./configure

    checking for grep that handles long lines and -e... /bin/grep
    checking for egrep... /bin/grep -E
    checking for a sed that does not truncate output... /bin/sed
    ```

```
checking for cc... cc
checking whether the C compiler works... yes
checking for C compiler default output file name... a.out
checking for suffix of executables...
checking whether we are cross compiling... no
checking for suffix of object files... o
checking whether we are using the GNU C compiler... yes
checking whether cc accepts -g... yes
checking for cc option to accept ISO C89... none needed
checking how to run the C preprocessor... cc -E
checking for icc... no
checking for suncc... no
checking whether cc understands -c and -o together... yes
checking for system library directory... lib
checking if compiler supports -R... no
checking if compiler supports -Wl,-rpath,... yes
checking build system type... i686-pc-linux-gnu
checking host system type... i686-pc-linux-gnu
checking target system type... i686-pc-linux-gnu
checking for PHP prefix... /usr
checking for PHP includes... -I/usr/include/php5 -I/usr/include/
php5/main -I/usr/include/php5/TSRM -I/usr/include/php5/Zend
-I/usr/include/php5/ext -I/usr/include/php5/ext/date/lib -D_
LARGEFILE_SOURCE -D_FILE_OFFSET_BITS=64
checking for PHP extension directory... /usr/lib/php5/20090626+lfs
checking for PHP installed headers prefix... /usr/include/php5
checking if debug is enabled... no
checking if zts is enabled... no
….
```

6. Build it by running the make command:

   ```
   make

   /bin/bash /home/dynamicguy/Desktop/xdebug-2.1.0/libtool
   --mode=compile cc   -I. -I/home/dynamicguy/Desktop/xdebug-2.1.0
   -DPHP_ATOM_INC -I/home/dynamicguy/Desktop/xdebug-2.1.0/include
   -I/home/dynamicguy/Desktop/xdebug-2.1.0/main -I/home/dynamicguy/
   Desktop/xdebug-2.1.0 -I/usr/include/php5 -I/usr/include/php5/
   main -I/usr/include/php5/TSRM -I/usr/include/php5/Zend -I/usr/
   include/php5/ext -I/usr/include/php5/ext/date/lib -D_LARGEFILE_
   ```

```
SOURCE -D_FILE_OFFSET_BITS=64  -DHAVE_CONFIG_H  -g -O0    -c /home/
dynamicguy/Desktop/xdebug-2.1.0/xdebug.c -o xdebug.lo

…. . . .

Build complete.

Don't forget to run 'make test'.
```

7. Install the extension now by running this command:

   ```
   sudo make install
   Installing shared extensions:      /usr/lib/php5/20090626+lfs/
   ```

8. Now open /etc/php5/cli/conf.d/xdebug.ini and replace the content with the following:

   ```
   zend_extension=/usr/lib/php5/20090626+lfs/xdebug.so

   xdebug.remote_enable=on

   xdebug.remote_log="/var/log/xdebug.log"

   xdebug.remote_host=localhost

   xdebug.remote_handler=dbgp

   xdebug.remote_port=9000

   xdebug.remote_mode=req

   xdebug.default_enable = On

   xdebug.show_exception_trace = On

   xdebug.show_local_vars = 1

   xdebug.max_nesting_level = 50

   xdebug.var_display_max_depth = 6

   xdebug.dump_once = On

   xdebug.dump_globals = On

   xdebug.dump_undefined = On

   xdebug.dump.REQUEST = *

   xdebug.dump.SERVER = REQUEST_METHOD,REQUEST_URI,HTTP_USER_AGENT
   ```

9. Repeat the previous step for the `/etc/php5/apache2/conf.d/xdebug.ini` file.
10. Save the `xdebug.ini` file and restart your Apache:

    sudo /etc/init.d/apache2 restart

11. You can check the Xdebug status now from the terminal of the `phpinfo()` page.

    php -i | grep xdebug

    ```
    /etc/php5/cli/conf.d/xdebug.ini,
    xdebug
    xdebug support => enabled
    xdebug.auto_trace => Off => Off
    xdebug.collect_assignments => Off => Off
    xdebug.collect_includes => On => On
    xdebug.collect_params => 0 => 0
    xdebug.collect_return => Off => Off
    xdebug.collect_vars => Off => Off
    xdebug.default_enable => On => On
    xdebug.dump.COOKIE => no value => no value
    xdebug.dump.ENV => no value => no value
    xdebug.dump.FILES => no value => no value
    xdebug.dump.GET => no value => no value
    xdebug.dump.POST => no value => no value
    xdebug.dump.REQUEST => * => *
    xdebug.dump.SERVER => REQUEST_METHOD,REQUEST_URI,HTTP_USER_AGENT
    => REQUEST_METHOD,REQUEST_URI,HTTP_USER_AGENT
    xdebug.dump.SESSION => no value => no value
    xdebug.dump_globals => On => On
    xdebug.dump_once => On => On
    xdebug.dump_undefined => On => On
    xdebug.extended_info => On => On
    xdebug.file_link_format => no value => no value
    xdebug.idekey => dynamicguy => no value
    xdebug.manual_url => http://www.php.net => http://www.php.net
    xdebug.max_nesting_level => 50 => 50
    xdebug.overload_var_dump => On => On
    xdebug.profiler_aggregate => Off => Off
    xdebug.profiler_append => Off => Off
    ```

Debugging and Unit Testing

```
xdebug.profiler_enable => Off => Off
xdebug.profiler_enable_trigger => Off => Off
xdebug.profiler_output_dir => /tmp => /tmp
xdebug.profiler_output_name => cachegrind.out.%p => cachegrind.
out.%p
xdebug.remote_autostart => Off => Off
xdebug.remote_connect_back => Off => Off
xdebug.remote_cookie_expire_time => 3600 => 3600
xdebug.remote_enable => On => On
xdebug.remote_handler => dbgp => dbgp
xdebug.remote_host => localhost => localhost
xdebug.remote_log => /var/log/xdebug.log => /var/log/xdebug.log
xdebug.remote_mode => req => req
xdebug.remote_port => 9000 => 9000
xdebug.scream => Off => Off
xdebug.show_exception_trace => On => On
xdebug.show_local_vars => On => On
xdebug.show_mem_delta => Off => Off
xdebug.trace_format => 0 => 0
xdebug.trace_options => 0 => 0
xdebug.trace_output_dir => /tmp => /tmp
xdebug.trace_output_name => trace.%c => trace.%c
xdebug.var_display_max_children => 128 => 128
xdebug.var_display_max_data => 512 => 512
xdebug.var_display_max_depth => 6 => 6
PWD => /home/dynamicguy/Desktop/xdebug-2.1.0
_SERVER["PWD"] => /home/dynamicguy/Desktop/xdebug-2.1.0
```

12. Additionally, you can check it in an error prone PHP page.

13. The last step of this recipe is to modify the core Magneto code so that we can see the errors in Magento with Xdebug. Open the `Mage.php` file from the `app` directory and replace the `run` method with this one:

    ```
    /**
     * Front end main entry point
     *
     * @param string $code
     * @param string $type
     * @param string|array $options
    ```

```php
*/
    public static function run($code = '', $type = 'store',
$options=array())
    {
      if (!self::getIsDeveloperMode()) {
        try {
          Varien_Profiler::start('mage');
            self::setRoot();
            self::$_app = new Mage_Core_Model_App();
            self::$_events = new Varien_Event_Collection();
            self::$_config = new Mage_Core_Model_Config();
            self::$_app->run(array(
               'scope_code' => $code,
               'scope_type' => $type,
               'options' => $options,
            ));
            Varien_Profiler::stop('mage');
        } catch (Mage_Core_Model_Session_Exception $e) {
            header('Location: ' . self::getBaseUrl());
            die();
        } catch (Mage_Core_Model_Store_Exception $e) {
            require_once(self::getBaseDir() . DS . 'errors' . DS .
'404.php');
            die();
        } catch (Exception $e) {
            if (self::isInstalled() || self::$_isDownloader) {
              self::printException($e);
              exit();
            }
            try {
              self::dispatchEvent('mage_run_exception',
array('exception' => $e));
                if (!headers_sent()) {
                   header('Location:' . self::getUrl('install'));
                } else {
                   self::printException($e);
                }
            } catch (Exception $ne) {
            self::printException($ne, $e->getMessage());
            }
        }
      } else {
        Varien_Profiler::start('mage');
        self::setRoot();
```

Debugging and Unit Testing

```
        self::$_app = new Mage_Core_Model_App();
        self::$_events = new Varien_Event_Collection();
        self::$_config = new Mage_Core_Model_Config();
        self::$_app->run(array(
          'scope_code' => $code,
          'scope_type' => $type,
          'options' => $options,
        ));
        Varien_Profiler::stop('mage');
    }
}
```

14. Now if we change the code of the `app/design/frontend/base/default/template/catalog/product/view.phtml` file and put some PHP error prone code (try this: `<?php echo ?>`) deliberately, we should see a page something like this:

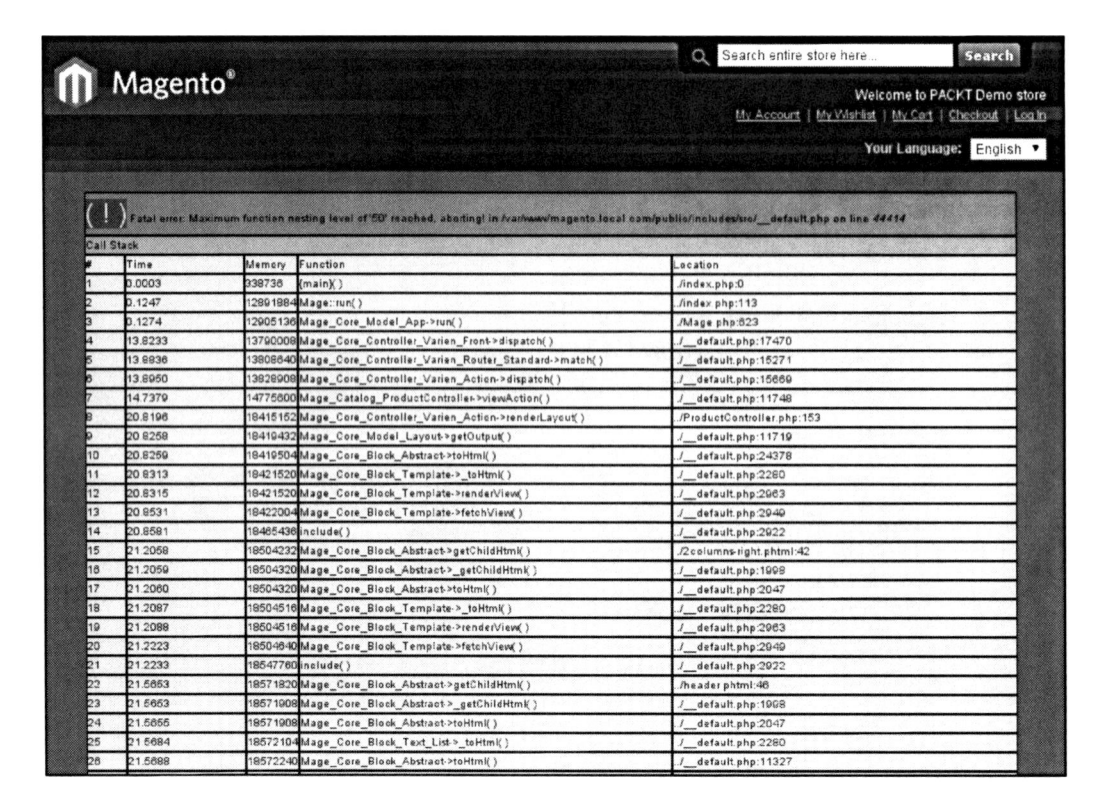

> If you want your errors to be colorful, don't forget to set the `html_errors = On` in your `php.ini` file. In an Unix OS, it should be in `/etc/php5/apache2/php.ini`.

How it works...

In this recipe, we installed the Xdebug from source. We grabbed the Xdebug's source code from their online repository. Then we compiled it. This is pretty similar for any typical PHP extension—**phpize | configure | make | make install**. After installation, we configured the Xdebug ini configuration both for CLI and Apache. The configuration parameters could be different, as you please. You can see more configuration options on http://xdebug.org/docs/all_settings.

Finally, we set a condition in the Mage.php's run() method to print the exceptions in the developer mode only. We checked that with self::getIsDeveloperMode() method. If you are curious to see how the developer mode is set, have a look at the index.php file and look for the following lines:

```
if (isset($_SERVER['MAGE_IS_DEVELOPER_MODE'])) {
    Mage::setIsDeveloperMode(true);
}
```

You can set the developer mode via htaccess or Apache site config. For htaccess, put the following line in your htaccess:

```
setEnv MAGE_IS_DEVELOPER_MODE true
```

There's more...

Let's say, to compute a Fibonacci number your terminal conditions are incorrect, the application can run for a very long time before it runs out of memory or time. You can set the xdebug.max_nesting_level parameter to limit the depth of recursion. For example, xdebug.max_nesting_level = 50 limits recursion to a depth of 50 nested calls before the application is forced to terminate. To demonstrate, run the code with Xdebug enabled. This is how we set up some configuration directives to debug our Magento script.

Using FirePHP with Zend Wildfire plugin

FirePHP is a Firebug add-on for Firefox browser, which is useful for debugging a PHP script. FirePHP could be used via installing it from the PEAR repository or from the Zend Framework's library. Magento CMS is built on top of Zend Framework, which has got rich PHP libraries and plugins. Zend Wildfire plugin FirePHP is one of them. This recipe will help you use this plugin in Magento.

Debugging and Unit Testing

Getting ready

We will be using Firebug and the FirePHP console, thus we got to install these two add-ons and of course, Firefox itself.

- `https://addons.mozilla.org/en-US/firefox/addon/1843/`
- `https://addons.mozilla.org/en-US/firefox/addon/6149/`

How to do it...

1. Fire up your Magento project in your favorite PHP IDE.
2. Add the following code snippet on line number 70 of `index.php`:

```
// -----------------------------------------------------------
// wildfire plugin calling function
// -----------------------------------------------------------

/**
 * Logs variables to the Firebug Console
 * via HTTP response headers and the FirePHP Firefox Extension.
 *
 * @param  mixed   $var    The variable to log.
 * @param  string  $label OPTIONAL Label to prepend to the log event.
 * @param  string  $style  OPTIONAL Style of the log event.
 * @param  array   $options OPTIONAL Options to change how messages are processed and sent
 * @return boolean Returns TRUE if the variable was added to the response headers or buffered.
 * @throws Zend_Wildfire_Exception
 */
function toFirePHP($var, $label = 'Magento vars', $style = 'INFO', $options=array())
{
  if (Mage::getIsDeveloperMode()) {
    $httpRequest = new Zend_Controller_Request_Http();
    $httpResponse = new Zend_Controller_Response_Http();
    $channel = Zend_Wildfire_Channel_HttpHeaders::getInstance();
    $channel->setRequest($httpRequest);
    $channel->setResponse($httpResponse);
    ob_start();
    Zend_Wildfire_Plugin_FirePhp::send($var, $label, $style, $options);
    $channel->flush();
    $httpResponse->sendHeaders();
  } else {
    return null;
  }
}
```

```
            }
// ---------------------------------------------------------------
// wildfire plugin calling function ends
// ---------------------------------------------------------------
```

3. Save and close `index.php`.
4. Make sure the Magento profiler and developer's mode is **ON**.
5. You can call the `toFirePHP` function from anywhere in Magento CMS. Let's give it a try with `view.phtml` from the `app/design/frontend/base/default/template/catalog/product/` directory.
6. Add this line in `view.phtml` at line number 38 and run it:

   ```
   <?php toFirePHP($_product->debug());?>
   ```

7. You should see a page something like the following screenshot, if you have Firebug and FirePHP console enabled:

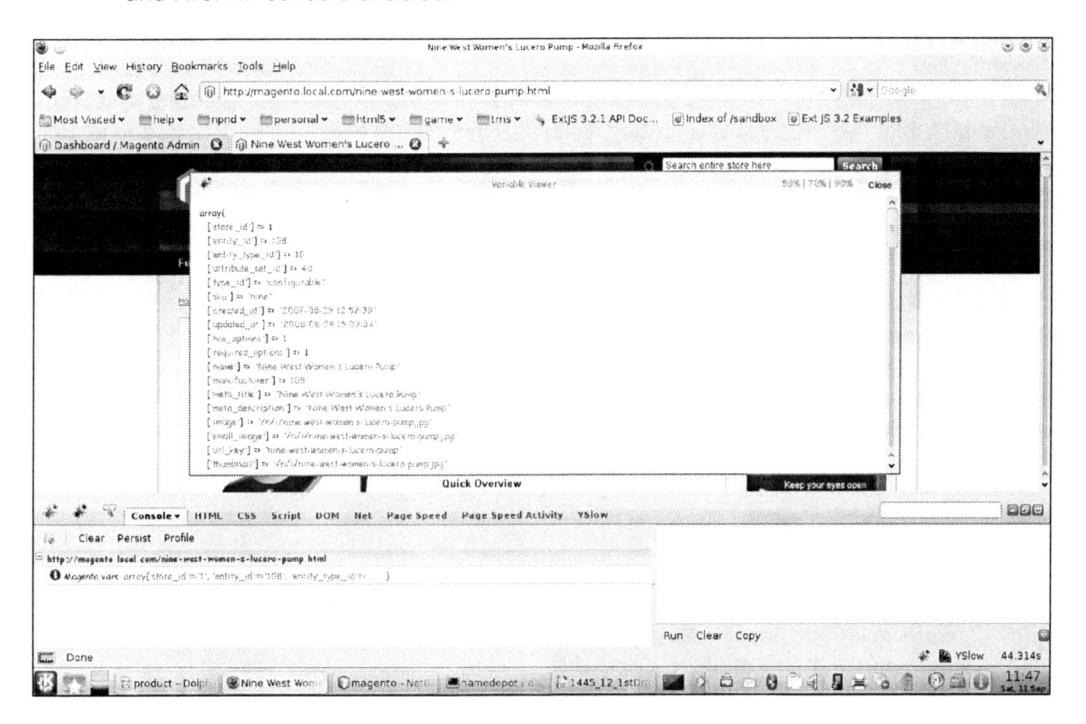

Debugging and Unit Testing

How it works...

We wrote a `toFirePHP()` function to pass a variable to the FirePHP console with different options. We can pass it as `LOG`, `INFO`, `WARN`, `ERROR`, `EXCEPTION`, `TRACE`, `TABLE`, `DUMP`, `GROUP_START`, or `GROUP_END` via the third parameter of the `toFirePHP()` function. While the first one is the placeholder for the dumping variable to be shown in the console, the second one is for the label in the console.

Make sure to add your Magento domain in FirePHP

To make it work with FirePHP, you ought to add your domain in FirePHP as white list. You can add/block a domain by clicking on the **FirePHP** icon and then the **Allowed Sites...** link.

Installing PHPUnit and necessary PHP CLI binaries

PHPUnit is the tool that we will be using for unit testing. Installation of PHPUnit is pretty straightforward as we will be using PEAR installer. It's recommended to install it via PEAR. PEAR is shipped with every release of PHP since version 4.3.0. In Unix-like operating systems, PEAR is added to the executable directory, such as `/usr/bin`, `/usr/local/bin`, and so on. Thus, a PEAR command is accessible from any location. A pear package could be installed via the following command:

```
apt-get install php-pear
```

If you are in Windows and using XAMPP, you should see an `exe` file named `pear.exe` in the `\xampp\php` folder. If you don't see `pear.exe`, you should run the `pear.bat` file to install it. You can see more instructions here: http://pear.php.net/manual/en/installation.getting.php. After installing PEAR, you should navigate (`cd C:\\xampp\php`) the php directory before issuing the commands shown in the following *How to do it...* section.

How to do it...

1. The PEAR channel (`pear.phpunit.de`) is used to distribute PHPUnit. This channel needs to be registered with the local PEAR environment. Issue the following command in the terminal to discover it:

   ```
   pear channel-discover pear.phpunit.de
   ```

2. There are some components in (`components.ez.no`) channel that PHPUnit depends on. So our next channel to discover is:

   ```
   pear channel-discover components.ez.no
   ```

3. A component that PHPUnit depends upon is hosted on the Symfony Components PEAR channel (`pear.symfony-project.com`). This is the last channel to discover:

   `pear channel-discover pear.symfony-project.com`

4. Okay, it is time to install PHPUnit itself:

   `pear install phpunit/PHPUnit`

5. This will install all necessary dependencies and PHPUnit from the internet.

6. The next tool to be installed is PHP5-CLI. You can install it via the terminal by using the following command:

   `sudo apt-get install php5-cli`

How it works...

PHPUnit is the member of XUnit family for PHP. It's the predecessor of popular unit testing framework for Java JUnit.

PEAR channels are the repository for various PEAR packages. These channels are used to distribute PEAR packages. We discovered the channels with the channel-discover command.

Finally, we issued the installation command to install PHPUnit via the PEAR installer. You can test your PHPUnit installation in the terminal by issuing the following command:

`phpunit --version`

The previous command should return a text something like the follPHPUnit 3.5.5 by Sebastian Bergmann.

There's more...

Alternatively, you can install it from archive:

1. Download a release archive from `http://pear.phpunit.de/get/` and extract it to a directory that is listed in the `include_path` of your `php.ini` configuration file.

2. Prepare the `phpunit` script:
   - Rename the `phpunit.php` script to `phpunit`.
   - Replace the `@php_bin@` string in it with the path to your PHP command-line interpreter (usually `/usr/bin/php`).
   - Copy it to a directory that is in your path and make it executable (`chmod +x phpunit`).

3. Prepare the `PHPUnit/Util/PHP.php` script:
   - Replace the `@php_bin@` string in it with the path to your PHP command-line interpreter (usually `/usr/bin/php`).

243

Debugging and Unit Testing

Writing your first Magento test case

Test Driven Development (TDD) has become a popular and widely accepted practice today. This is related to test-first programming concepts of extreme programming. Though in TDD the test cases should be written first, in this recipe, we will be writing test cases for legacy codes.

Magento is built on top of Zend Framework, which itself is tested and encourages Test Driven Development. In Magento, we can write unit tests using PHPUnit for our own module or any other existing modules for better acceptance. This recipe will guide you through to write your first test case for Magento. In this recipe, we will be writing tests for the News model of the News module.

Getting ready

Install PHPUnit, Xdebug, and PHP5-CLI binaries. Make sure that you created the News module as we had described it in *Chapter 8, Creating a Module* of this book.

How to do it...

1. Create a new folder in your Magento root and name it as `tests`.
2. Create a new PHP file in the `tests` folder named `autoload.php`.
3. The following is the content for `autoload.php`. This file contains some `ini` settings and instantiation of a Magento application that will be used in unit tests:

```php
<?php

ini_set('include_path', ini_get('include_path') . PATH_SEPARATOR
. dirname(__FILE__) . '/../app' . PATH_SEPARATOR . dirname(__FILE__));

//code coverage generation requires lots of memory
ini_set('memory_limit', '512M');

//autoloading will work as we set the inlcude path earlier
require_once 'Mage.php';

//creating the Magento application instance
Mage::app('default');

//so we don't get "Headers already sent message" in case of error,
can also var_dump now...
session_start();
```

4. Create a new XML file in the `tests` folder and name it `phpunit.xml`.
5. Now put the following content in it. The contents are for setting up a test suite for Magento:

```xml
<?xml version="1.0" encoding="UTF-8" ?>

<phpunit backupGlobals="false"
  backupStaticAttributes="false"
  colors="true"
  convertErrorsToExceptions="true"
  convertNoticesToExceptions="true"
  convertWarningsToExceptions="true"
  processIsolation="true"
  stopOnFailure="false"
  syntaxCheck="true"
  bootstrap="./autoload.php"
>

  <testsuite name="Magento Test Suite">
    <directory>./</directory>
  </testsuite>

  <filter>
    <whitelist>
      <directory>../app/code/local</directory>
    </whitelist>
  </filter>

</phpunit>
```

6. Create the required folders, as the following screenshot depicts:

```
> app
> downloader
> errors
> includes
> js
> lib
> media
> nbproject
> pkginfo
> shell
> skin
v tests
  v app
    v code
      v local
        v Packt
          v News
            Model
```

Debugging and Unit Testing

> If you are in a Linux box, you can create all the directories through a single command (assuming you are in the tests directory): `mkdir -p app/code/local/Packt/News/Model/`.

7. Now create a new PHP file in the `tests/app/code/local/Packt/News/Model/` folder and name it as `NewsTest.php`.

8. Let's put the content of `NewsTest.php` as follows:

```php
<?php

require_once 'PHPUnit/Framework.php';

class NewsTest extends PHPUnit_Framework_TestCase
{

   protected $_newsModel;

   public function setUp()
   {
      echo 'Starting test for ', $this->getName(), '() method';
      Mage::app('default');
         $this->_newsModel = Mage::getModel('news/news');
   }

   protected function tearDown()
   {

   }

   public function testGetAllNews()
   {
      $newses = $this->_newsModel->getCollection();
      $this->assertEquals(2, sizeof($newses));
   }

}
```

9. Now open your terminal and navigate to the `tests` directory. Write `phpunit` in the terminal and hit enter.

   phpunit

10. You should see a screen similar to the following:

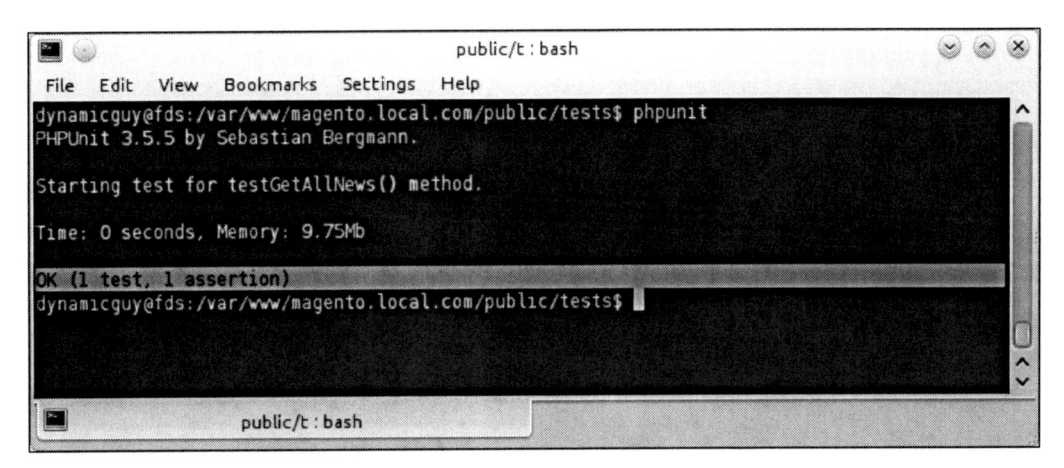

```
dynamicguy@fds:/var/www/magento.local.com/public/tests$ phpunit
PHPUnit 3.5.5 by Sebastian Bergmann.

Starting test for testGetAllNews() method.

Time: 0 seconds, Memory: 9.75Mb

OK (1 test, 1 assertion)
dynamicguy@fds:/var/www/magento.local.com/public/tests$
```

How it works...

The very first task to accomplish in this recipe is to create the required file structure and an instance of the Magento application. We did it as per the given screenshot and created a new `autoload.php` file. Here we have most of the job done, because all required Mage features are bootstrapped. You can use any controller, model, call Mage core functions, helpers, and so on that come under the specified directory in `phpunit.xml`.

The `phpunit` test suite's configurations reside in the `phpunit.xml` file. We specified the test directory, white list filter for sources to be tested and some PHPUnit attributes such as colors, bootstrap file, syntaxCheck, and so on.

The last step was about writing the test case itself. We included the PHPUnit framework at the beginning. We wrote a class named `NewsTest`, which extended `PHPUnit_Framework_TestCase`. The `setUp()` and `tearDown()` methods are called before running every test. We have assigned the News model via Mage in the `setUp()` method. The `testGetAllNews()` is the test case for News model, which checks whether the News model returns two rows or not. We are assuming that our news table has two entries. If News model returns two rows, then it will pass the test or fails otherwise. You can and are strongly encouraged to write more tests in this way.

Debugging and Unit Testing

There's more...

You can fully automate the testing by using the `setUp` and `tearDown` methods. Let's say we first emptied the news table and added two rows in it via News model in `setUp()`.

After checking these two rows in test cases, we remove those inserted two rows in the `tearDown` method to make the database as it were.

See also

- Installing PHPUnit and necessary PHP CLI binaries
- Installing and configuring Xdebug

Index

Symbols

_generateServiceLink() method 195
<global> block 68

A

ab (ApacheBench)
 about 200, 201, 207
 Magento, benchmarking with 202, 203
accepted payment banner
 adding, at footer 61, 62
Active Record 132
addAttributeToFilter() method 132
addFilterAtributes routine 134
Alternative PHP Cache. *See* **APC**
APC
 about 215
 installing 215
 URL 220
apt-get command 13
Artisan System 117

B

backend
 shipping module, adding 181, 183
blocks
 about 167
 adding, for News module 159-168
blog, Magento 48
brute-force approach 232
bundle product
 adding 95, 96

C

caching
 disabling 24
catalog optimization, Magento store 112
Catalog Price Rules
 about 79
 setting up 80
Catalog system defaults
 setting up 87-89
category optimization, Magento store 112
CMS
 contact form, placing 38-40
CMS Page optimization, Magento store 113
CMS template
 about 32
 adding 34
Comma Separated Values. *See* **CSV**
Concurrent Version System *See* **CVS**
configurable product
 about 97, 101
 creating 97-100
config.xml file
 about 149, 179, 188, 190
 blocks 152
 creating, for modules 149-152
confirmation page
 Google AdWords tracking code, adding 31, 32
contact form
 about 38
 placing, in CMS 38-40
controller
 about 140
 creating, for modules 140-148
 working 148

core_write privilege 130
Create, Read, Update, and Delete. *See* CRUD
credit card icons
  about 61
  adding, to skin image directory 61, 62
Cross-Site Request Forgery attack. *See* CSRF attack
CRUD 142
CSRF attack
  about 117
  preventing, in Magento 117, 119
CSV 94
custom admin theme
  about 84
  creating 85
custom variable
  creating 76-78
  using, on e-mail templates 76-78
CVS 11

D

database connection, Magento 122-124
Database Repair Tool 132
database replication, Magento
  master slave setup, used 124-129
debugging 231-232
debug_zval_dump() function 231
directories
  creating, for modules 138

E

EAccelerator
  URL 220
EAV 66, 121
EAV design, Magento
  about 132
  working 133, 134
e-mail templates
  custom templates, using on 76-78
empty class
  creating, for module 190, 191
empty module
  creating 186-188
  creating, with Module Creator 136, 137
enabler file
  creating 186-188

Entity-Attribute-Value. *See* EAV
error page
  customizing 28, 30

F

Facebook 90
featured product
  creating 81-84
  displaying, on homepage 81-84
FirePHP
  about 239
  using, with Zend Wildfire plugin 241, 242
footer
  accepted payment banner, adding 61, 62
FQDN
  about 8
  using 8
frontend
  shipping module, adding 183, 184
frontend block
  about 185
  creating, for widget 192-195
Fully Qualified Domain Name *See* FQDN

G

getCollection() method 132
get command
  issuing 216
gnuplot-file 202
Google AdWords tracking code
  about 31
  adding, to confirmation page 32
Google Analytics
  about 78
  using, for Magento 78, 79
Google Website Optimizer. *See* GWO
GTmetrix
  about 200, 201, 207
  Magento, benchmarking with 207
  URL 207
GWO
  about 73
  homepage 74, 75
  using 75
  working 76

H

helper
  creating, for News module 153
home link
  adding, to menu bar 23-26
homepage
  featured product, displaying on 81-84

I

IndexController class 148
installation, Apache
  command 8
installation, APC 215
installation, Magento 1.4
  in PHP 5.3.2 106-110
installation, Memcached 216
installation, MySQL
  command 9
installation, PHP5
  command 8
installation, PHP CLI binaries 243
installation, PHPUnit 242, 243
installation, Xdebug 232-239

J

jQuery
  about 51
  support, adding to Magento 52-55
  URL 52
jQuery.noconflict() function 51
js frameworks, Magento 51
JW Image Rotator 3.17
  integrating, in Magento 40-43
  working 43

L

Lightbox 55
Lightbox2
  about 60
  adding, in Magento 55-60
'Like' plugin, Facebook
  adding, in product pages 90, 91
  URL 91

LongTail Ad Solutions
  URL 43

M

Magento
  about 7, 23, 87
  benchmarking, with ab (ApacheBench) 202, 203
  benchmarking, with GTmetrix 207
  benchmarking, with Magento Profile 204
  benchmarking, with Page Speed 201, 206
  benchmarking, with Siege 203, 204
  benchmarking, with WebPagetest 207
  benchmarking, with YSlow 205, 206
  blog 48
  CSRF attack, preventing 117, 119
  database connection, managing 122-124
  database replication, master slave setup used 124-129
  error page, customizing 28, 30
  file structure 20
  Google Analytics, using for 78, 79
  GWO 73
  jQuery support, adding 52-55
  js frameworks 51
  JW Image Rotator 3.17, integrating 40-43
  LightBox2, adding 55-60
  modules, activating 139
  MySQL tools, setting up 15, 16
  new page, creating 49, 50
  orders, deleting 70, 72
  page title, changing 26-28
  PayPal Website Payments Pro, implementing 114-116
  platform, developing with vhost 8-11
  resource 122-124
  Singleton design pattern, using 129, 130
  SVN, setting up 11-13
  template tags 50
  WordPress, integrating into 45-47
Magento 1.4
  acquiring, via SVN 13, 14
  installing, in PHP 5.3.2 106-110
Magento 1.4.x, product types
  about 101
  bundle 101

configurable 97-101
downloadable 101
grouped 101
simple 101
virtual 101
Magento CMS 50
Magento code
working with 20, 21
Magento configurations
about 213
tuning up 214-219
Magento Connect
about 70
working 72
Magento database
optimizing 208
repairing 130-132
Magento Developer 7
Magento EAV design
about 132
working with 133, 134
Magento profiler
about 200, 201
Magento, benchmarking with 204
Magento project
setting up, with NetBeans 17-19
Magento store
catalog optimization 112
category optimization 112
CMS Page optimization 113
product optimization 113
search engine optimization 110, 114
Table Rates, adding 91-94
template optimization 113
Magento test case
writing 244-247
Magento widgets 185
make command 233
max_execution_time setting 220
max_input_time setting 220
mcrypt module 106
Memcached
installing 216
memory_limit setting 220
menu bar
home link, adding to 23-26

model adapter class
writing, for shipping module 180, 181
models
about 180
creating, for modules 154, 155
module configuration
initializing 171-179
Module Creator
about 136
empty module, creating 136, 137
working 137
modules
about 135, 136
activating 139
config.xml file, creating for 149-152
controller, creating for 140-148
directories, creating for 138
empty class, creating for 190, 191
models, creating for 154, 155
mysql> mysqladmin extended -i100 -r command 210
MySQL server
optimizing 208-210
MySQL server tuning
wrong units 210
mysql> SHOW GLOBAL STATUS; command 210
mysql> SHOW INNODB STATUS; command 210
mysql> SHOW LOCAL STATUS; command 210
mysql> SHOW STATUS; command 210
mysql> SHOW VARIABLES; command 210
MySQL tools
setting up 15, 16

N

NetBeans
about 16
Magento project, creating 17-19
new page
creating 49, 50
News module
blocks, adding for 159-168
helper, creating for 153
SQL, setting up for 156, 157
template, designing for 157, 158

O

orders
  deleting, in Magento 70, 72
output_buffering setting 220

P

Page Speed
  about 200-208
  Magento, benchmarking with 206
  online documentation, URL 229
page title
  changing, in Magento 26-28
PayPal 114
PayPal Website Payments Pro
  implementing, in Magento 114-116
PEAR channels
  about 242
  working 243
PHP 5.3.2
  Magento 1.4, installing 106-110
PHP accelerators 220
PHP CLI binaries
  installing 243
php.ini configuration
  about 220
  accelerating 221
PHPUnit
  about 242
  installing 242, 243
  working 243
phpunit.xml file 247
platform
  developing, with vhost 8-11
price rules, Magento
  catalog 79
  shopping cart 80
print_r() function 231
product
  adding, by Magento product ID 94
  adding, by SKU 97
  adding, to cart with Querystring 94-96
  shipping 171
product detail
  YouTube video, embedding in 101-104
product optimizations, Magento store 113

product page
  Facebook 'Like' plugin, adding to 90, 91
product types, Magento 1.4.x
  about 101
  bundle 101
  configurable 97-101
  downloadable 101
  grouped 101
  simple 101
  virtual 101

Q

Querystring
  product, adding to cart 94-96

R

registration form
  Twitter handle field, customizing in 65-70
resource, Magento 122, 124
RSS feed
  about 36
  adding 36, 37

S

Search Engine Optimization, Magento store 114
self::getIsDeveloperMode() method 239
shipping
  about 91, 171
  product 171
shipping module
  adding, in backend 181, 183
  adding, in frontend 183, 184
  model adapter class, writing 180, 181
Shopping Cart Price Rules
  about 80
  setting up 80
Siege
  about 200-207
  Magento, benchmarking with 203, 204
Singleton design pattern
  using, in Magento 129, 130
SKU
  product, adding with 97

source model
  creating, for services 191, 192
SQL
  setting, up for News module 156, 157
style.css content 46
SVN
  about 11
  Magento 1.4, acquiring 13, 14
  setting up 12, 13
system.xml file 179
Subversion *See* **SVN**

T

Table Rates
  adding, for Magento shop 91-94
tagoSphere plugin
  URL 52
TDD 244
template
  about 198
  creating 196, 198
  designing, for News module 157, 158
template optimization, Magento store 113
template tags, Magento 50
Test Driven Development. *See* **TDD**
testGetAllNews() function 247
TinyMCE 50, 104
TortoiseSVN client
  downloading, URL 11
Twitter handle field
  customizing, in registration form 65-70

U

Urchin on Demand 78

V

var_dump() function 231
vhost
  platform, developing 8-11
virtual host *See* **vhost**

W

WebPagetest
  about 200, 201
  Magento, benchmarking with 207
web server configuration
  optimizing 210-213
widgets
  about 186
  declaring 188-190
  frontend block, creating for 192-195
widget.xml file 188, 190
WordPress
  about 45
  integrating, in Magento 45- 47
WYSIWYG editor 101

X

XAMPP package
  downloading, URL 9
XCache
  URL 220
Xdebug
  about 231
  installing 232-239
  website link 232
XML files 179

Y

YouTube video
  embedding, in product details 101-104
YSlow
  about 200-221
  Magento, benchmarking with 205, 206
  online documentation, URL 229
  rules, applying 222- 227

Z

Zend Framework 8
Zend Wildfire plugin
  FirePHP, using 241, 242

Thank you for buying
Magento 1.4 Development Cookbook

About Packt Publishing

Packt, pronounced 'packed', published its first book "*Mastering phpMyAdmin for Effective MySQL Management*" in April 2004 and subsequently continued to specialize in publishing highly focused books on specific technologies and solutions.

Our books and publications share the experiences of your fellow IT professionals in adapting and customizing today's systems, applications, and frameworks. Our solution based books give you the knowledge and power to customize the software and technologies you're using to get the job done. Packt books are more specific and less general than the IT books you have seen in the past. Our unique business model allows us to bring you more focused information, giving you more of what you need to know, and less of what you don't.

Packt is a modern, yet unique publishing company, which focuses on producing quality, cutting-edge books for communities of developers, administrators, and newbies alike. For more information, please visit our website: www.packtpub.com.

About Packt Open Source

In 2010, Packt launched two new brands, Packt Open Source and Packt Enterprise, in order to continue its focus on specialization. This book is part of the Packt Open Source brand, home to books published on software built around Open Source licences, and offering information to anybody from advanced developers to budding web designers. The Open Source brand also runs Packt's Open Source Royalty Scheme, by which Packt gives a royalty to each Open Source project about whose software a book is sold.

Writing for Packt

We welcome all inquiries from people who are interested in authoring. Book proposals should be sent to author@packtpub.com. If your book idea is still at an early stage and you would like to discuss it first before writing a formal book proposal, contact us; one of our commissioning editors will get in touch with you.

We're not just looking for published authors; if you have strong technical skills but no writing experience, our experienced editors can help you develop a writing career, or simply get some additional reward for your expertise.

Magento 1.3: PHP Developer's Guide

ISBN: 978-1-847197-42-9　　　　Paperback: 260 pages

Design, develop, and deploy feature-rich Magento online stores with PHP coding

1. Extend and customize the Magento e-commerce system using PHP code
2. Set up your own data profile to import or export data in Magento
3. Build applications that interface with the customer, product, and order data using Magento's Core API
4. Packed with examples for effective Magento Development

Magento: Beginner's Guide

ISBN: 978-1-847195-94-4　　　　Paperback: 300 pages

Create a dynamic, fully featured, online store with the most powerful open source e-commerce software

1. Step-by-step guide to building your own online store
2. Focuses on the key features of Magento that you must know to get your store up and running
3. Customize the store's appearance to make it uniquely yours
4. Clearly illustrated with screenshots and a working example

Please check www.PacktPub.com for information on our titles

Magento 1.3 Theme Design

ISBN: 978-1-847196-64-4   Paperback: 188 pages

Customize the appearance of your Magento e-commerce store with Magento's powerful theming engine

1. Give your Magento stores a unique branded look and feel by creating your own Magento themes
2. Use design techniques to reinforce your brand message and increase sales
3. Customise your Magento theme's look, feel, layout, and features
4. Promote and improve your Magento store with the use of social media such as Twitter, social bookmarks, and so on

Magento 1.3 Sales Tactics Cookbook

ISBN: 978-1-849510-12-7   Paperback: 292 pages

Solve real-world Magento sales problems with a collection of simple but effective recipes

1. Build a professional Magento sales web site, with the help of easy-to-follow steps and ample screenshots, to solve real-world business needs and requirements
2. Develop your web site by using your creativity and exploiting the sales techniques that suit your needs
3. Provide visitors with attractive and innovative features to make your site sell

Please check www.PacktPub.com for information on our titles

Lightning Source UK Ltd.
Milton Keynes UK
04 January 2011

165167UK00001B/25/P